Management in Developing Countries

Organizational Behaviour and Management Series
Edited by Robert Goffee

Management in Developing Countries

Edited by

Alfred M. Jaeger

and

Rabindra N. Kanungo

London and New York

First published 1990
by Routledge
11 New Fetter Lane, London EC4P 4EE

Simultaneously published in the USA and Canada
by Routledge
a division of Routledge, Chapman and Hall, Inc.
29 West 35th Street, New York, NY 10001

Laserset by
NWL Editorial Services, Langport, Somerset TA10 9DG

**Printed and bound in Great Britain by
Biddles Ltd, Guildford and King's Lynn**

British Library Cataloguing in Publication Data
Management in developing countries.
   1. Developing countries. Organizations. Management
   I. Jaeger, Alfred M, *1950–*   II. Kanungo, Rabindra N.
(Rabindra Natu)   III. Series
658.4′009172′4

ISBN 0–415–03505–8

Library of Congress Cataloging in Publication Data
Management in developing countries / edited by Alfred M.
Jaeger and Rabindra N. Kanungo
         p.   cm. – (Organizational behaviour and
management series)
   Includes bibligraphical references.
   ISBN 0–415–03505–8
   1. Management–Developing countries.   2. Organizational
behavior–Developing countries.   I. Jaeger, Alfred M.
   II. Kanungo, Rabindra N.   III. Series.
   HD70.D44M35   1990
   658′009172′4–dc20   90–31655
                                                                          CIP

*To those who cherish the missionary vision for
international development*

Contents

Contents

Figures

Tables

Contributors

Pullin K. Garg is Samskark and a founder member of the Indian Society for Individual and Social Development, Ahmedabad, India.

Cynthia Hardy is Associate Professor in the Faculty of Management at McGill University, Montreal, Canada.

Alfred M. Jaeger is Associate Professor of Organizational Behaviour in the Faculty of Management at McGill University, Montreal, Canada.

Jan J. Jørgensen is Associate Professor in the Faculty of Management at McGill University, Montreal, Canada.

Rabindra N. Kanungo is Professor of Organizational Behaviour in the Faculty of Management at McGill University, Montreal, Canada.

Pradip N. Khandawalla is L & T Professor of Organizational Behaviour at the Indian Institute of Management, Ahmedabad, India.

Moses Kiggundu is Associate Professor at the School of Business at Carleton University, Ottawa, Canada.

Sitakant Mahapatra is in the Indian administrative service, New Delhi, India.

Manuel Mendonca is Lecturer in the Faculty of Management at McGill University, Montreal, Canada.

Indira J. Parikh is Professor of Organizational Behaviour at the Indian Institute of Management, Ahmedabad, India.

Fritz Rieger is Assistant Professor at the University of Windsor, Ontario, Canada.

J.B.P. Sinha is Professor at the ANS Institute of Social Studies, Patna, India.

Kalburgi M. Srinivas is Professor of Organizational Behaviour at the Faculty of Commerce and Business Administration at the University of Regina, Regina, Canada.

Arthur M. Whitehill is Professor of International Management at the College of Business Administration of the University of Hawaii at Manoa, Hawaii, USA.

Durhane Wong-Rieger is Associate Professor at the University of Windsor, Ontario, Canada.

James Woycke is Research Fellow at the University of Toronto, Toronto, Canada.

Shirley C. Zhuang is Graduate Research Assistant at the College of Business Administration of the University of Hawaii, Hawaii, USA.

Preface

As the world becomes increasingly interdependent and the economic future of developed countries hinges more and more on success in meeting the problems facing the Third World, interest in management in developing countries has heightened. In their search for help in understanding and facing their problems, managers in developing countries are confronted with a scarcity of resources, not only physical resources, but intellectual resources as well. Relatively little is written about the unique human and organizational problems facing managers in the developing world, be they indigenous managers of domestic organizations or expatriates from large multinational firms. This book brings together a set of readings which directly address the questions and needs of managers of organizations in the developing countries.

The book covers a series of topical areas. They range from the 'macro' organizational (organization–environment interaction) level of analysis to the 'micro' individual behaviour (human resources in an organizational context) level of analysis. Several chapters are also devoted to the discussion of the limitations of Western management theories and techniques in the developing country context. Both theoretical analysis of problems and empirical findings are included within each of these topical areas. The contributors have tried to identify several key issues facing managers in developing countries, and summarize the lessons which have been learned and often indicate where work remains to be done. One important area not covered in this book is the area of management training and development. The omission of this area is deliberate. The emerging literature in the area of training and development of human resources in developing country organizations is so rich and varied that we thought it would require separate treatment in another volume. While this book is primarily devoted to macro- and micro-level basic issues of organizational behaviour and related indigenous management approaches suitable for developing countries, another complementary volume dealing exclusively with the management development and training area is currently in preparation.

This book is designed for use in both in-house managerial training programmes and university teaching programmes on management of organizations in the Third World. Although management courses on organization theory (OT) and organizational behaviour (OB) exist in industrial and educational training institutions throughout the world, trainers and participants in such programmes are acutely aware of the lack of a single source text that deals with the human resource and organizational issues of the Third World. The book attempts to fill this void by providing a comprehensive overview of the issues facing managers of organizations in developing countries. The book also brings together several contributions on the most current research on management issues in the Third World. We hope that not only trainers but also researchers in the field (OB and OT) will benefit from the book.

We should like to express our sincere thanks to Jean Hepworth whose admirable composure and skills helped in the preparation of the manuscript, and to Minati Kanungo and Zinette Khan whose support led to the completion of the project.

Montreal
                                    Rabindra N. Kanungo
                                    Alfred M. Jaeger

Chapter one

Introduction: the need for indigenous management in developing countries

Rabindra N. Kanungo and Alfred M. Jaeger

Introduction

Organizations are socio-technical systems with specific objectives of producing goods and services for their clientele. In order to manage such organizations effectively, it is necessary to understand how these systems work. Social scientists working in the field of organizational behaviour have proposed many theories and techniques that have helped management practitioners not only to understand the complexities of organizational systems but also to manage them effectively in order to achieve their production and service objectives.

Most widely dispersed management theories and techniques have their origin in the industrialized countries of the West. Many organizations in these industrialized countries have benefited from their prescriptions. As a result, Western management thought and practice have turned into 'sacred cows' for industrial development. Countries in the developing world are advised, and feel themselves, that they must strive to adopt Western thought and practices to achieve economic prosperity within the shortest possible time. Hence many organizational practices and management training programmes in the developing countries in modern times are based on 'an uncritical emulation and extrapolation from the experiences of the economic growth model of western countries, grossly disregarding the fundamental differences in socio-cultural constraints and local conditions and circumstances' (Sinha and Kao 1988: 11). Uncritical transfer of management theories and techniques based on Western ideologies and value systems has in many ways contributed to organizational inefficiency and ineffectiveness in the developing country context.

Managing organizations is a complex act. It requires a thorough understanding of the dynamic relationships within the socio-technical system (the internal environment) and the relationship to the external environment with which the system is in constant interaction. Since the external environment of organizations in the developing countries is different from that of the Western industrialized countries, management theories and practices developed in the developed country context may have only limited applicability in the context of the developing world. If one accepts the above premise, it becomes clear that there is a need to develop indigenous management theories and practices for use in the developing country context. This book represents an effort at exploring this perspective and an attempt at providing some outlines of management approaches appropriate for the environments found specifically in developing countries.

The need for indigenous management

Every organization must deal with the management of its internal and external environments, i.e. the management of the people and technology within the organization as well as the management of relations with the environment external to or outside the organization.

Every organization has the basic purpose of achieving two sets of objectives with respect to the management of its human resources. The first set has to do with improving the performance of organizational members to deliver goods and services for which the organization is formed in the first place. Productivity of a given organization – whether it is measured in terms of units produced, volume of sales accomplished, quality of services rendered, amount of profit margin, or cost effectiveness of the operation – is largely dependent on the performance of organizational members, be they managers or rank and file workers.

The second set of objectives has to do with developing and maintaining the human potential that serves as the backbone of the organization. The capacity of an organization to survive and to respond to competitive challenges from time to time can only be sustained and mobilized when the organization has highly competent and motivated manpower. Thus the effectiveness of the management of an organization is very much dependent on the nature of the human resources it possesses. In other words, an effective organization is one that has members who exhibit high levels of both work-related motivation (job and organizational commitment) and work performance.

Viewing organizational effectiveness in this way presupposes the existence of a system of management practice and employee behaviour that is conducive to high levels of work motivation and performance. Furthermore, such management practice and employee behaviour within an organization in large part results from managerial and employee values, attitudes, and beliefs regarding work and organizations. In other words, every organization has an internal work culture of its own which influences the behaviour or practices of both the management and the workers. The organizational work culture represents a form of organizational reality that shapes both the micro-level individual processes (day-to-day practices and behaviours of organizational members) and macro-level organizational processes (design of organizational structure, technologies employed, and strategic activities).

As a set of shared values, beliefs, and norms about the nature of work and organization, the work culture is constantly influenced by the environment in which the organization operates. In fact, the survival and growth of an organization depends on its developing an appropriate corporate culture that can adequately respond to external environmental forces. Just as the effectiveness of an individual depends on how adequately he or she copes with the surrounding environmental demands, the effectiveness of an organization also depends on how it adapts to its environmental demands by developing an appropriate corporate culture. In developing the appropriate coping strategies, organizations must be sensitive to environmental constraints and opportunities. Such sensitivity implies identifying and responding to three major aspects of the environment: (a) economic and technological, (b) political and legal, and (c) socio-cultural.

The economic–technological environment provides constraints and opportunities with respect to the technological, material, monetary, and human resource procurement necessary for the organization to function effectively. For instance, organizations must respond adequately to the prevailing labour market conditions. Management must plan the manpower needs of the organization according to the availability and flexibility of labour. Manpower planning effectiveness depends on whether management has a free hand in hiring, firing, retraining, or retrenching workers with minimal legal and political interference. Effectiveness in manpower planning for increased productivity and better service also depends on wage levels and the flexibility with which wages can respond to existing realities. For example, if economic or market conditions necessitate lower wage levels, or a moderate increase in wages, or even a wage freeze or reduction, then organizational effectiveness is enhanced to the extent that the ethos governing wages permits a flexible response to these conditions. The success of the organization would also depend on its adequate response to the challenges to its financing activities posed by economic conditions such as the availability of investment capital, inflation rates, interest rates, taxes, etc.

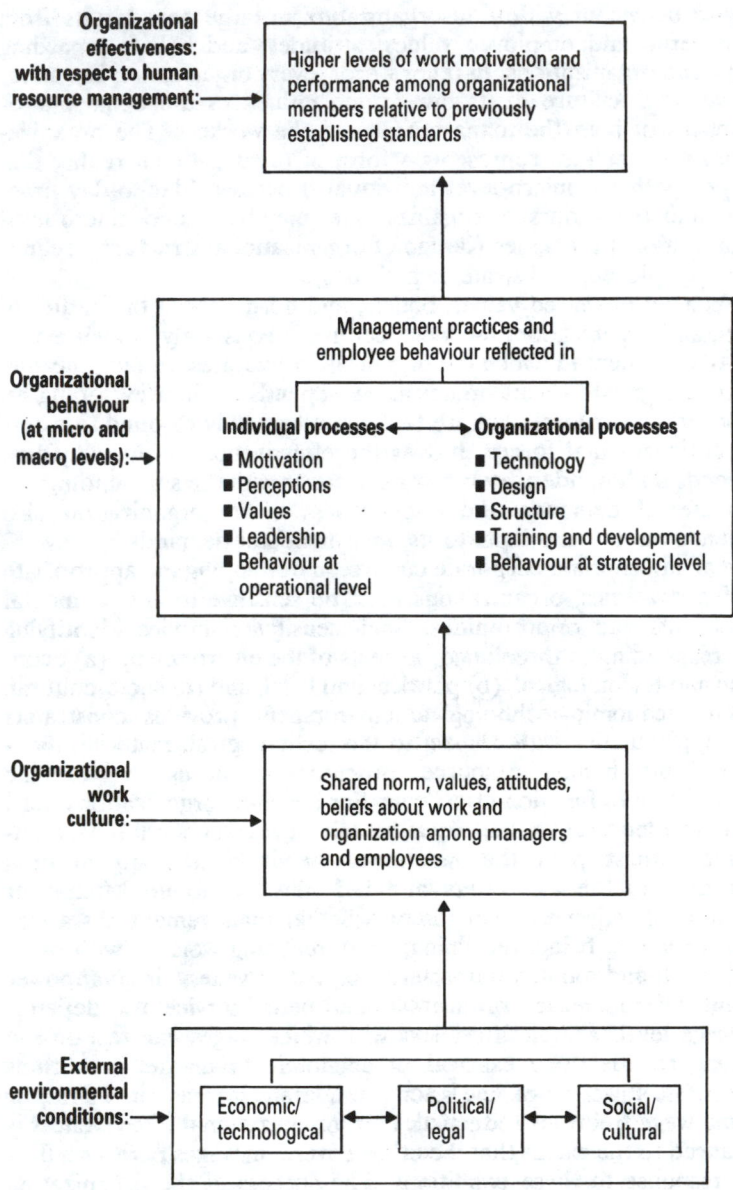

Figure 1.1 External and internal environmental factors influencing organizational effectiveness

Furthermore, the level of technology available for carrying out the organization's tasks is an important consideration for the organization's success. Important also is the development of an infrastructure which facilitates the procurement of materials, the location of suppliers, and distribution outlets. When the prospects of financing the organization, of obtaining the appropriate technology, and of finding the right markets are either inadequate or uncertain, organizational effectiveness suffers.

Besides the economic and technological environment, the political and legal environment also provides either facilitatory or inhibitory conditions for the successful operation of organizations. For instance, the stability of governments (local, regional, and/or national) creates business confidence. Legal systems which provide protection from foreign competition and establish specific labour mores and practices either promote or inhibit healthy organizations. Political interference in the management of organizations and the bureaucratic hurdles that management often encounters are widely known to contribute to organizational failure.

Finally, the socio-cultural environment provides challenges for dealing with human resources (a product of the socio-cultural environment) within the organization and for dealing with the clients (customers, community served) outside the organization. The socio-cultural environment of any given society determines collective norms and values, and individual beliefs, attitudes, and action preferences. Since organizational functioning depends on the behaviour and attitudes of people within a given society, organizational behaviour is profoundly influenced by the socio-cultural environment within which the organization operates. Sensitivity to the socio-cultural environment is particularly important for effective human resource management in organizations. The preceding discussion is summarized in Figure 1.1, which depicts the external environmental and internal organizational forces that influence organizational effectiveness with respect to human resource management.

Both international business and cross-cultural management studies recognize the importance of environmental variables, particularly those relating to the socio-cultural environment as a major determinant of organizational effectiveness both within a given country (Kanungo 1980) and across various countries in the world (Kanungo and Wright 1983; Adler 1986). However, in the context of developing countries, systematic explorations of what these environmental and cultural variables are and how management can deal with them for greater organizational effectiveness are just beginning to take place (Kiggundu *et al.* 1983; Sinha and Kao 1988).

Most of our knowledge and technology about how best to manage human resources within organizations stems from the social science research and management theories and practice of the developed world, particularly North America. North American based knowledge and technology have been imported by developing countries with the hope that what has worked for American economic and human resource development will work for development in the rest of the world.

Such uncritical acceptance of Western development strategies is based on the belief that the socio-cultural features of developing societies commonly referred to as 'traditionalism' are inimical to economic development. For instance, it has been argued that the lack of a Protestant work ethic, religiosity, and consequent fatalism, dependence, familism, etc. are the common socio-cultural constraints on economic development in the context of developing societies (Weber 1958) – hence the perceived need for change and modernization through the emulsification of Western experiences of organizational efficiency and entrepreneurship (Lewis 1955; McClelland and Winter 1969).

Unfortunately, the proven knowledge and technology in one socio-cultural context does not necessarily work effectively in another context, primarily because of the potent role of the contextual variables in determining organizational functioning and effectiveness. Developmental strategies that utilize socio-cultural features of the given society may actually be more desirable for overall organizational effectiveness. This is clearly seen in the case of newly industrialized Asian countries such as South Korea, Taiwan, Singapore, and Hong Kong, as well as in Japan. The success of organizations in these countries is 'widely attributed to both management styles and work attitudes that are rooted in Confucian values, familism, and institutional structures that are not necessarily Euro-American' (Sinha and Kao 1988: 12).

Uncritical adaptation of Western management strategies is neither necessary nor desirable for managing organizations in developing countries. What is needed is to develop relevant management theories and practices based on the local conditions and circumstances, and socio-cultural forces. Thus it is important to recognize explicitly the context of economic, political, and cultural differences between the developed and the developing countries and appropriately to develop and modify the knowledge and technology that is best suited to managing organizations in these areas.

Characterization of environments of developed and developing countries

At this point one might ask: how can we characterize the economic, political, and cultural differences between the developed Western industrialized and developing Third World countries? How do these differences impact the internal work culture and the management practices and employee behaviour in organizations in developing countries? What can managers do to improve the handling of human resources within the specific environmental and cultural constraints? What are the facilitating and inhibiting conditions inherent in the environmental contexts for the effective utilization of human resources? These are some of the complex issues that have no easy solutions. However, some general notions with respect to such differences can give a better appreciation of the need for indigenous management in developing countries and may provide some clues as to what forms it might take.

Although organizations in each country of the world have to adapt to the unique features of their own environment, for the convenience of analysis we shall look at the environment of organizations in two commonly understood clusters: those located in Western industrialized countries and those located in Third World or developing countries.

Organizations found in each cluster have some commonalities. The two clusters differ on several dimensions with respect to their external environment and internal work culture which influence both micro- and macro-level organizational behaviour. These dimensions can be grouped into three categories: dimensions relating to the economic and political environment, dimensions relating to the socio-cultural environment, and dimensions relating to the internal work culture. A listing of the dimensions on which the two clusters differ is presented in Table 1.1.

Economic and political environment

The economic–technological and the political–legal environments with which organizations interact can be characterized in terms of two critical factors suggested by Triandis (1984): (a) the predictability of future environmental events and (b) the difficulty in obtaining resources from the environment. Variations in the environment on these dimensions have a significant impact on overall organizational behaviour as well as on the behaviour of individuals and groups within the organization. As Triandis points out, 'predictability has implications for the difficulty of the environment. Very predictable environments are easier than very unpredictable, and

Table 1.1 Dimensions on which organizations in developed and developing countries differ

Dimensions	Developed countries	Developing countries
A Characterization of economic and political environment		
Predictability of events	Relatively high	Relatively low
Difficulty of obtaining resources from environment	Relatively easy	Relatively difficult
B Characterization of socio-cultural environment		
Uncertainty avoidance	Relatively low	Relatively high
Individualism–collectivism	Relatively high individualism	Relatively low individualism
Power distance	Relatively low	Relatively high
Masculinity–femininity	Relatively high masculinity	Relatively low masculinity
Abstractive–associative	Relatively high abstractive/low associative thinking	Relatively low abstractive/high associative thinking
C Characterization of internal work culture (management values and climate of beliefs and assumptions)		
Descriptive assumptions about human nature		
Causality and control of outcomes	Internal	External
Creative potential	Unlimited	Limited
Malleability	Malleable	Fixed
Time perspective	Future oriented	Past and present oriented
Time units for action	Long term	Short term
Prescriptive assumptions about guiding principles of behaviour within organization		
Task orientation	Proactive	Passive/reactive
Success orientation	Pragmatism	Moralism
People orientation	Collegial/participative	Authoritarian/paternalistic
Environment orientation	Context independent	Context dependent

both very simple and very complex societies live in very predictable environments' (p. 83).

The Western industrialized environment represents a high degree of complexity: a multitude of firms are engaged in producing a vast array of products and services. Their characterization as 'developed' means that the infrastructure is developed, the supply of a trained labour supply is developed, the capital markets are developed, and business–government relations are developed to the point of facilitating commerce or at least not hindering it. Thus the difficulty of obtaining resources is comparatively low and predictability is on average relatively high.

The developing country environment represents complexity of a different kind. Developing countries no longer represent the traditional agrarian society but are on the way to industrialization and modernization. Very often, the developing country environment becomes complex because of the non-availability of resources to meet the high aspirations for development. Thus, complexity is the result not just of what is, but what 'is not'. Organizational means and goals tend to be incongruous and create difficulties for effective management. Furthermore, the developing country environment can be characterized as being on average relatively more unpredictable. The political and legal climates in most developing countries are perceived to be relatively less stable. Very often they also represent certain characteristics of 'loose societies' where 'norms are not well developed', and where lawless corrupt practices are more the rule than an exception. This type of environment also poses problems for obtaining the required economic, technological, and skilled human resources. Thus the challenge facing the manager in a developing country is qualitatively very different from that facing his or her counterpart in the developed world. Hence, managing organizations in a developing country requires some very different approaches and skills in order to be successful.

In response to difficult and unpredictable economic and political environments in developing countries, organizations adopt various coping strategies such as lack of planning for the future with a long-term goal perspective, lack of time management, lack of entrepreneurship and moderate risk taking, and behaviour reflective of a lack of trust 'in the system'. These dysfunctional coping strategies act as barriers to organizational effectiveness. Indigenous management theories need to address this issue.

In the context of development, significant changes in the environment are necessary to make it more predictable and easy. These include the supply of adequate financing, vocational training programmes, technology development, political non-interference, judiciary and executive reforms, etc., and in the realm of organizational behaviour, management training and development, time management, reward system reforms to reinforce appropriate behaviour, etc.

Socio-cultural environment

By differentiating developed and developing countries along cultural lines, one can say that they comprise two distinct cultural groups. To understand better what this means, one must examine what is meant by culture. Most management researchers subscribe to a view of culture which sees it as a set of ideas shared by members of a group. A useful definition of culture from this perspective is provided by the anthropologist Roger Keesing (1974). He describes culture as being an individual's theory of what his fellows know, believe, and mean, his theory of the code being followed, the game being played. Culture is therefore not an individual characteristic but rather denotes a set of common theories of behaviour or mental programmes that are shared by a group of individuals.

To connect culture to management, it is helpful to look to an empirical model of culture developed by Hofstede (1980a) along with a dimension from Glenn and Glenn (1981) suggested by Kedia and Bhagat (1988). These dimensions provide us with a framework for understanding cultural variation in an organizational context.

Hofstede carried out an empirical analysis that resulted in a concise framework of dimensions for differentiating national cultures. Although the framework has some limitations, it is most widely used by researchers and is recognized as a significant landmark in cross-cultural research (Triandis 1982).

Hofstede used a forty-country questionnaire survey of employees of one multinational organization; 116,000 questionnaires were administered in two waves (1968 and 1972). From these data, four dimensions were found to differentiate national cultures: power distance, uncertainty avoidance, individualism (collectivism), and masculinity (femininity). These were described by Hofstede as follows:

- Power distance is 'the extent to which a society accepts the fact that power in institutions and organizations is distributed unequally' (1980b: 45).
- Uncertainty avoidance is 'the extent to which a society feels threatened by uncertain and ambiguous situations by providing career stability, establishing more formal rules, not tolerating deviant ideas and behaviours, and believing in absolute truths and the attainment of expertise' (1980b: 46).
- Individualism 'implies a loosely knit social framework in which people are supposed to take care of themselves and their immediate families only, while collectivism is characterized by a tight social framework in which people distinguish between in-groups and out-groups; they expect their in-group (relatives, clan, organ-

izations) to look after them, and in exchange for that they feel they owe absolute loyalty to it' (1980b: 45).

● Masculinity expresses 'the extent to which the dominant values in society are "masculine" that is, assertiveness, the acquisition of money and things, and not caring for others, the quality of life, or people' (1980b: 46).

The cultural dimensions manifest themselves in organizations in a number of ways. For example, associated with high masculinity is a performance rather than a people orientation. The existence of low uncertainty avoidance implies a willingness to take risks and accept organizational change. An individualist believes that involvement with organizations is calculative, whereas a collectivist believes involvement with organizations has a moral basis. If power distance is low, subordinates consider superiors to be 'people like me' and vice versa.

A fifth dimension, that of abstract versus associative thinking, is also particularly useful in understanding cultural differences between developed and developing countries. This dimension can be summarized as follows: 'In associative cultures, people utilize associations among events that may not have much logical basis, whereas in abstractive cultures, cause–effect relationships or rational Judeo-Christian types of thinking are dominant' (Kedia and Bhagat 1988: 566). Associative and abstractive cultures also tend to differ on the predominant mode of communication and persons' relationship to their context. In associative cultures, the context plays an important role in determining an individual's perceptions, attributions, and behaviours. In contrast, in abstractive cultures these tend to be influenced more by abstract rules and principles applied equally to every situation. In addition, in associative cultures communication tends to be more face to face and is between people who share a large body of historical information from their culture and society. In contrast, in abstractive cultures, communication through technological mechanisms such as the mass media as well as individual electronic media such as telephone and electronic mail tend to be emphasized (Kedia and Bhagat 1988).

Most importantly, we should point out the ways in which culture affects the interaction of individuals. On the one hand, culture *facilitates* certain behaviours. Members of a cultural group share complementary behavioural programmes which regulate their interaction. Associated with these programmes are values and ideology which provide a guide and a meaning to what they are doing. Implicit in this view is the fact that a culture also *inhibits* other behaviours, behaviours which run counter to the values or practices of the culture.

A culture also provides a guide for perception and attribution of others' behaviour. Thus, within a cultural group, certain behaviours will generate a feeling and response that is positive while others will generate a negative feeling and response.

One example which can illustrate these phenomena in an organizational context is the behaviour of 'bypassing', i.e. a subordinate making direct contact with the superior of his boss. In a situation of low power distance, this behaviour would be more likely to occur and would not be viewed very negatively. In a situation of high power distance, this behaviour would be unlikely to occur and, if it did, would be viewed very negatively. Thus, in the latter situation, bypassing behaviour would not only be inhibited, but would in effect be punished, and thus be unlikely to recur.

Work culture within organizations

The preceding discussion on the influences of the external environment and the dimensions of national cultures suggests that peoples' assumptions, beliefs, and values about different aspects of their world are shaped by these environmental forces. Members of an organization in a given environment therefore would share a common set of assumptions, beliefs, and values that in turn would guide their modal pattern of behaviour in the organization. In other words, the external environmental forces shape the internal work culture of an organization.

Analysing culture from a broader perspective, Schein (1985, 1988) has described three levels of culture: basic assumptions and premises; values and ideology; and artifacts and creations. The first level includes such things as the relationship of man to nature, time orientation, beliefs about human nature, the nature of man's relationship to man, and man's concept of space and his place in it. These are usually taken for granted by members of a cultural group and are 'preconscious'. But it is these taken-for-granted assumptions that determine values and ideologies (indicating ideals and goals as well as paths for 'getting there') and the cultural artifacts and creations (such as manifest behaviour, language, technology, and social organization). Schein therefore argues that, in order to understand how organizations work, one needs to understand the internal work culture, particularly the taken-for-granted assumptions of organizational members.

In Table 1.1, part C, we can see the contrast between the developing countries and developed countries on the dimensions of work culture. The various culture-determined assumptions that affect the work behaviour of organizational members can be broadly categorized under two headings: descriptive assumptions about human nature and prescriptive assumptions about guiding principles of human conduct. The two sets of assumptions are different in the sense that the former describes what human beings are like whereas the latter provides normative guidelines for engaging in and judging the appropriateness of behaviour.

The work cultures of organizations in developed and developing countries differ with respect to the assumptions regarding the nature of causation and control over outcomes (pleasant and unpleasant) which one experiences in life. Rotter (1966) suggested that individuals differ in this respect. Some tend to believe that they are responsible for the outcomes, or their behaviour causes and controls the outcomes (internal locus of control). Others tend to believe that the outcomes they experience in life are determined by forces outside themselves (external locus of control). The locus of control beliefs in developing countries tends to be more external, indicating more of a sense of fatalism in the internal work culture.

Another difference in work culture can be traced to the difference in beliefs about human potential and malleability. Within organizations in developing countries, human capabilities are often viewed as more or less fixed with limited potential. Hence career planning and progression with supporting training facilities are extremely limited. In the developed countries, however, organizations emphasize malleability and unlimited creative potential of human resources. Thus the internal work culture in the developing countries is more conducive to the Theory X (carrot and stick) model of management (McGregor 1960), whereas in the developed countries the Theory Y (participative) model is relatively more suitable.

The unpredictable and difficult environment in developing countries has created a time perspective that excludes future orientation and long-term planning (Triandis 1984). In a predictable environment, being future oriented or having a long-term perspective favours planning, whereas in an unpredictable environment a short-term past and present orientation seems more desirable and hence would not favour planning.

With regard to the normative assumptions guiding one's day-to-day behaviour, several interesting differences are noticed. For example, organizations in developed countries value and encourage a proactive stance while dealing with a given task. This reflects high masculinity of the socio-cultural environment and internal locus of control beliefs. In developing countries, however, a passive stance in relation to tasks is judged to be more desirable. Individuals are encouraged to change themselves to meet environmental pressures (or task demands) rather than to bring about changes in the environment (or the task) to meet their own needs (see Rothbaum *et al.*, 1982, for an interesting discussion on the issue of controlling self versus controlling the environment). Organizational members therefore seem to reflect non-assertive and non-aggressive task orientations.

The success in task-related behaviour is often judged by pragmatic considerations in the developed countries. The individualistic achievement orientation of the Western world coupled with high masculinity has encouraged the use of pragmatic norms. In the developing countries, on the other hand, high collectivism and femininity have encouraged the use of moralism based on traditions and religious beliefs as the norm for judging the success of an individual's behaviour. People are judged successful not because of their entrepreneurship or material prosperity, but because of their nurturant and moral stand to serve interpersonal well-being (rather than personal well-being).

The characterization of people orientation in developing country organizations as authoritarian and paternalistic indicates a high power distance, whereas the collegial–participative nature of relationships in developed countries is indicative of a relatively lower power distance. In the superior–subordinate relationship, paternalism and dependence are valued and encouraged in developing countries. The trend is quite the opposite in developed countries. Finally, the behaviour orientation towards the environment reveals context dependence in developing countries. This is indicative of the associative mode of thinking. The context independence of the developed countries reflects an abstractive mode of thinking. Abstract principles, rules, and procedures are considered absolutes and transcend contextual forces in guiding behaviour in the developed country context. In developing countries, such principles are only relative and contextual forces override principles when the two are in conflict.

Indigenous management theories need to address the impact of these cultural factors on individual behaviour in organizations. One assumption implicit in most work in the area of comparative or cross-cultural management, and one shared by the authors, is that the organization is indeed an 'open system' and cultural values from the environment are brought into the work place and have a very strong impact on the organization's work culture.

Future prospects

Two conclusions are apparent from what has been discussed so far. First, organization theories and practices advocated in the Western industrialized world context can have serious limitations when applied to organizations in the developing countries. For instance, most theories of management originating in the developed world make the assumption that individuals will hold the values of relatively low uncertainty avoidance, relatively high individualism, relatively low power distance, relatively high masculinity, and relatively high abstractive thinking (Hofstede 1980b; Jaeger 1986). One example of a management practice which fits with these values of the developed world is management by objectives (MBO). Hofstede (1980b) describes MBO as 'perhaps the single most popular management technique "made in USA"'. He states that MBO presupposes the following underlying value orientations:

(1) that subordinates are sufficiently independent to negotiate meaningfully with the boss (not-too-large power distance);
(2) that both are willing to take risks (weak uncertainty avoidance);
(3) that performance is seen as important by both (high masculinity).

These values are in line with those found in North America, but are clearly at odds with what is often the case in developing countries. As a result, one would expect any attempts at using MBO to be less than successful. In fact, one can imagine a situation where the use of MBO would be clearly dysfunctional, ultimately causing mistrust and suspicion between a superior and his subordinates, the former essentially trying to force the latter to interact in a manner distinctly foreign to the local culture while at the same time not really willing to accept that type of behaviour.

The second conclusion that follows from the discussion of environmental and cultural differences in the developed and developing countries is the need for indigenous theories and techniques to manage organizations in the Third World effectively. Several chapters in this volume attempt to fulfil this need. The chapters address the nature of the work cultures likely to be found in developing countries and possible effective ways of working within them.

An overview

Addressing the issue of indigenous management, the book is organized into three parts. Part I deals with macro-level perspectives analysing different ways in which organizations in developing countries need to respond strategically to their environment. In Chapter Two Khandwalla makes the point that organizational behaviour research has not paid sufficient attention to our understanding of strategic developmental organizations in the developing countries. He argues that, in order to be socially responsive, we need to focus on the study of these organizations, and he provides both a typology and a critical analysis of their characteristics. In Chapter Three Kiggundu discusses the notion of structural adjustment necessary for the organizations in the developing countries to cope successfully with environmental demands. Kiggundu provides a useful framework for both understanding and implementing such structural adjustments. In Chapter Four Jørgensen examines the history and performance of transport and telecommunications firms in East Africa. He proposes measures with which to measure their efficiency and overall performance and then analyses the influence of industry culture and other environmental factors in the performance of these firms. Hardy, in Chapter Five, also takes a historical look at organizational growth and development. She describes the remarkable record of the University of Campinas which managed to thrive in the very turbulent and potentially threatening environment of Brazil in the 1970s and 1980s. In the last chapter in Part I, Rieger and Wong-Rieger present a conceptual analysis of organizational forms from a cultural perspective. They propose a configurational model of organizational types which fit with certain value systems in developed and developing countries. To illustrate these configurations, they describe a field study which examined the presence of these organizational types in the international airline industry.

Part II of the book contains several contributions that specifically identify the limitations of Western techniques for managing organizations in developing countries. In Chapter Seven, Jaeger identifies a set of common American management practices and techniques and analyses their cultural appropriateness to developing countries. He finds that most of these practices imply a value orientation alien to the culture of the Third World. In Chapter Eight, Kiggundu takes an in-depth look at the socio-technical systems approach to organizational analysis and design. Similarly to the analysis in the previous chapter, he finds that many of the values underlying the socio-technical systems approach clash with the situation in developing countries. On the basis of this analysis, Kiggundu makes some suggestions as to how to make the socio-technical systems approach effective in these situations. Zhuang and Whitehill describe the history of management in the People's Republic of China and its key features. In this context, they explain why Western management techniques have not been utilized in China and look to the future of Chinese management. Chapter Ten is an analysis of the inherent value conflict encountered by persons in positions in large organizations in India. Parikh and Garg describe the traditional Indian role and value structure which has its origins in the villages. They then explain the unavoidable value conflict and dysfunctional impact that this causes in large formal organizations. This final chapter examines the value conflicts which have been described in one form or another in the preceding chapters of Part II and describes them from the point of view of the individual whose roots are firmly planted in the culture and society of a developing country.

In Part III, several recent attempts at developing indigenous perspectives at the micro level to influence organizational members' behaviour are discussed. Two major issues in organizational behaviour are addressed: work motivation and organizational leadership. Three chapters are devoted to motivation/performance issues and the remaining chapters are devoted to leadership/supervision issues. In Chapter Eleven Kanungo presents a model of worker motivation which helps us to understand what motivates and de-motivates workers in a developing country context. He also explains how and why many models of motivation from the developed world are inappropriate for the analysis of work motivation in the cultural and economic context of most developing countries. In the next chapter (Chapter Twelve) Srinivas identifies the inadequacy of conventional Western strategies and proposes a set of holistic strategies for worker delineation in developing countries. In Chapter Thirteen, Mendonca and Kanungo deal more specifically with the issue of motivation and performance management in organizations in developing countries. They suggest ways to improve performance management in organizations after analysing the facilitatory and inhibitory effects of cultural variables.

The three remaining chapters in Part III provide three different perspectives on leadership/supervision relevant to developing countries. First, Sinha in Chapter Fourteen describes an effective leadership/supervision model consistent with culture-based expectations of both superiors and subordinates in Indian organizations. Second, Mahapatra in Chapter Fifteen discusses the issue of culture and leadership in tribal communities in India and describes both successful and unsuccessful intervention attempts by government agencies for tribal development. Finally, Woycke in Chapter Sixteen describes the characteristics of leaders responsible for managing political modernization and economic development at a national level. The three chapters taken together provide useful insight into leadership characteristics in traditional tribal, modern organizational, and national political levels.

The final chapter provides a summary statement. It identifies the commonalities in the thinking of various contributors, highlights the unique indigenous management approaches that have been described, and suggests directions for future investigation and development of indigenous management techniques.

References

Adler, N. J. (1986) *International Dimensions of Organizational Behavior*, Boston, MA: Kent Publishing Co.

Glenn, E. S. and Glenn, C. G. (1981) *Man and Mankind: Conflict and Communication Between Cultures*, Norwood, NJ: Ablex.

Hofstede, G. (1980a) *Culture's Consequences: International Differences in Work-related Values*, Beverly Hills, CA: Sage.

Hofstede, G. (1980b) 'Motivation, leadership, and organization: do American theories apply abroad?', *Organizational Dynamics* 9,1: 42–62.

Jaeger, A.M. (1986) 'Organization development and national culture: where's the fit?', *Academy of Management Review* 11, 1: 178–90.

Kanungo, R. N. (1980) *Biculturalism and Management*, Toronto: Butterworths.

Kanungo, R. N. and Wright, R. W. (1983) 'A cross-cultural comparative study of managerial job attitudes', *Journal of International Business Studies*, Fall: 115–29.

Kedia, B. L. and Bhagat, R. S. (1988) 'Cultural constraints on transfer of technology across nations: implications for research in international and comparative management', *Academy of Management Review* 13, 4: 559–71.

Kessing, R. (1974) 'Theories of culture', *Annual Review in Anthropology* 3: 73–97.

Kiggundu, M. N., Jørgensen, J. J., and Hafsi, T. (1983) 'Administrative theory and practice in developing countries: a synthesis', *Administrative Science Quarterly* 28, 1: 66–84.

Lewis, W. A. (1955) *Theory of Economic Growth*, London: Allen & Unwin.

McClelland, D. C. and Winter, D. G. (1969) *Motivating Economic Development*, New York: Free Press.

McGregor, D. (1960) *The Human Side of Enterprise*, New York: McGraw-Hill.

Rothbaum, F. M., Weisz, J. R., and Snyder, S. S. (1982) 'Changing the world and changing self: a two process model of perceived control', *Journal of Personality and Social Psychology* 42: 5–37.

Rotter, J. B. (1966) 'Generalized expectancies for internal versus external control of reinforcement', *Psychological Monographs* 80 (1, whole no. 609).

Schein, E. H. (1985) *Organizational Culture and Leadership*, San Francisco, CA: Jossey-Bass.

Schein, E. H. (1988) 'Innovative cultures and adaptive organizations', Working Paper, Sloan School of Management, Massachusetts Institute of Technology, Cambridge, MA.

Sinha, D. and Kao, H. S. R. (1988) 'Introduction: value-development congruence', in D. Sinha and H. S. R. Kao (eds) *Social Values and Development: Asian Perspectives*, New Delhi: Sage.

Triandis, H. C. (1982) 'Review of culture's consequences: international differences in work-related values', *Human Organization* 41, 86–90.

Triandis, H. C. (1984) 'Toward a psychological theory of economic growth', *International Journal of Psychology* 19, 79–95.

Weber, M. (1958) *The Religions of India: The Sociology of Hinduism and Buddhism*, Glencoe, IL: Free Press.

Part one

Managing organizations in a developing country environment: macro-level perspectives

Chapter two

Strategic developmental organizations: some behavioural properties

Pradip N. Khandwalla

Introduction

The field of organizational behaviour (OB) in India, and possibly in the Third World as a whole, has not been notably socially responsive. Indian OB research abounds in replications of Western research (Padaki 1987), notably of the two-factor theory (Herzberg 1966), hierarchy of needs (Maslow 1954), need satisfaction models (Porter and Lawler 1968), achievement motivation (McClelland 1961), motivational climate (Litwin and Stringer 1968), authoritarian-participative leadership (Likert 1961), etc. There has been far less emphasis on how such staples of Third World reality as poverty, scarcity, social stratification, kinship orientation, traditionalism, political interference, corruption, and state regulation affect micro-OB and macro-OB behaviour (Khandwalla 1987a). The vast social change and development experiments initiated by the government as well as by private institutions and enterprises have also, by and large, escaped the attention of OB professionals. In particular, there has been neglect of the organizational dynamics of a socially highly significant organizational type, the strategic developmental organization, that is the centre-piece of national developmental strategies in the Third World.

State-supported socio-economic development has been a notable feature of many Third World mixed economies. In India, for instance, the volume of government investment, adjusted for inflation, has risen from around US$5 billion a year in the 1950s to around US$ 30 billion a year in the late 1980s (there has also been a corresponding growth in private sector investment). The bulk of this investment in nation-building industrialization, infrastructure development, and development of human resources has been channelled through a host of organizations specially set up by, or funded by, the state. These include federal as well as state-level planning agencies, industrial capital lending banks, various governmental agencies, a large number of state-owned enterprises, and a variety of cooperative societies, research and educational institutions, voluntary organizations, etc. These are called strategic developmental organizations because of their strategic long-term significance for such dimensions of socio-economic development as faster economic growth, greater self-reliance for the economy, greater social equity, enlargement of opportunities to citizens for personal growth, etc. As an example of the mushrooming of these developmental organizations, federal-government-owned enterprises increased in India from 5 to 219 between 1951 and 1981 (Bureau of Public Enterprises 1981), and countries such as Mexico, Brazil, Tanzania, Pakistan, and Peru have also recorded comparable increases (Pillai 1986).

The purpose of this chapter is to identify some distinctive characteristics of strategic developmental organizations, to indicate a working typology of these organizations, and to develop several ideas concerning their strategic and operating behaviour.

The strategic developmental organization

The strategic developmental organization may be defined as an organization that is given, or assumes on its own, the responsibility for the growth and development of the domain in which it operates (Khandwalla 1988–9). This responsibility is over and above any commitments its management may have for the organization's own growth, profitability, image, etc. Thus, the Planning Commission in India has the mandate of speeding up the growth rate of the Indian economy; the Industrial Development Bank of India has the responsibility for channelling an ever larger volume of resources into corporate investment; the federal Indian Ministry of Human Resource Development has the mandate to improve the health and longevity of the people, their literacy, and their skills. Similarly, there are a number of institutions in the private sector that have adopted some developmental mission or other. These include apex societies for cooperative work such as the National Dairy Development Board; various institutes of science, technology, and management; research institutions; a number of development-oriented voluntary organizations; and even private corporations that adopt such goals as the development of backward areas, import substitution, technology development, or pioneering into the country entirely new lines of products, and thereby founding new industries.

Not all government agencies, public or private sector corporations, cooperatives, voluntary organizations, or educational institutions, etc. are strategic (or equally strategic). Only those of the above that have or adopt responsibility for the growth and development of the domains they operate in would be called strategic developmental organizations. Thus, government agencies and ministries concerned primarily with law and order, national security, revenue collection, or other routine administrative matters would not be considered strategic; nor would academic institutions, cooperative societies, or corporations that pursue primarily the interests of either their owners or members or clients. The existence of a strong domain-related public purpose, and that, too, concerning the future growth and development of the particular domain served or operated in, is the essence of the strategic developmental organization considered in this chapter.

There have been numerous studies of Third World government, development and other agencies (Sajo 1970; Hopper 1972; Torczyner 1972; Mathur and Bhattacharya 1975; Abramson 1978; Pai Panandikar and Kshirsagar 1978; Salinas 1978; Bagadion and Korten 1980; Guess 1982; Paul 1982; HRD Unit 1984; Ickis *et al.* 1986; Srivastava 1986), government-owned corporations (V.V. Bhatt 1978; Chaudhuri and Khandwalla 1983; Khandwalla 1986; Ramamurti 1986; Shiva Ramu 1986), cooperative societies (Baviskar 1980; Balaji 1985; Phansalkar and Srinivasan 1985; Singh *et al.* 1985), voluntary organizations (Natarajan 1977; Chattopadhyay and Pareek 1984; Subramanian 1984; D'Souza 1988), academic institutions (Pareek and Rao 1970; Ramos 1971; Ganesh 1980; Devadoss and Muth 1984), community development programmes and organizations (De Sousa 1979; Tandon and Brown 1981; Soares 1984), etc. However, there are virtually no reported studies of strategic developmental organizations as a genre. Given the importance of these organizations in Third World development, theory construction and research pertaining to them are critically needed.

Types of strategic developmental organizations

There are at least three types of strategic developmental organizations (Khandwalla 1988–9). One type is the sectorally apex developmental organization. This has coordinative and regulatory responsibilities *vis-à-vis* the sector served. There are several Indian examples of this type, with analogues throughout the Third World. The Planning Commission is one example. Currently, with the help of fifty-odd sectoral task forces, it is in the process of finalizing the next 5-year socio-economic development plan that may cost around US$500 billion, aiming at an overall growth rate of 6 per cent per annum, with specific targets in a great variety of sectors. The Reserve

Bank of India which regulates the entire banking system for controlling inflation, setting priorities between different sectors for the supply of credit, etc. is another example. The Reserve Bank of India is not just one more central bank: it has a strong developmental focus. For instance, it gives priority to agricultural finance, small-scale industries, industries in backward areas, priority industries, etc. Several central government and state government ministries, notably the ministries of finance, industry, energy, transportation, human resource development, etc., are also apex developmental organizations in their respective sectors. Their aims are not just administrative. They are the engines of regulated growth in their respective spheres, initiating development programmes, disbursing funds to various private and public agencies involved in development, monitoring performance, taking corrective action, etc. Although a variety of Indian organizations have been studied (Sinha 1981; Ganesh and Rangarajan 1983; Khandwalla 1987a), there is virtually no research available on these critically important apex strategic developmental organizations.

Another category of strategic developmental organizations is the one that spearheads developmental effort in a particular sector without playing an apex monitoring, supervisory, or coordinative role. The spearhead developmental organizations usually have somewhat narrower, more specific missions; they are often partially autonomous, even when they are government-owned or controlled; and they also often encounter competition. The most common kind of spearhead strategic developmental organization is the public enterprise. It is usually created by Third World governments to assume 'commanding heights' in a particular industry or sector, force the pace of development in it, strive for import substitution, and raise the growth rate of output in the industry. The public enterprise is a vital element of the industrialization strategy of Third World countries. In India public enterprises account for the bulk of output of such basic and strategic industries as heavy machinery, metals (including steel), oil, coal, power, petrochemicals, and basic and heavy chemicals (Bureau of Public Enterprises 1985).

In addition to public enterprises, there are many other semi-autonomous spearhead strategic developmental organizations. For instance, educational institutions have been created to train scarce technological and managerial manpower needed for speeding up industrialization. Examples in India are the institutes of technology and the institutes of management. Specialized financial institutions have been set up to increase the flow of financial resources for industrial and agricultural investment (Indian examples are several term lending institutions, nationalized banks, and the National Bank for

Agricultural and Rural Development). Many research institutions and laboratories have been set up to increase research and development in key sectors, such as, in India, the national physical laboratories, industry-specific research organizations, etc. Large development programmes (Paul 1982) for increasing milk supply through cooperativization, for example, or for slowing population growth through family planning or for increasing adult literacy or for raising the rural masses from dire poverty by making available to them means for generating additional income, etc. are also spearhead organizations.

In India, at least, there has been far more research on spearhead strategic organizations than on apex strategic organizations. Some useful work has been reported on strategic public enterprises (V. V. Bhatt 1978; Chaudhuri and Khandwalla 1983; Kulkarni *et al.* 1983; Khandwalla 1986; Ramamurti 1986; Shiva Ramu 1986), on strategic academic/training/research institutions (Chowdhry 1968; Chowdhry and Sarabhai 1968; Chowdhry *et al.* 1972; Gangjee 1978; Ganesh 1980; Chaudhuri 1986), and on development projects and programmes (Moulik 1980; Khanna and Subramanian 1982; Paul 1982; Murthy 1986; Srivastava 1986).

Finally there is a potpourri of non-official developmental organizations that range across private enterprises, cooperative societies, voluntary organizations, action groups, associations, lobbies, etc. For convenience they may be called catalytic strategic developmental organizations. They are strategic regionally more often than at the national level and they are development oriented by choice rather than by government directive. Lacking in large resources and official authority, they usually seek to catalyse development through networking, persuasion, and beneficiary participation in their decision making. In India, some of the development-minded private business groups such as the Lalbhais, the Mafatlals, etc. have sought to catalyse rural development through setting up rural development foundations. Other enterprises such as those belonging to the Tata Group have sought to catalyse industrial development by moving into the 'core' sector of the economy, i.e. into those relatively 'high-tech' industries where returns are not assured, the gestation period of the investment is long, the technology and markets are relatively unfamiliar, and the products are imported or in short supply. While many cooperative societies are not social development oriented, some are (Baviskar 1980; Phansalkar and Srinivasan 1985). A number of voluntary organizations have been playing social change agent roles (Natarajan 1977; Subramanian 1984; D'Souza 1988). Several associations, especially of private sector industry, seek to play developmental roles by undertaking policy studies to advise the government in the formulation of development-oriented public policy.

Despite the enormous variety in the types of organizations that could be labelled strategic developmental, they share some common distinguishing characteristics (Khandwalla 1988–9). First, they have or assume a developmental mission *vis-à-vis* the sector in which they operate. The concern for profitability or financial viability tends to be secondary. Second, they tend to have moderate to high resource dependence on the government, at least in the Third World where private funds for altruistic social development are rather scarce. This resource dependence (Pfeffer and Salancik 1978) implies substantial influence of the government on the operations of these organizations. Since the operating culture of the government tends to be bureaucratic (Mathur and Bhattacharya 1975; HRD Unit 1984), the government monitors of these organizations tend to transmit bureaucratic norms and practices to the dependent organizations. Third, their youth, their developmental mission, and their change agent role usually imply that their tasks are unfamiliar, non-routine, and risk laden. This combination of characteristics helps them attract scarce national (and even international) resources. But it also tends to institutionalize conflicting operating styles: bureaucratic conformity to government rules and regulations because of resource dependence on the government, as well as an entrepreneurial (Mintzberg 1973) and organic (Burns and Stalker 1961) mode of management to cope with daunting missions and operating uncertainty. These contrary pulls create a fascinating genre bedevilled by a sort of complexity not normally encountered in Western corporate organizations. The strategic and operating behaviour of these organizations therefore differs, in some respects strikingly, from that of Western corporate organizations.

Strategic behaviour of strategic developmental organizations

Western strategic management has revolved mostly around diversification and vertical integration (Egelhoff 1982; Daniels *et al.* 1984; Palepu 1985), and competitive product, niche, and cost-advantage strategies (Hall 1980; Porter 1980; Scherer 1980). While appropriate to corporate organizations, these strategic options are far less relevant to Third World strategic developmental organizations. Other strategic elements, discussed below, seem to be far more relevant to the latter.

Domain compliance

Strategic developmental organizations in the Third World tend to pursue national priorities such as a greater output of essential goods and services, import substitution and greater national self-reliance, greater equity, etc. Since they are expected to play a pace-setter role, obtaining the compliance of the domain served to national priorities becomes an important goal of strategic developmental organizations. This is a particular concern of apex strategic organizations. The Indian Planning Commission for example develops national as well as sectoral growth targets and monitors their achievement by the various ministries, governmental agencies, state governments, etc. Since target setting is in part a gaming exercise, one commonplace strategy pursued by apex organizations appears to be to pitch high targets in the hope that actual achievement may be close to the secret real targets. Another strategy appears to be to reward the good performers through speedier sanctions and more munificent allocation of resources for their projects. Often domain compliance is sought through the participation of representatives of the domain, such as by sponsoring conferences of sub-strategic organizations to evolve criteria for evaluating the latter's performance, co-opting prominent beneficiary organizations onto the governing boards of strategic developmental organizations, etc. Deputing representatives of the strategic organization onto the governing boards of sub-strategic organizations, developing a cadre of professional managers for the sector through a central training institute set up by the strategic organization, organizing periodic performance reviews of sub-strategic organizations by desk officers of the strategic organization, etc. are other means of control commonly used by strategic developmental organizations. In India, these options are known to be employed by the government monitors of public enterprises (Khandwalla 1986). The domain compliance alternatives may be usefully contrasted with the price leadership, collusion, etc. means employed by dominant corporations for securing compliance of rivals (Scherer 1980).

Learning strategy

Strategic developmental organizations often operate in relatively unfamiliar terrains. They therefore face a real danger of initiating long-term projects or actions that are ill conceived in hindsight. Because of the power over domain of these organizations (especially the power of the apex and spearhead ones), these ill-conceived actions may result in vast waste of resources or suffering. The Indian public sector abounds in stories of expensive projects that turned out to be duds (Khandwalla 1986; Ramamurti 1986). Unfamiliarity with technology and the needs of the clientele can aggravate flawed initial choices. Studies of successful Third World public programmes and public sector enterprises (Paul 1982; Khandwalla 1986) indicate that they tend to pursue vigorous learning strategies, e.g. starting small and growing fast only after mastering technological and marketing intricacies; starting with only one goal and only later adding other goals; starting with one product and diversifying only later; starting with a pilot project and only later scaling up; entering in a small way the most difficult market segment and then going in a big way into the easier markets (Patil 1982); phasing expansions, etc. Another learning strategy commonly followed is to team up with one or more enterprises or institutions in the developed countries for technology transfer. Thus, in the 1950s HMT, an Indian public enterprise, teamed up with Oerlikon of Switzerland to transfer machine tool technology to India (Patil 1982); BHEL, another public enterprise, later teamed up with Siemens; and two Indian management institutes secured management technology from Harvard and Massachusetts Institute of Technology.

Innovation diffusion

Given the responsibility for the growth and development of the domain, the strategic organization is particularly concerned that an innovation or an improved practice is diffused throughout the domain served as quickly as possible. This is in sharp contrast with the corporate practice of protecting an innovation by defensive patenting or other means (Scherer 1980). The strategic organization tries to diffuse innovation by publicizing it, by deputing teams to organizations served to try and institutionalize it in them (Gangjee 1978), by training change agents working in these institutions (Hill *et al.* 1973); by codifying 'good' management practices in a sector in the form of guidelines (BPE and BHEL 1976), etc.

Autonomy-seeking strategy

Many strategic developmental organizations seek respite from bureaucratic pressures and political pressures in order to pursue their missions more forcefully. Their bureaucratic and political masters also seem to have begun to realize that operating autonomy to pursue public policy objectives is essential for mission accomplishment. Thus, a number of strategic options have begun to emerge for increasing their autonomy without decreasing their accountability for mission accomplishment. One idea is the holding company device, in which several strategic developmental organizations report to a holding company (or equivalent) rather than directly to the government (Murthy and Nath 1988). In this way direct political and bureaucratic interference may be minimized. A second idea is the memorandum of understanding device (Sreedhar Sharma 1982) under which the government and the strategic developmental organization sign a formal document setting forth their respective obligations towards one another. A third idea is to bring the culture of the well-managed strategic developmental organization into the governmental bureaucracy, by seconding its chief executive to a monitoring role in the government (Khandwalla 1986). Several Indian public enterprises have learnt to increase their autonomy by building up their credibility with government monitors. They seek this by involving government monitors in their problems, by keeping them regularly posted on their actions, by networking with important officials and politicians within the government structure, and by showing good performance *vis-à-vis* strategic goals of the government (Khandwalla 1986). Some have sought to decrease their financial dependence on the government by resorting to national and even international capital markets or funding agencies.

Domain development strategy

Since domain development (rather than market exploitation) is a major objective of strategic developmental organizations, they need to develop a number of options for this. One option is networking with a number of institutions in the domain in order to develop a domain development strategy (Paul 1982; Ganesh and Joshi 1985). As an example, Indian term lending institutions, mostly government owned, have created an inter-institutional meeting forum to coordinate their activities with a view to channelling capital to the private manufacturing sector. Public enterprises in India have created an institution called the Standing Committee for Public Enterprises (SCOPE) for sharing problems and concerns.

A second option is one of institution building, i.e. of helping existing sub-strategic organizations with training, resources, etc. to build up their capacity for developmental action (Gangjee 1978; Ganesh 1980). As an example, the Indian Institute of Management at Ahmedabad has helped a number of other MBA programmes in India and other Third World countries to get going; the Ahmedabad Textile Industry's Research Association (Gangjee 1978) conducts a variety of technical and operations-related studies in textile mills with a view to improving their efficiency, productivity, etc.

A third option is for strategic developmental organizations to start one or more special purpose organizations, each playing a specialized role in the overall developmental strategy for the sector. For example, the Industrial Development Bank of India, the apex term lending institution in India, has helped set up the Entrepreneurial Development Institute for training entrepreneurs and entrepreneurship trainers; in association with governments of various Indian states, it has also formed state-level subsidiaries for channelling term finance to small- and medium-scale enterprises. Major nationalized Indian banks have collaborated in setting up the National Institute of Bank Management to train bankers and conduct banking-related research. Several large Indian public enterprises such as BHEL and the State Bank of India have set up staff colleges for training purposes. HMT, a well-known Indian public enterprise, took the lead in the setting up of the Central Machine Tool Research Institute. The Behavioural Research Centre has been setting up village cooperatives of low caste persons in Gujarat to increase their self-reliance; the National Dairy Development Board has been playing a major role in setting up 'Anand pattern' cooperative dairies in other parts of India. A number of voluntary organizations such as the Self-employed Women's Association and Tilonia (Roy 1986–7) have assisted in their replication in other parts of India.

These domain development strategies may be usefully contrasted with the 'secure market domination to cream the market' strategies pursued by corporate organizations (Porter 1980).

General management mode of strategic developmental organizations

The distinctive peculiarity of many strategic developmental organizations, particularly the apex and spearhead ones, is that they have to practise apparently contradictory modes of management. As they are embedded in bureaucratic governmental systems or dependent upon them, they are forced to be conservative and mechanistic. As mission-charged ventures in often unfamiliar terrain they have to be entrepreneurial and organic. As instruments for achieving national priorities they are often subject to pressures from the government to adopt high targets. This in turn often leads to participative posturing but authoritarian goal setting at lower management levels.

The State Bank of India, a spearhead bank formed by nationalizing the privately owned Imperial Bank of India in the 1950s, illustrates these contrary pulls. The State Bank's mission was to break the stranglehold of big business houses on Indian banks and make credit available to smaller industrialists and businessmen and to break the stranglehold of money-lenders in the Indian countryside and make banking facilities available to millions of farmers and rural craftsmen. The State Bank today is a vast organization of some 10,000 branches and 280,000 employees (Sarkar 1988). By one count the bank's operations are subject to 20,000 externally or internally mandated regulations and the bank must abide by the guidelines, about how much credit to give at what interest rates to which sectors, that are issued from time to time by the Reserve Bank of India and the Indian Ministry of Finance to which it administratively reports. Operating targets for the year are evolved in meetings between executives and their subordinates; but, reportedly, the process is more authoritarian than participative, with the targets being announced by the boss rather than evolved after a full and frank discussion. The bank is a huge bureaucracy, with many levels and specialist departments, and yet it is widely considered to be one of the more dynamic, better managed, and innovative of Indian banks. For instance, it has ventured into merchant banking and leasing, mutual fund, housing finance, export promotion, and dissemination of technology-related information; it has currently a very high Moody's rating; its reorganization in the 1970s was highly participative and effective (Goyal 1982); from 500 offices in 1955 the number has grown to 8,000 in 1987 (Sarkar 1988); it has achieved a spectacular penetration of the Indian rural areas; and it has set up a large number of branches overseas.

How do these organizations manage to institutionalize opposing practices? One way is to oscillate between opposing stances over a period of time – turn conservative for a while if too many new initiatives have been taken, and vice versa; turn bureaucratic if too much looseness is felt in structure and processes, and vice versa. Another way is to present a different face for each significant stakeholder. For instance, appear to abide by rules and regulations to government monitors; appear to be dynamic to politicians and social pressure groups that want the organization to respond to social needs; appear participative in internal pronouncements; turn authoritarian when targets have to be achieved, etc. A third strategy seems to be to develop distinctive managerial structures to play different modes of management. For example, the personnel chief plays the participation and human resource development card; the operations chief plays the hit-targets-at-any-cost card; the corporate planning chief plays the entrepreneurial card; the organization and methods chief, the internal auditor, and the financial controller play the efficiency, systems, standardization card. Frequent reorganization is another way that glaring internal contradictions are partially straightened out (for the time being) (e.g. Goyal 1982). In-house training is a major device for institutionalizing the meet-all-contingencies Janus-faced culture. What emerges is a schizoid organization that meets at least minimally the contrary pressures upon it. It is often impressive in its numerical achievements but poor in the quality of its work and deficient in its true social impact. Many spearhead Indian industrial finance corporations, set up to provide industrial capital to small- and medium-scale units in different Indian states, have done an impressive job in terms of the number of firms funded, but their portfolios are full of irrecoverable loans, and in the case of several of these corporations the true bad and doubtful debts reportedly exceed by several times the paid-up capital and reserves. A strength of the schizoid organization is that multiple operating cultures create variegated experiences, thereby enriching the repertory of action alternatives available to management. This enhances the coping capability and the survivability of the organization.

Research on the way successful Third World public enterprises, development programmes, and academic institutions are managed (Ganesh 1980; Paul 1982; K. S. Bhatt 1985; Khandwalla 1986; Ramamurti 1986) and on the way sick strategic organizations are revived (A. Bhatt 1984; Khandwalla 1986, 1988b) indicates that a participatory but proactive form of professional management at the top is highly suitable for strategic developmental organizations (Khandwalla 1987b). The key elements of this sort of management are structures for workers' as well as managers' participation in decision making (through such devices as works councils and performance review meetings of departmental heads) and their effective use; calculated risk taking; an accent on rapid, often opportunistic, organizational growth; emphasis on innovation, experimentation, and pioneering; and the setting up of tailor-made 'professional' planning, financial control, personnel, and operations management systems. It appears that these intrinsically schizoid organizations, tossing between the Scylla of bureaucracy and the Charybdis of mission-oriented development, need to resort to further anomalies to perform well, namely a combination of creative entrepreneurship and hard-nosed systems-oriented professional management. The trick is apparently to convert the pressure for bureaucratic satisficing on conflicting goals by minimum acceptable performance on each into an adaptive sort of professional systems-oriented management. The latter seeks optimization across several conflicting objectives and generates the slack to pursue conflicting objectives through entrepreneurship. Where the management fails to make this sort of creative response to the intrinsic contradictions in the working of strategic developmental organizations, the performance tends to be poor.

Organizational behaviour issues in strategic developmental organizations

The resource dependence of strategic developmental organizations on the government and governmental agencies and their developmental missions generate some interesting OB issues (Khandwalla 1988–9). Resource dependence on the government predisposes them to a bureaucratic mode of functioning which in turn breeds rigidity, alienation, inter-departmental conflicts, etc. (Crozier 1964). The application of government pay norms makes it difficult for strategic developmental organizations to get the best professional managers in the market (Vathsala and Kumar 1979). On the other hand, their missionary goals potentially can attract committed managers, technologists, and other staff, and the superordination of these goals potentially can foster collaboration (Sherif 1963). The apex and the spearhead strategic developmental organizations especially function as mission-oriented bureaucracies. Their schizoid character may well nurture schizoid personality traits in their staff members. An added complication in pluralistic societies like India is the commonplace insistence on representation of different regions, religious groups, and economic classes on the staff, either on the basis of explicit quotas or on the basis of unwritten norms. This tends to create a checkerboard of small cliques and impedes collaboration and team work.

A special kind of leadership is needed in strategic developmental organizations to overcome the intrapersonal paralysis caused by contrary orientations and the interpersonal barriers caused by sub-cultural cliques. In addition to the usual task-oriented and people-oriented leadership recommended by Western human relations experts (Blake and Mouton 1964; Bowers and Seashore 1966), the leader must accentuate superordinate goals including patriotism to overcome his subordinates' intrapersonal contradictions and interpersonal blocks. Credible and persistent articulation of the organization's (or department's) mission, vision of excellence, and core values (Burns 1978; Peters and Waterman 1982; Bennis and Nanus 1985) is needed for this purpose. This has to be supplemented by an enormous communications effort involving communications with both external and internal stakeholders. As an example, during a recent attempt at turning SAIL (India's massive public sector steel giant with a staff of 250,000) around, the new chief executive Mr Krishnamurthy spent the first four or five months talking to an estimated 25,000 officials, managers, union leaders, workers, etc. (Khandwalla 1988). A third feature of leadership not commonly encountered in Western prescriptions is the need for the leader to build up credibility. Strategic developmental organizations, partly because of their bureaucratic anchors and partly because of their daunting tasks, tend to fail (40 per cent of India's public sector enterprises are loss making (Khandwalla 1988)). Thus leaders are often held in some scorn by their followers. Turnaround research on public sector enterprises (Khandwalla 1986) indicates that leaders that are able to generate a stream of modest but quick payoff actions tend to earn credibility. This calls for opportunism and dynamic action. Thus the model of top management leadership that seems relevant for strategic developmental organizations seems to differ in significant respects from popular Western models such as the human relations one (Likert 1961; Bowers and Seashore 1966), the Fiedler model (1971), or the contingency model of Vroom (Vroom and Yetton 1973).

Organizational leaders have also to contend with another fact of life. Strategic developmental organizations in the Third World tend to be staffed by 'Westernized' managers and technocrats in the higher echelons and by people from the ranks of the far more traditional lower middle class and the poor in the lower non-managerial echelons. These organizations also tend to have as their 'clients' the poor and the disadvantaged. The gulf in identities and world views between the organizational rank on the one hand and the organizational file and the organizational clientele on the other tends to be vast. Indian studies of the psychology of the poor suggest that they tend to have short-time orientation, a low achievement ethic, a high distrust of others, fatalism, low capacity to collaborate for common interests, high dependence on the powerful, etc. (Moulik 1981). Industrial relations problems tend to be commonplace in these organizations, as do adversarial relations between the organization and its intended beneficiaries. A result is frequent time and cost overruns of development projects, under-achievement of targeted benefits, and benefits not reaching the target clientele but instead being pre-empted by the better off (A. Bhatt 1984; Subramanian 1986). A nurturant, paternalistic but task-oriented leadership has been suggested as a necessary transitional form to a participative leadership in Third World societies (Sinha 1984; Ahiauzu 1989). Such a leadership style could also be used for attracting the poor among the intended beneficiaries of these organizations.

Another idea is for the organizational élites to drop their 'Western' alien manners and mores and go native, i.e. adopt indigenous mores without, of course, giving up developmental objectives (Roy 1986–7). A variant is to search for vital indigenous institutions of conflict resolution, community participation, psycho-social support in times of grief, celebration, etc. and to institutionalize them after suitable modifications in strategic developmental organizations (Garg and Parikh 1986–7). A third variant is for the organizational élites to draw upon indigenous spiritual orientations and to spiritualize the staff, especially the decision makers, so that their purity and nobility can transform the character of human relations within the organization (Chakraborty 1985).

Concluding comments

Strategic developmental organizations are amongst the most important in the Third World. They are intended to be megaton weapons in the battle against poverty, backwardness, and inequity. They often fail to perform well because of their inherent contradictions – their stifling bureaucratic anchorages versus their missionary transformational social objectives. In their global importance for human growth they far outrank multinational corporations. Yet they have been ignored by Western OB scholars and neglected by Third World OB scholars. They offer exceptional sites for socially relevant OB research, and indeed, given their complexity and distinctiveness, especially *vis-à-vis* the Western corporate organization, they also offer rich sites for research that can lead to paradigm shifts in OB. In this chapter some of their more interesting and distinctive strategic and operational behaviours, as well as some of their behavioural problems and leadership implications, have been briefly outlined. Several hypotheses on mission performance by strategic developmental organizations have already been developed (Khandwalla 1988–9); much more theoretical work needs to be done *vis-à-vis* their birth and death rates (Starbuck and Nystrom 1981), their life cycles (Cameron and Whetten 1981), their domain compliance, learning, innovation diffusion, domain development, and autonomy-seeking strategies, their modes of management, their structures, and their leadership, conflict resolution, internal change, and motivational modes. Research on strategic developmental organizations could become a treasure trove for all of OB.

References

Abramson, R. (1978) *An Integrated Approach to Organization Development and Performance Improvement*, West Hartford, CT: Kumarian.

Ahiauzu, A. (1989) 'Theory A system of work organization for the modern African workplace', *International Studies of Management and Organization*, 19(1): 6–27.

Bagadion, B. and Korten, F. F. (1980) 'Developing viable irrigators' associations: lessons from small scale irrigation in the Philippines', *Agricultural Administration* 7: 273–87.

Balaji, C. (1985) 'Organizational commitment and satisfaction of professionals and non-professionals in cooperatives', *Vikalpa* 10: 35–42.

Baviskar, B. (1980) *The Politics of Development: Sugar Cooperatives in Maharashtra*, Delhi: Oxford University Press.

Bennis, W. and Nanus, B. (1985) *Leaders: The Strategies for Taking Charge*, New York: Harper.

Bhatt, A. (1984) 'Creation out of calamity: the case of a training institution', *Vikalpa* 9, 4: 374–8.

Bhatt, K. S. (1985) Research report on corporate planning in public enterprises, Hyderabad: Institute of Public Enterprises (mimeo).

Bhatt, V. V. (1978) 'Decision making in the public sector: a case study of Swaraj Tractors', DFD study no. 48, PPFDDED, World Bank, Washington, DC.

Blake, R. and Mouton, J. (1964) *The Managerial Grid*, Houston, TX: Gulf Publishing.

Bowers, D. and Seashore, S. (1966) 'Predicting organizational effectiveness with a four-factor theory of leadership', *Administrative Science Quarterly* 11, 2: 238–63.

BPE and BHEL (1976) *Government Policy for the Management of Public Enterprises*, New Delhi: Government of India, Ministry of Finance, BPE, and BHEL.

Bureau of Public Enterprises (1981, 1985) *Public Enterprises Survey*, vol. 1, New Delhi: BPE, Ministry of Finance, Government of India.

Burns, J. (1978) *Leadership*, New York: Harper.

Burns, T. and Stalker, G. M. (1961) *The Management of Innovation*, London: Tavistock.

Cameron, K. and Whetten, D. (1981) 'Perceptions of organizational effectiveness over organizational life cycles', *Administrative Science Quarterly* 26: 525–44.

Chakraborty, S. K. (1985) *Human Responses in Organizations: Towards the Indian Ethos*, Calcutta: Vivekananda Nidhi.

Chattopadhyay, S. and Pareek, U. (1984) 'Organization development in a voluntary organization', *International Studies of Management and Organization* 14: 46–85.

Chaudhuri, S. C. (1986) 'Technological innovation in a research laboratory in India: a case study', *Research Policy* 15: 89–103.

Chaudhuri, S. C. and Khandwalla, P. N. (1983) 'Management of diversification in public enterprises', *Institute of Public Enterprises Journal* 6: 41–66.

Chowdhry, K. (1968) 'Institution building and social change: the case of ATIRA', *Indian Journal of Public Administration* 14, 4: 943–61.

Chowdhry, K. and Sarabhai, V. (1968) 'Organization for development task: Atomic Energy Commission of India', *Indian Journal of Public Administration* 14, 1: 1–22.

Chowdhry, K., Gaikwad, V., and Bhattacharya, S. (1972) *An Organization*

Study of the Indian Council of Agricultural Research, Ahmedabad: IIMA.

Crozier, M. (1964) *The Bureaucratic Phenomenon*, Chicago, IL: University of Chicago Press.

Daniels, J. D., Pitts, R.A., and Tretter, M.J. (1984) 'Strategy and structure of U.S. multinationals: an exploratory study', *Academy of Management Journal* 27, 2: 292–307.

De Sousa, P. (1979) 'IRD and the agent of change', *Indian Journal of Social Work* 39: 425–30.

Devadoss, M. and Muth, R. (1984) 'Power, involvement and organizational effectiveness in higher education', *Higher Education* 13, 4: 379–91.

D'Souza, K. C. (1988) 'Organizations as agents of social change: policy orientation and organizational design', unpublished doctoral dissertation, IIMA, Ahmedabad.

Egelhoff, W. G. (1982) 'Strategy and structure in multinational corporations: an information processing approach', *Administrative Science Quarterly* 27: 435–58.

Fiedler, F. (1971) 'Validation and extension of the contingency model of leadership effectiveness: a review of empirical findings', *Psychological Bulletin* 76, 2: 128–48.

Ganesh, S. R. (1980) 'Performance of management education institutions: an Indian sampler', *Higher Education* 9: 239–53.

Ganesh, S. R. and Joshi, P. (1985) 'Institution building: lessons from Vikram Sarabhai's leadership', *Vikalpa* 10, 4: 399–413.

Ganesh, S. and Rangarajan, T. (1983) 'Research review: organization behaviour research in India: a critique of the last decade', *Organization Studies* 4, 3: 357–74.

Gangjee, Z. (1978) 'The process of technology transfer in the Ahmedabad textile industry', unpublished doctoral dissertation, IIMA, Ahmedabad.

Garg, P. and Parikh, I. (1986–7) 'Values, design and development of strategic organizations', presented at the International Conference on Organizational and Behavioural Perspectives on Social Development, IIMA, Ahmedabad, 29 December 1986 to 2 January 1987.

Goyal, R. (1982) 'Managing change in a large organization', in S. Chattopadhyay and U. Pareek (eds) *Managing Organizational Change*, New Delhi: Oxford and IBH.

Guess, G. M. (1982) 'Institution-building for development forestry in Latin America', *Public Administration and Development* 2: 309–24.

Hall, W. K. (1980) 'Survival strategies in a hostile environment', *Harvard Business Review*, September/October: 75–85.

Herzberg, F. (1966) *Work and the Nature of Man*, New York: World.

Hill, T., Haynes, W., and Baumgartel, H. (1973) *Institution Building in India: A Study of International Collaboration in Management Education*, Boston, MA: Division of Research, Harvard Graduate School of Business Administration.

Hopper, J. R. (1972) 'Management training in developing countries: a sectoral approach', *Training and Development Journal* 26, 6–10.

HRD Unit (1984) 'Towards organization development in government: an empirical study', *International Studies of Management and Organization* 14, 2–3: 30–45.

Ickis, J., de Jesus, E., and Maru, R. (eds) (1986) *Beyond Bureaucracy: Strategic Management of Social Development*, West Hartford, CT: Kumarian.

Khandwalla, P. N. (1986) 'Performance determinants of public enterprises: significance and implications for multinationalisation', in A. Negandhi, H. Thomas, and K. Rao (eds) *Research in International Business and International Relations*, vol.1, Greenwich, CT: JAI Press.

Khandwalla, P. N. (1987a) 'Organizational behaviour research in India: a review', Working paper 667, IIMA, Ahmedabad.

Khandwalla, P. N. (1987b) 'Organizations of the future: a strategic organization perspective', in National Productivity Council, *Productivity Through People in the Age of Changing Technology*, New Delhi: National Productivity Council.

Khandwalla, P. N. (1988) 'Dynamics of corporate regeneration', L and T Chair paper presented at IIMA, Ahmedabad, 12 September 1988.

Khandwalla, P. N. (1988–9) 'OB for social development: a position paper', *International Studies of Management and Organization* 18, 4, Winter: 6–44.

Khanna, I. and Subramanian, A. (1982) 'Lessons from Antyodaya for integrated rural development', *Vikalpa* 7: 227–34.

Kulkarni, S., Prakasam, R., and Nangia, R. (1983) *Personnel Policies in Banks: An Employee Opinion Survey*, Bombay: NIBM.

Likert, R. (1961) *New Patterns of Management*, New York: McGraw-Hill.

Litwin, G. H. and Stringer, R. A. (1968) *Motivation and Organizational Climate*, Boston, MA: Division of Research, Harvard University.

McClelland, D. (1961) *The Achieving Society*, Princeton, NJ: Van Nostrand.

Maslow, A. (1954) *Motivation and Personality*, New York: Harper & Row.

Mathur, K. and Bhattacharya, M. (1975) *Administrative Response to Bureaucracy*, New Delhi: Concept.

Mintzberg, H. (1973) 'Strategy making in three modes', *California Management Review* 16, Winter: 44–53.

Moulik, T. (1980) 'Action research on rural development for rural poor: the Dharampur Project', *National Labour Institute Bulletin* 6: 57–75.

Moulik, T. (1981) 'Psychology of poverty in India', in U. Pareek (ed.) *A Survey of Research in Psychology 1971–76 Part II*, Bombay: Popular Prakashan.

Murthy, K. R. S. and Nath, N. C. B. (1988) 'Can a holding company be an effective buffer for government enterprise', *Vikalpa* 13, 3: 3–15.

Murthy, N. (1986) 'Family planning programme: lessons from management interventions', *Vikalpa* 11, 3: 205–12.

Natarajan, N. (1977) 'Role of voluntary organization in the development of backward area: Nagaland', *Indian Journal of Public Administration* 23, 3: 355–69.

Padaki, R. (1987) 'Job attitudes', Ahmedabad: ATIRA (mimeo).

Pai Panandikar, V. and Kshirsagar, S. (1978) *Bureaucracy and Development Administration*, New Delhi: Centre for Policy Studies.

Palepu, K. (1985) 'Diversification strategy, profit performance and the entropy measure', *Strategic Management Journal* 6: 239–55.

Pareek, U. and Rao, T. V. (1970) 'The pattern of class room influence – behaviour of class teachers of Delhi', *Indian Educational Review* 5, 1: 55–70.

Patil, S. M. (1982) *HMT Over Three Decades*, New Delhi: Documentation Centre for Corporate and Business Policy Research.

Paul, S. (1982) *Managing Development Programmes: The Lessons of Success*, Boulder, CO: Westview Press.

Peters, T. and Waterman, R. (1982) *In Search of Excellence: Lessons From America's Best Run Companies*, New York: Harper & Row.

Pfeffer, J. and Salancik, G. (1978) *The External Control of Organizations: A Resource Dependence Approach*, New York: Harper.

Phansalkar, S. and Srinivasan, R. (1985) 'Multicoops: parameters for success', *Vikalpa* 10, 1: 52–64.

Pillai, R. (1986) 'Privatisation: a loaded issue', *Business India*, 20 October –2 November: 76–9.

Porter, L. W. and Lawler, E. (1968) *Managerial Attitudes and Performance*, Homewood, IL: Irwin.

Porter, M. E. (1980) *Competitive Strategy*, New York: Free Press.

Ramamurti, R. (1986) 'State-owned enterprises in high-technology industries: a comparative study in the capital goods sector', in A. Negandhi, H. Thomas, and K. Rao (eds) *Research in International Business and International Relations*, vol. 1, Greenwich, CT: JAI Press.

Ramos, C. P. (1971) 'The use of modern management techniques in the public administration of developing countries', *Philippine Journal of Public Administration* 15: 15–20.

Roy, S. (1986–7) 'The Tilonia model as a new approach', presented at the International Conference on Organizational and Behavioural Perspectives for Social Development, IIMA, Ahmedabad, 29 December 1986 to 2 January 1987.

Sajo, T. A. (1970) 'Sensitivity training: a report on an application of a change technique in the Philippine bureaucracy', *Philippine Journal of Public Administration* 14: 284–7.

Salinas, A. D. R. (1978) 'An OD experience in the Latin American public sector through the instrument of collective organizational programming', *Public Personnel Management* 7: 272–8.

Sarkar, K. (1988) 'State Bank of India: leading the pack', *Business India*, 30 May–12 June: 40–8.

Scherer, F. M. (1980) *Industrial Market Structure and Economic Performance*, Chicago, IL: Rand McNally.

Sherif, M. (1963) 'Experiments in group conflict', in W. W. Charters and N. L. Gage (eds), *Readings in the Social Psychology of Education*, Boston, MA: Allyn & Bacon.

Shiva Ramu (1986) 'Public enterprises in developing countries: move toward internationalisation', in A. Negandhi, H. Thomas, and K. Rao (eds) *Research in International Business and International Relations*, vol. 1. Greenwich, CT: JAI Press.

Singh, M., Verma, D., and Yadav, J. (1985) 'Analysis of operational efficiency structure of UP milk cooperatives', *Indian Cooperative Review* 22, 4: 397–402.

Sinha, J. B. P. (1981) 'Organizational dynamics', in U. Pareek (ed.) *A Survey of Research in Psychology*, part II, pp. 415–75, New Delhi: ICSSR.

Sinha, J. B. P. (1984) 'A model of effective leadership styles in India', *International Studies of Management and Organization* 14, 2–3: 86–98.

Soares, K. C. (1984) 'Improving the quality of life in Caribbean villages: participatory approaches in development', *Organization Development Journal* 2: 5–11.

Sreedhar Sharma, J. (1982) 'The enterprise contract system in public enterprise management – the French experience', *IPE Journal* 5, 4: 69–76.

Srivastava, U. K. (1986) 'Organization innovation and training of personnel: a key to better utilization of irrigation potential', *Vikalpa* 11,1: 27–37.

Starbuck, W. H. and Nystrom, P. C. (1981) 'Designing and understanding organizations', in P. Nystrom and W. Starbuck (eds) *Handbook of Organization Design*, vol.1, New York: Oxford University Press.

Subramanian, A. (1984) 'Designing development programmes: some pointers from voluntary agencies', *Abhigyan*, Autumn: 16–36.

Subramanian, A. (1986) 'Strategies for changing agency-centered development programs', in J. Ickis, E. de Jesus, and R. Maru (eds) *Beyond Bureaucracy: Strategic Management of Social Development*, West Hartford, CT: Kumarian.

Tandon, R. and Brown, L. D. (1981) 'Organization-building for rural development: an experiment in India', *Journal of Applied Behavioral Science* 17, 2: 172–89.

Torczyner, J. (1972) 'The political context of social change', *Journal of Applied Behavioral Science* 8: 287–317.

Vathsala, S. and Kumar, K. (1979) 'Top executives pay parity', *Lok Udyog* 13, 3: 41–6.

Vroom, V. and Yetton, P. (1973) *Leadership and Decision Making*, Pittsburgh, PA: University of Pittsburgh Press.

Chapter three

Managing structural adjustment in developing countries: an organizational perspective

Moses N. Kiggundu

Introduction

The economies of developing countries and the organizations therein face uncertain and changing environments. In such situations structural adjustment often becomes necessary periodically for the continued survival of these entities.

What is structural adjustment? Structural adjustment means different things to different people. To the Minister of Finance, it means budget cuts and deficit reductions. To the urban poor, it means the removal of food subsidies and a rising cost of living. To the US Agency for International Development, it means public policy reform and privatization. To the International Monetary Fund (IMF) it means the manipulation of monetary and financial instruments to promote external trade and domestic production. To the non-government organizations (NGOs), it is the need to protect the poor and the weak and to ensure a satisfactory level of social services in areas such as education, health, employment, and refuge services. Yet, for the newly born, it casts doubts as to whether he or she will live long enough to celebrate the fifth birthday.

These different conceptualizations are not surprising because structural adjustment is a complex set of multilevel organizational and inter-organizational interventions with multiple goals and objectives, a wide range of active and passive actors, and many intended and unintended consequences. Elsewhere, I have defined structural adjustment as a 'process of identifying, creating, changing, developing, nurturing, and sustaining a wide range of public and private sector organizations for the effective management of the economy and its constituent sectors' (Kiggundu 1989: 472).

While most of the discussions on structural adjustment tend to focus on the appropriateness and effectiveness of the IMF approach, its conditionalities (Ravenhill 1986), and its negative consequences (Cornia *et al.* 1987), this chapter will focus on the organization and

Table 3.1 A partial list of the major organizations in the management of structural adjustment in Uganda

1. Public Sector

The Executive Branch:	the President's Office
Line ministries:	finance, agriculture, transport, power and communications, cooperatives, commerce, industry and technology, health, education
Central coordinating agencies:	Prime Minister's Office, Ministry of Planning and Economic Development, Bank of Uganda
Crop marketing boards:	Coffee Marketing Board, Lint Marketing Board
Security forces:	the National Resistance Army, Uganda Police
Stated-owned enterprises:	Uganda Development Corporation and subsidiaries, Uganda Railways

2. Private Sector

Financial institutions:	commercial banks, others
Indigenous private sector:	small-scale enterprises
Foreign-owned enterprises:	agricultural estates, construction firms, small-scale manufacturing, trading companies
Joint ventures:	hotels, mining, sugar estates, banks

3. Regional organizations

The Preferential Trade Area (PTA) and associated institutions

Regional financial institutions:	the African Development Bank, the East African Development Bank
Regional management institutes:	Eastern and Southern African Management Institute

4. International organizations

The IMF, the World Bank and affiliates
International development and funding agencies
United Nations agencies: UNDP, UNIDO, ILO, FAO, WHO, UNICEF
International business investment and trading organizations, e.g. SGS

5. New organizations

Rehabilitated state-owned enterprises, e.g. hotels
Indigenous non-government (self-help) organizations
Indigenous private sector organizations
Multilateral Investment Guarantee Agency (MIGA) of the World Bank, African Project Development Facility (APDF), Enhanced Structural Adjustment Facility (ESAF), Compensatory Financing Facility (CFF), Programmes of Action to Mitigate the Social Effects of Adjustment (PAMSCAD)

management of structural adjustment. In taking this approach it is recognized that, although the economics theory behind structural adjustment programmes is internally consistent, it often runs into problems of implementation and sustainability due, at least in part, to lack of effective management resources. This in turn leads to a wide range of negative consequences rending the fabric of society, and aggravating the human condition. Structural adjustment is a comprehensive restructuring and coordination of a country's public, parastatal, and private sector organizations. It is pervasive and requires the active support of local and international organizations and groups. It requires a more effective and socially sensitive mobilization, distribution, and utilization of scarce productive resources such as foreign exchange, public funds, investment capital, and technical and managerial skills. Unfortunately, most of the countries on structural adjustment programmes, whether nationally conceived or in collaboration with the World Bank, the IMF, and the donor community, have limited managerial capacity to design and implement policy. Accordingly, it is argued here that structural adjustment programmes will not produce the intended economic results and could even aggravate the negative consequences until and unless the participating countries have significantly improved their capacity to organize and manage such complex sets of interventions in the public, parastatal, and private sectors on a sustainable basis.

For a structural adjustment programme ultimately to succeed, the participating organizations whether public or private (Bozeman 1987; Roth 1987), domestic or international (Kiggundu 1989), must have the capacity to perform their respective technological and managerial tasks. This is particularly important for strategic organizations.

Strategic organizations can be defined as those macro-level organizations which are directly involved in promoting social and economic development and which are responsible for the development of other organizations operating in similar sectors (Khandwalla and Rao 1987). They are the organizations whose performance is absolutely critical for the success and sustainability of the structural adjustment programme.

Examples of strategic organizations include the ministries of finance, agriculture, and industry, the central bank, exporters such as the Cocoa Marketing Board in Ghana, security forces, and the international funding and donor agencies. Table 3.1 lists some of the major organizations involved in the management of structural adjustment in Uganda. These can be grouped into four categories: public sector, private sector, regional organizations, and international organizations. In this chapter we focus on the public sector and international organizations, the two most important groups in many programmes of structural adjustment.

A framework for organization and management

In order to understand the challenges of implementing structural adjustment programmes, it is necessary to understand the concepts of organization and management especially as they relate to the various domestic and international sectors actively involved or affected by these programmes. This section outlines a conceptual model of organization and management and shows how this relates to the major activities of structural adjustment programmes. Any organization can be conceptualized as being made up of two task subsystems: the critical operating tasks and the strategic management tasks.

The *critical operating tasks* (COTs) are the basic tasks of the organization which it must perform to justify its existence and through which it strives to achieve its charter, mission, goals, and objectives. They involve acquiring the necessary inputs, organizing the production units to transform the inputs into finished goods or services, distributing them to the intended consumers or clients, providing technical and administrative support to other parts of the organization, disposing of its waste and byproducts, and obtaining information and feedback from the environment concerning its input and output transactions and conduct.

The *strategic management tasks* (SMATs), in contrast, are managerial and leadership tasks which define the uniqueness of the profession and its dynamic relationships with other organizations, client systems, and the outside environment. They include the development of the organization's charter and mission statement, giving it the image of its uniqueness, legitimizing that image, formulating strategies for the effective achievement of its mission, communicating the mission, philosophy, and shared values to its members, clients, and the general public, managing the external environment to take advantage of emerging opportunities, and protecting the organization and its internal and external stakeholders against potential threats.

The integrating mechanisms

The (COTS and SMATS do not exist in isolation but are integrated in a living dynamic functioning organization. This integration takes place at three different levels: (i) integration within the COTs through several routine integrating mechanisms (RIMs); (ii) integration within and between the COTs and SMATs through various complex integrating mechanisms (CIMs); and (iii) integration between the organization and the rest of the world through what I have elsewhere called collaborative institutional arrangements (Kiggundu 1989).

RIMs are programmed methods of coordinating various parts of the organization. They are designed to deal with simple repetitive predictable task requirements between two or more aspects of the organization. The three most commonly used RIMs in most organizations are establishing a hierarchy of authority and supervision, establishing standard operating procedures (SOPs), and developing alternative forms of work organization.

CIMs are designed to integrate or bring together in a systematic and purposive way the more complex tasks of the organization. They are usually used for integrating the organization's tasks associated with the SMATs. The more complex the organization's requirements are in terms of both its internal organization and management and the complexity, uncertainty, or hostility of the external environment, the more the need for more complex integrating mechanisms. CIMs are highly labour intensive, require clinical or intuitive judgement rather than routine application of standard procedures, and are relatively more expensive to utilize effectively. They require highly skilled and experienced personnel and effective managers. Therefore they should not be used in situations where the organization and its major stakeholders are better off using the less expensive RIMs.

Most commonly used CIMs include establishing lateral relationships, direct contacts, deliberations, task forces, teams, and matrix designs.

Organizations must perform their critical operating and strategic management tasks and their respective integrating mechanisms with economy, efficiency, and effectiveness. The purpose of structural adjustment programmes is to assist participating organizations to improve their productivity by enhancing their capacities to perform their critical operating and strategic management tasks.

Illustrations from an African central bank

The concepts of organization and management developed above can be illustrated using information recently obtained from a management resource audit of an African central bank. The purpose of this study was to find out the extent to which the bank's institutional resources were sufficient for the mandate and tasks that it was expected to perform (Kiggundu and Sekinobe-Musoke 1988). It was found that the central bank's critical operating tasks include issuance of currency, discarding old currency notes, banking for government, regulating the money supply, banking for and supervising commercial banks and other financial institutions, administration of public debt, exchange control and foreign exchange regulations, analysing the impact of government policy on various financial and economic sectors, providing security, and developing sustainable and effective SOPs. Like other central banks in most developing countries, the bank's COTs include supervising the implementation of various development projects. The most consuming critical operating tasks for this African central bank included currency and banking, foreign exchange allocations, public debt administration, banking supervision, providing security, and acquiring and maintaining scarce resources such as highly trained and experienced personnel, bullion vehicles, computers, and domestic and international data flows in usable form.

The bank's strategic management tasks include internal supervision and coordination of the functions of all its departments, developing and articulating the bank's mission and management philosophy consistent with the existing legislative mandate and government policy, articulating and communicating that philosophy to all its stakeholders, and managing a complex network of domestic and international linkages in both the public and private sectors. The most time-consuming strategic management tasks for this bank for the 1980s and perhaps well into the 1990s are related to the current economic crisis and efforts to implement economic recovery programmes. Specifically, the most challenging tasks for senior management include formulation of effective and acceptable monetary and financial policies, the management of the public debt, the effective allocation and utilization of scarce foreign exchange resources, and acting as a central coordinating agency for the implementation of structural adjustment programmes.

The governor of the bank, the chief executive officer, and his senior staff hold regular meetings with the chief executives of other financial institutions, senior officials of the economic ministries such as finance and economic planning, agriculture, industry, and commerce, export crop marketing boards such as the Coffee Marketing Board, private sector business executives, and senior members of the ruling regime. A lot of executive time and energy is spent preparing for and meeting with advisors and consultants from the IMF, the World Bank and its agencies, and several other donor and international funding agencies.

The bank also maintains active linkages with the rest of the world by means of various international collaborative institutional arrangements. These are structural and behavioural arrangements designed to bring about sustainable improvements in the performance of its COTs and SMATs. Examples of such linkages include frequent contacts with other central banks, coin makers and currency (note) printers, consulting companies, SGS, and several international investment companies. All these linkages are designed and must be assessed in terms of their positive contributions to the bank's performance of its COTs and SMATs.

The management resource audit found that, in order for this bank to perform its COTs and SMATs with economy, efficiency, and effectiveness, it needed highly sophisticated intellectual, technical, administrative, physical, and managerial resources and the capacity to utilize them effectively. At the time of the management resource audit, the bank did not have such resources. Accordingly, it was experiencing serious difficulties in the performance of its COTs arising out of its statutory mandate, and gradually management was losing the capacity to manage the bank as an effective central coordinating public financial institution.

Organizational aspects of structural adjustment

Structural adjustment is a nation-wide process involving many organizations in the private and public sectors both within the country and internationally. Table 3.1 gives a partial list of the major organizations directly involved in various aspects of the management and coordination of Uganda's Economic Recovery Programme which was initiated in May 1987. Each of these organizations must perform its COTs and SMATs effectively in order to contribute positively to the reform or recovery process. In addition, their individual activities must be effectively coordinated by the central coordinating agencies such as the Central Bank of Uganda, the Ministry of Planning and Economic Development, or the Prime Minister's Office.

The problems of management and coordination of the participating organizations for the policy formulation, and implementation, of the structural adjustment programmes are so serious that they threaten the overall integrity of such programmes. These problems are common in many developing countries (Kiggundu 1989). For example, a US Agency for International Development working document on the problems of Zambia's structural adjustment programme observed that:

> many of these negative impacts are inherent in the minimal capacity of government to manage restructuring effectively. Clearly, there is a need to improve management systems for the coordination and for decision-making in order to carry on with the process.
>
> (USAID 1986: 8)

These problems became so severe that in May 1987 Zambia broke off from the IMF structural adjustment programme and introduced its own home-grown Interim National Development Plan (INDP). According to Hedges (1988) and Young (1988), Zambia's problems have not abated partly because of the inherent difficulties of management and coordination of structural adjustment and partly because of inadequate foreign exchange inflows. Using the framework developed above, this means that the strategic organizations for the formulation and implementation of the structural adjustment programme have not performed their respective critical operating and strategic management tasks well enough to make a significant positive impact on the overall performance of the economy. Examples of such strategic organizations in Zambia include the Cabinet Office, line ministries, the Bank of Zambia and the Foreign Exchange Management Committee (FEMAC), Zambia Consolidated Copper Mines (ZCCM), and the international funding and aid agencies led by the IMF and the World Bank.

Public sector reform and structural adjustment

A major part of structural adjustment involves the introduction of a wide range of reforms aimed at bringing about improvements in the performance of public institutions. Typical reform strategies include streamlining and improving public sector management, partial or complete divestiture, liquidation or closure of public enterprises, decentralization, and creating more effective business organizations in the private sector. In this section, some of these strategies are discussed with particular emphasis on the extent to which they contribute positively to the improvement of the performance of the COTs and SMATs of the domestic participating organizations.

Internal management improvements

Structural adjustment interventions based on a broad macroeconomic level of analysis have been unsuccessful because of the failure to pay adequate attention to the specific organizations through which implementation would take place. These interventions are best understood and implemented if they are specified right down to the level of the participating organizations such as a line ministry department, a central coordinating or regulatory agency, or a public enterprise. If the public sector is inefficient and ineffective, this means that specific organizations are lacking the capacity, motivation, or support systems to perform their respective COTs and SMATs with efficiency, economy, and effectiveness, over a sustained period of time.

According to the 1983 World Development Report of the World Bank, problems of public sector management in developing countries include inappropriate macroeconomic policies such as exchange rates and excessive borrowing, distorted incentives, low-yielding investments, investment delays and rising costs, low capacity utilization, and poor maintenance. An internal IMF review of the adjustment experiences of African countries for the period 1980–3 concluded that 'the expected improvements did not materialize mainly because of the limited administrative capabilities of the government to effect requisite changes' (Zulu and Nsouli 1985: 16). A recent sessional paper on Kenya's economic management and growth concluded that the 'Central government has reached the limit of its ability to manage competently a growing number of parastatals and development projects' (Government of Kenya 1986: 19). Each of these problems can be traced to the responsible organizations within which reform strategies should be anchored. It should also be possible to specify whether internal management improvements should be focused at the COTs, the SMATs, or both. For example, a recent management resource audit of an African central bank concluded that improvements were urgently needed in the performance of both the bank's COTs and its SMATs (Kiggundu and Sekinobe-Musoke 1988; Kiggundu 1989).

Public enterprises and structural adjustment

Public enterprises are the antithesis of structural adjustment. They are criticized not only for a persistent record of poor performance but for a wide range of social, economic, and political problems. For example, Balassa *et al.* (1986) blame most of the current problems in Latin America on state capitalism. They blame state capitalism for a wide range of problems including public sector deficits, domestic and foreign borrowing, misallocation and under-utilization of resources, and general weakening of public institutions. Others (Shirley 1983; Aharoni 1986; Hafsi *et al.* 1987; Roth 1987) agree. Accordingly, public enterprises are always targets of structural adjustment interventions aimed at improving their internal management, downsizing, partial or complete divestiture, or total closure. It is partly because of this and partly because of the realization of the important role that public enterprises play in the economic lives of most countries that organizations such as the International Labour Office in Geneva are committed to understanding (Fernandes 1986) and improving (Powell 1987) public enterprise performance.

Both improved understanding and performance of public enterprises can be enhanced by conceptualizing each such enterprise as an organization with both COTs and SMATs which must be performed and integrated using, respectively, routine and complex integrating mechanisms. Specific interventions such as operator training, supply

51

of tools, equipment, and machinery, and management development can then be designed and implemented focused on specific task subsystems of specific public enterprises.

Executives and policy makers of public enterprises can use this organizational framework to assess the possible effects of various structural adjustment interventions on specific public enterprises. For example, if the impact of a proposed set of interventions cannot be traced down to the specific COTs and SMATs of the target public enterprise(s), it is unlikely that such interventions will have any effects on enterprise performance and management. Therefore, they should not be undertaken unless justified on other grounds. Likewise, interventions with maximum positive effects on the performance of the enterprise's COTs and SMATs should not be rejected unless they are associated with known negative consequences.

Divestiture

A major aspect of structural adjustment is a redefinition of the role of government in the management of the economy. The objective is to reduce government involvement, especially through enterprise ownership and control, to increase the role of the private sector, both domestic and international, to eliminate internal structural market imperfections, and to allow competitive forces to play a bigger role in the decisions affecting the allocation and utilization of economic resources. This whole process is quite complicated and must therefore be adequately managed. For example, the formulation of liberalizing economic policies requires a well functioning government bureaucracy. The implementation is even more demanding because it is predicated both on a committed and understanding public sector, including the parastatal sector, and the existence of a viable private sector.

Divestiture is the strategy by which economic reforms are introduced. It is a collective term which refers to different methods of reorganizing economic enterprises. The overall objectives for all these methods are to bring about reforms in public enterprises and to increase the role of the private sector in the ownership, management, and control of the economy. Divestiture can be partial or complete. Partial divestiture means that the public enterprise still has a role to play in partnership with the private sector. Examples of partial divestiture include contracting, leasing, domestic and international joint ventures, franchising, and management contracts. Complete divestiture means that the public institution in question has completely divested itself from the ownership, management, and control of an enterprise. Examples include privatization, assets or equity liquidation, closures, and decentralization.

As has been emphasized before (Kiggundu 1989), all these methods of divestiture need to be effectively managed in order for the benefits of structural adjustment to begin to flow and to be sustained. Space does not allow for a complete discussion of the management requirements for each of these methods. Only two, privatization and contracting, will be briefly discussed.

Privatization

Effective management of privatization requires a double coincidence of wants and abilities. The public enterprise must be well managed so as to be attractive to potential buyers. Likewise, the private sector's willingness to buy must be backed up by demonstrable capacity to provide better operations and management for the privatized enterprise. In many developing countries, especially those in serious economic situations, these conditions do not exist and therefore privatization is difficult to implement.

Privatization is undertaken for various economic, social, and political reasons. Regardless of the reason, the public enterprise targeted for privatization should have the capacity to perform its COTs efficiently or its SMATs effectively. If its COTs are poorly performed, the enterprise will show a loss on its operations, its return on investment will be poor, and its assets will be undervalued. There will be fewer interested buyers and the pressures will be on the government for liquidation or closure. Yet, available evidence suggests that in developing countries privatization has tended to be concentrated on money-losing or marginal areas (Nellis 1986; Kiggundu 1989).

If the public enterprise targeted for privatization does not have good strategic managers, again the value of the enterprise and the final purchase price will tend to be quite low. Public enterprises operate under conditions of market imperfections. There are no competitive forces in the pricing of their products or assets. Therefore the sale of such enterprises must be done through negotiations, and managers lacking in strategic management abilities cannot be effective negotiators because they lack the experience as well as the necessary knowledge from the external environment. This was the case in Togo when, according to Nellis (1986), the government leased a near-defunct publicly owned steel mill to a foreign entrepreneur on very generous terms. The general lesson from these experiences is that it helps if the performance of its COTs and SMATs is enhanced before a public enterprise is listed for privatization.

Equally important is the quality of the private sector enterprise that is taking over the privatized public enterprise. The private sector can be domestic or international. With the exception of a few newly industrializing countries such as South Korea, India, and Brazil, most developing countries have a relatively small indigenous private sector dominated by small-scale enterprises. The international private sector, however, is dominated by large multinational corporations in mining, agriculture, transport, finance, and manufacturing. This gives the international private sector advantage in competing for the privatized public enterprises. At the same time, it must be realized that the domestic private sector firms may be so small as to be lacking in the financial, technological, and management resources to take over the operations and management of the privatized enterprises effectively. Yet governments tend to prefer privatization through domestic rather than foreign private sector firms. The implications from these observations are clear: effective implementation of privatization requires assistance to the indigenous private sector organizations so that those intending to take over the privatized enterprises have COTs and SMATs advanced enough to take on added responsibilities.

Contracting

Unlike privatization, contracting leaves the public enterprise intact but organizations in the private sector are invited to provide assistance in the performance of the public enterprise's COTs, SMATs, or both. Here the objective is not to change the ownership of the public enterprise but to enhance its capacity to fulfil its mandate to deliver goods and services to the public. Contracting takes many different forms but the most common types include management contracts (Kiggundu 1989), contract farming (Glover 1986), contracting out (Moore *et al.* 1987), international subcontracting (Germidis 1980), and technical cooperation (Ozgediz 1983).

Management contracts are especially common in mechanized large-scale agricultural enterprises such as sugar estates. Major multinational corporations such as Booker McConnell, Tate & Lyle, and Lonrho have management contracts with various public enterprises in developing countries in the tropics. For example, Booker Agriculture International, an affiliate of Booker McConnell, manages the Mumias outgrower sugar scheme in Western Kenya. Under the contract, the international company is expected to assist Mumias in the performance of its COTs from the growing of sugar cane to the production and marketing of sugar, perform some of the SMATs, and advise government in other areas such as global changes with future effects on the production and marketing of sugar on the international market. It is also expected that it will facilitate technology transfer and the development of an indigenous private sector. In return, the international company receives three types of income: (i) a fixed fee for expatriate salaries and related overhead costs, (ii) a commission on sales of sugar, and (iii) a small share of net profits.

With contract farming, the multinational corporation agrees to buy, process, and market specified quantities and quality of farm produce at preset prices. These arrangements, commonly used in the production of fruits and vegetables in Central America, help bring the multinational corporations together with small growers, cooperatives, peasants, and local governments. These arrangements assist the farmers to enhance the performance of their COTs while the multinational performs the SMATs on behalf of all the farmers.

Contracting out is becoming an increasingly popular method of privatization in both industrialized and developing countries. Here the government department or public enterprise specifies the work that needs to be done and sends out a request for proposal (RFP) to prospective private sector bidders. Each bidder responds to the RFP by providing evidence of its technical and management capabilities to perform the required work and the price that it will charge. The immediate objective for contracting out is to provide the public institution with outside assistance in the performance of specified COTs or SMATs. Strategically, it can also be used to assist in the development of the indigenous private sector by assisting them to get contracts which they would be unable to win on the open market. This can be done for firms in specifically targeted sectors or underdeveloped regions of the country. Examples of service contracts include road and vehicle maintenance, medical laboratory work, distribution of agricultural inputs such as fertilizers and outputs such as export promotion, and general government services such as printing, production and distribution of utilities, social services, transport, and telecommunications.

Very little research has been done on the effects of contracting out on the management of structural adjustments. A recent study in Honduras (Moore *et al.* 1987), however, examined the effects of government contracting out of construction services in housing, rural primary schools, and rural roads. The results were rather discouraging because contracting out did not give the government better service from the private sector in terms of better quality of construction, better turnaround time, or lower costs. The private sector firms in Honduras were not able to perform their respective construction COTs better than government departments and public enterprises had done before. These results were explained in terms of the firms' own internal weaknesses in the performance of their COTs and SMATs as well as the inability or unwillingness of the government to remove various bureaucratic obstacles associated with malpractices and market imperfections.

Structural adjustment as an international collaborative institutional arrangement

Structural adjustment is made that much more difficult to manage because of its international dimensions. In its comprehensive form, it is best conceptualized as a network of domestic and international collaborative institutional arrangements involving different levels of government and public enterprises, foreign governments, multinational corporations and small-scale enterprises, domestic and international NGOs, the United Nations system of organizations, the IMF, the World Bank and affiliates, and international donor agencies. Unfortunately, the burden of organizing, coordinating, and managing these complex and asymmetrical domestic and international collaborative institutional arrangements falls on the developing country recipient government. These governments, already riddled with economic, social, and political problems associated with the implementation of structural adjustment programmes, are often ill equipped for these added responsibilities.

Several international collaborative institutional arrangements such as contract farming and management contracts have been discussed above. Here, two special types of such arrangements are briefly discussed in connection with the role they play in the management of structural adjustment: (i) international subcontracting, and (ii) the IMF and the World Bank development agencies.

International subcontracting

International subcontracting is one of the non-equity arrangements by which international organizations can facilitate implementation of structural adjustment through privatization. It is a contractual arrangement whereby the international organization such as a multinational corporation subcontracts one of several local firms to undertake certain aspects of the production of its finished or semi-finished products. In this way the multinational corporation is exporting parts of its COTs and is using its technological expertise to enhance the local firms' capacity to perform their respective COTs. According to Germidis (1980), many developing countries openly promote international subcontracting as the official industrial development strategy. This is because of the expectation that such subcontracting facilitates the development of the private sector by contributing to the local firms' technological development, management capabilities, and access to international markets. The experience from various developing countries, however, shows that the overall effects of international subcontracting to the economy are quite limited in scope, magnitude, and duration (Germidis 1980).

The International Monetary Fund and the World Bank

In the minds of many observers in developing countries, structural adjustment is synonymous with the IMF and the World Bank. Indeed, most discussions of structural adjustment are almost exclusively focused on these powerful institutions (Killick 1983; Cornia *et al.* 1987). In this last section, the discussion is limited to the role these institutions play in the management of structural adjustment. The general observation made here is that because of the professional background and training of the dominant coalitions controlling these powerful institutions, they tend to focus on the formulation of sound structural adjustment policies but put little or no emphasis on the management of the implementation and substantiability of such complex, pervasive, and painful structural social changes. It is also important to mention that there is no intrinsic relationship between structural adjustment and these institutions. Indeed several countries do undertake structural adjustment programmes without these institutions' blessing or direct involvement.

What role do these institutions play in the management of structural adjustment programmes? First, they perform specialized SMATs for various government ministries such as finance, central coordinating agencies such as the central bank, private sector industrial organizations, regional organizations, and even some international organizations (see Table 3.1 above). In this way they enhance the capacity of the recipient government and its institutions in the performance of their respective SMATs. This is one of the areas of strength for these institutions because quite often they come up with internally consistent and sound economic analysis and policy recommendations.

Second, they assist the government to identify its strategic organizations, and attempt to help them in the performance of their respective COTs associated with the implementation of the structural adjustment programme. This is an area where these institutions are weak because they fail to map out a step-by-step implementing strategy for the participating organizations. Instead, they send in short-term foreign consultants whose effectiveness at the operating levels is often questionable for a variety of reasons (Kiggundu 1986, 1988).

Third, they assist the participating organizations in opening up international collaborative institutional arrangements. This is perhaps the most important source of power for these institutions. When they bless the structural adjustment programme of a country, as they are currently (1989) doing with countries such as Ghana, the Philippines, Jamaica, and Uganda, they bring with them many other international organizations both in the public and private sectors. When they pull out of a country, as they did in Zambia in May 1987, they take with them most of the same international organizations. They also create institutions specifically designed to assist only those countries whose economic behaviour conforms to their values and ideals. Examples include the Emerging Markets Growth Fund, the Multilateral Investment Guarantee Agency (MIGA), and the Programme of Action to Mitigate the Social Effects of Adjustment (PAMSCAD).

The Emerging Markets Growth Fund was created in 1985 by the International Finance Corporation, an affiliate of the World Bank, to accelerate the growth of capital markets in selected developing countries by investing in the local stock markets. MIGA was established in 1985 during the joint World Bank–IMF meeting in Seoul. Its purpose is to stimulate the flow of direct foreign investment into developing countries by issuing long-term guarantees protecting investors against non-commercial risks such as nationalization. PAMSCAD was established to provide direct assistance to those such as the poor, the sick, the uneducated, women, and children who are adversely affected by the harsh realities of structural adjustment. In all cases, these programmes are available only to those countries whose structural adjustment programmes are blessed by these powerful institutions.

Finally, these institutions provide resources such as foreign exchange, technical expertise, and international goodwill. Such resources are particularly critical for the participating organizations to be able to acquire the necessary inputs and perform their respective COTs and SMATs with economy and efficiency.

Despite all these contributions, there is increasing scepticism both within and outside the institutions as to the efficacy of their structural adjustment programmes in addressing the fundamental economic problems facing many developing countries. The criticisms involve two groups: those who ask for internal adjustment to the programmes by advocating, for example, more external resources, longer periods of adjustment, and debt amortization, and those who reject the programmes as being theoretical, irrelevant to domestic national realities, politically naive, and designed to appease Western interests. Within the framework developed here, the relevance of any structural adjustment programme, whether it is formulated by the IMF and the World Bank or whether it is home-grown, must be assessed in the context of its overall effects on the country's strategic organizations. If the programme does not make a significant and sustainable impact on the performance of these organizations' respective COTs and SMATs, it cannot contribute to the economic recovery of that country.

Summary and conclusion

Structural adjustment is defined as a long-term strategy of identifying, changing, developing, nurturing, and sustaining a wide range of public and private sector organizations so as to bring about more effective management of the economy and efficient allocation and utilization of resources. The organization is conceptualized as having two interrelated task subsystems. These are the COTs and the SMATs which are focused at the operating and management levels of the organization respectively. The two task systems are in turn integrated by various RIMs and CIMs respectively.

This organizational conceptualization is used to discuss the challenges associated with the management and coordination of the various implementation strategies associated with structural adjustment programmes. Using illustrations from various developing countries, it is emphasized that the lack of operational and managerial resources for the strategic organizations is a major bottleneck for the successful implementation and sustainability of structural adjustment programmes. The same conceptual framework is used to discuss some of the most common methods of bringing about public sector reforms through structural adjustment programmes. These include public enterprise reforms, divestiture, privatization, contracting out, and international subcontracting. The chapter is concluded by examining the role of the IMF and the World Bank in the management of structural adjustment programmes.

The general conclusion is that these powerful institutions fulfil a range of multiple roles on behalf of the recipient government and its institutions. The problem, however, is that in performing these roles the emphasis has been traditionally on strategic management or policy formulation tasks, and little attention has been paid to the operational implementation tasks. The challenge confronting international as well as domestic organizations in developing countries is therefore to reform some of their resources and efforts on the more routine operational aspects of their strategies for structural adjustment.

References

Aharoni, Y. (1986) *The Evolution and Management of State-owned Enterprises*, Cambridge, MA: Ballinger.

Balassa, B., Bueno, G. M., Kuczynski, P., and Simonsen M. H. (1986) *Toward Renewed Economic Growth in Latin America*, Washington, DC: Institute for International Economics.

Bozeman, B. (1987) *All Organizations are Public: Bridging Public and Private Organizational Theories*, San Francisco, CA: Jossey-Bass.

Cornia, G. A., Jolly, R., and Stewart F. (1987) *Adjustment with a Human Face: Protecting the Vulnerable and Promoting Growth*, Toronto: Oxford University Press.

Fernandes, P. (1986) *Management Relations Between Government and Public Enterprises: A Handbook for Administrators and Managers*, Geneva: International Labour Office.

Germidis, D. (ed.) (1980) *International Subcontracting: A New Form of Investment*, Paris: Development Centre, Organization for Economic Cooperation and Development.

Glover, D. J. (1986) 'Multinational corporations and third world agriculture', in T. H. Moran (ed.) *Investing in Development: New Roles for Private Capital?*, Washington, DC: Overseas Development Council.

Government of Kenya (1986) *Sessional Paper No. 1 on Economic Management for Renewed Growth*, Nairobi: The Government Printer.

Hafsi, T., Kiggundu, M. N., and Jørgensen, J. J. (1987) 'Strategic apex configurations in state-owned enterprises', *Academy of Management Review* 12, 4: 714–30.

Hedges, T. (1988, December) 'Zambia's autonomous adjustment', *Africa Recovery* 2, 4: 6–13 (New York: United Nations Department of Public Information).

Khandwalla, P. N. and Rao, R. M. (1987) *International Conference on Organizational Behavioral Perspectives or Social Development*, 29 December 1986 to 2 January 1987, Report on the Papers, Keynote Addresses, Panel Discussions and Presentations, Ahmedabad: Indian Institute of Management.

Kiggundu, M. N. (1986) 'Limitations to the application of sociotechnical systems in developing countries', *Journal of Applied Behavioural Science* 22, 3: 341–53.

Kiggundu, M. N. (1988) 'International consulting to developing countries: challenges for the expatriate national', School of Business, Carleton University, Ottawa: (mimeo).

Kiggundu, M. N. (1989) *Managing Organizations in Developing Countries: An Operational and Strategic Approach*, West Hartford, CT: Kumarian Press.

Kiggundu, M. N. and Sekinobe-Musoke (1988) *Management Resource Audit of the Bank of Uganda*, The International Business Group Studies, School of Business, Carleton University, Ottawa, Canada.

Killick, T. (1983) 'The role of the public sector in the industrialization of African developing countries', *Industry and Development* 7: 57–83

(New York: United Nations).

Moore, R. J., Swanson, D. A., Lim, G. C., Burke, M. A., Greenstein, J., and Fehnel, R. A. (1987) *Contracting Out: A Study of the Honduran Experience*, Washington, DC: National Association of Schools of Public Affairs and Administration.

Nellis, J. R. (1986) 'Public enterprises in Sub-Saharan Africa', World Bank Discussion Paper No. 1, Washington, DC.

Ozgediz, S. (1983) 'Managing the public service in developing countries: issues and prospects', World Bank Staff Working Paper No. 583, Management and Development Series No. 10, Washington, DC.

Powell, V. (1987) *Improving Public Enterprise Performance: Concepts and Techniques*, Geneva: International Labour Office.

Ravenhill, J. (ed.) (1986) *Africa in Economic Crisis*, New York: Columbia University Press.

Roth, G. (1987) *The Private Provision of Public Services in Developing Countries*, New York: Oxford University Press.

Shirley, M. N. (1983) *Managing State-owned Enterprises*, World Bank Staff Working Paper No. 577, Management and Development Series No. 4, Washington, DC.

USAID (1986) 'Redesign of human and institutional resources development project (Zambia)', unpublished discussion paper, Project No. 611-0206.

Young, R. (1988) *Zambia: Adjusting to Poverty*, Ottawa: The North–South Institute.

Zulu, J. B. and Nsouli, S. M. (1985) *Adjustment Programs in Africa: The Recent Experience*, Washington, DC: International Monetary Fund, April.

Chapter four

Organizational life-cycle and effectiveness criteria in state-owned enterprises: the case of East Africa[1]

Jan J. Jørgensen

Introduction

State-owned enterprises (SOEs) occupy key positions in most developing economies, and so their performance is subject to intense scrutiny and frequent debate. This chapter offers a new approach to the performance debate by positing that effectiveness criteria vary over time depending on the relative strength of three levels of culture in and around the SOE: societal, industry, and organizational. Their relative strength is in turn linked to phases – cooperative, adversarial, and autonomous – in the life-cycle of the SOE–government relationship. The approach is tested against qualitative and quantitative data from eleven state-owned transport and communications firms in eastern Africa: Ethiopia, Kenya, Tanzania, and Uganda.

The socio-political environment of SOEs varies in eastern Africa. Ethiopia's Marxist government has relied heavily on SOEs for development, as has Tanzania's democratic socialist government. For the Kenyan and a succession of Ugandan governments, SOEs play a supporting role in a mixed public/private sector economy.

Despite these ideological contrasts, the importance of SOEs in the economies of these nations varies by a factor of only 2, as measured by the total number of SOEs and their share of fixed capital investment. Ethiopia in 1984 had 180 SOEs which together accounted for 36 per cent of gross fixed capital investment (Nellis 1986). Tanzania had 400 SOEs in 1981 (Nellis 1986), which accounted for 38 per cent of gross fixed capital formation in 1977 but only 28 per cent in 1984 (United Republic of Tanzania 1985). In 1982 the Kenyan government and its statutory boards had full or majority control of 83 enterprises, plus a minority interest in another 93, for a total of 176. SOEs accounted for 17 per cent of Kenya's gross fixed capital formation in 1978–9 (Nellis 1986). Uganda had 130 SOEs in 1985 (Nellis 1986) but their share of fixed capital formation is not known.[2]

Because SOEs play a major economic role, their performance is subject to intense scrutiny and debate. Although there are successful SOEs in the region, such as the Kenya Tea Development Authority, Tanesco (electricity, Tanzania), Ethiopian Airlines, and the Ethiopian Telecom Authority, these are exceptions in an overall pattern of weak and disappointing performance. For example, their profitability has been low, whether measured by operating profit, overall profit, return on investment, or economic benefits.

Of 196 Tanzanian commercial SOEs audited in 1978–9, 41 per cent suffered losses (Moshi 1980). Cumulative government investments and loan guarantees to Kenyan public enterprises in 1981 totalled about US$1.7 billion (18,000 million Kenya shillings), on which the government earned a return equal to a fraction of 1 per cent (Ndegwa 1982). In Uganda in 1979 the financial performance of 79 of 92 state-owned subsidiaries could be determined; of these, only 37 per cent were profitable (Seers *et al.* 1979). SOE performance on other criteria such as effectiveness and efficiency presents a similar mixed picture.

The causes of inadequate SOE performance have been the subject of several studies (Shirley 1983; Nellis 1986; Ayub and Hegstad 1987). According to an East African public enterprise workshop (Klaus 1980), they include the following factors:

(1) lack of clear objectives at all levels – the ministry, the SOE, and employees within the SOE;
(2) problems in the qualifications and motivation of managers;
(3) inefficient organizational structure – over-staffing, lack of job descriptions, lack of job evaluation;
(4) lack of communication between organizational levels and a tendency to suppress rather than manage internal conflicts;
(5) inadequate maintenance planning and lack of equipment inventory lists;
(6) lack of external incentives for increased sales;
(7) inadequate control systems and poor financial systems – inadequate cost accounting, high or even wasteful overheads, delays in preparing accounts, dependence on government subsidies;
(8) weak oversight by government, external audit delays, and weak inexperienced boards of directors;
(9) poor infrastructure – shortages of materials, spare parts, transportation, storage, and foreign exchange;
(10) political interference in staffing, recruitment, and promotion which reduces motivation and results in the hiring of under-qualified individuals;
(11) opportunistic misuse of SOEs by private individuals, bureau-

crats, or joint-venture partners;
(12) the inherent riskiness of state investment in sectors shunned by the private sector.

The poor performance by SOEs in developing countries has also been attributed to cultural factors (Kiggundu *et al.* 1983). The litany in Africa is familiar: over-centralized decision making, excessive hierarchy, lack of entrepreneurship, ethnic factionalism, mistrust, nepotism, and patron–client retinues (Moris 1977; Cohen 1981).

Yet within the same or similar societal cultures, some SOEs clearly perform better than others (Ayub and Hegstad 1987). Ethiopian Airlines thrives in a challenging societal culture. The performance of Kenya Airways has been less consistent in a seemingly benign societal culture. By some efficiency criteria, Uganda Posts and Telecommunications is leaner than Kenya Posts and Telecommunications, but the telecommunications service is far more effective in Kenya and even Tanzania than in Uganda. In contrast, Kenya Railways and Uganda Railways both seem to perform better than Tanzania Railways but on very different criteria. Kenya Railways enjoys higher productivity, stronger internal controls, and a small operating profit; Uganda Railways enjoys a better organization climate (cohesion and morale) and a positive evaluation by government agencies.

What constitutes good performance is neither constant nor clearcut. To understand the link between culture and performance, one must examine the variegated makeup of culture and of effectiveness criteria.

Variegated culture

In this study, culture is defined as a shared set of values and behavioural orientations (Jørgensen 1989). For SOEs, it is useful to distinguish three levels of culture: societal, industry, and organizational. The usual caveat applies: the cultural values described represent the dominant values within the organization, industry, or society – individuals may hold different values. When a set of individuals with different values is sufficiently large and homogeneous, it may be appropriate to refer to their values as a subculture or counter-culture.

Previous studies have focused on the societal culture's consequences for organizational culture (Hofstede 1983; Allaire and Firsirotu 1984; Adler and Jelinek 1986). The consequences of industry culture have been studied less frequently.

Industry culture

The link between societal and organizational culture is moderated by industry culture (Deal and Kennedy 1982). The organizational 'task environment' differs from one industry to another, giving rise to an industry culture that differs from societal culture (Child 1981). Regardless of differences in societal values, there will be some similar values between an airline in Tanzania and an airline in France or Malaysia arising from similarities in the task environment (Rieger 1986). Alternatively, regardless of identical societal values, there will be differences in values between an airline and a railway in Tanzania arising from differences in the task environment.

Industry culture's consequences can be studied in the diffusion of industry values to the organization through technology transfers, technological change, international training programmes, industry standards, and international and regional industry associations. For example, international industry associations can serve as strong reference points in setting effectiveness criteria and publishing performance data, as the International Air Transport Association does for airlines and the International Telecommunications Union for telecommunications. By contrast the international industry association for posts does not set criteria or publish performance statistics. Similarly, the Union of African Railways, a continental industry association for railways, offers training courses but does not regularly publish comparative performance data.

There can be industry cultural divisions within SOEs in the same industry. In railways there is conflict between traditional railwaymen and externally hired experts over orientation, structure, and policy. In posts and telecommunications there is conflict between the neglected postal side versus the powerful telecommunications engineers.

The changing balance between societal, industry, and organizational cultures

According to the life-cycle model of SOE–government relations (Hafsi *et al.* 1987), SOE autonomy is linked to the emergence of a strong organizational culture which helps to buffer the technical core from the societal culture. The model posits three phases in the SOE–government relationship: (a) the initial cooperative phase when the SOE is a start-up firm or is nationalized with little conflict; (b) the adversarial phase in which there are sharp conflicts between governmental objectives shaped by societal culture and technical–

commercial objectives shaped by industry culture and market forces; and (c) the autonomy phase in which the SOE's organizational culture predominates. Forces moving the relationship to the autonomy phase can include non-cultural factors, such as financial self-sufficiency, technical complexity, dynamic competition, and international operations (Sexty 1980; Ayub and Hegstad 1987; Ramamurti 1987).

Societal culture predominates in the initial *cooperative* phase. Industry culture and societal culture vie for dominance over organizational culture in the *adversarial* phase. Organizational culture and industry culture become more important than societal culture in the *autonomy* phase (Jørgensen 1989). In this study an autonomy index for the SOE is used to distinguish phases in the SOE–government life-cycle and the corresponding balance between societal, industry, and organizational cultures.

Variegated effectiveness criteria

Building on the life-cycle hypothesis that managerial priorities and performance criteria change over stages in the life-cycle (Quinn and Cameron 1983; Smith *et al.* 1985); Hafsi *et al.* (1987) hypothesized that effectiveness criteria for public enterprise change over phases in the relationship between the government and the individual firm.

Performance evaluation in public enterprise is complicated by the fact that the firm must pursue two competing sets of objectives: governmental objectives shaped by the political process and commercial objectives shaped by the market. Performance on commercial objectives seems to be evaluated on efficiency criteria, while performance evaluation on governmental objectives appears to centre on broader effectiveness criteria (Hafsi *et al.* 1987).

Efficiency is a productivity concept that can be defined as a ratio of outputs to inputs of a given quality. Although ostensibly objective, productivity measurement requires judgements regarding quality, overhead cost allocation, capital investment amortization, and cause–effect relationships. Effectiveness, by contrast, necessitates evaluating whether the organization is doing the right thing (Quinn and Rohrbaugh 1983).

Using multivariate analysis of judgements by organizational theorists and researchers, Quinn and Rohrbaugh demonstrate that commonly used effectiveness criteria, including efficiency, can be mapped onto a spatial model with three dimensions: (a) external versus internal orientation; (b) flexibility versus control; and (c) means versus ends (time horizon).

The external–internal and flexibility–control dimensions delineate effectiveness criteria into quadrants that match four approaches to organizational analysis: (a) human relations; (b) open systems; (c) internal processes; and (d) rational goals. Each has its own measures of effectiveness (Figure 4.1).

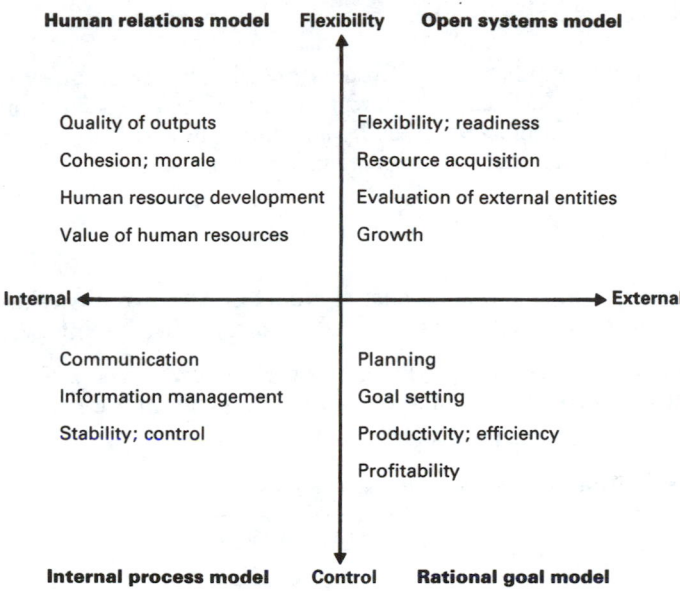

Human relations model Flexibility **Open systems model**

Quality of outputs

Cohesion; morale

Human resource development

Value of human resources

Flexibility; readiness

Resource acquisition

Evaluation of external entities

Growth

Internal ← → External

Communication

Information management

Stability; control

Planning

Goal setting

Productivity; efficiency

Profitability

Internal process model Control **Rational goal model**

Figure 4.1 Dimensions of effectiveness criteria
Source: Adapted from Quinn and Rohrbaugh 1983

Effectiveness criteria and the life-cycle

The salience of these effectiveness criteria varies by phases in the SOE–government life-cycle.

In the cooperative phase, starting operations is a key goal. Efficiency is not an important performance criterion at this point. As long as trains are able to carry vital coffee exports and petroleum imports, the Uganda government cares little about profitability or productivity in Uganda Railways. Rough calculations demonstrate to government that, despite obvious rail inefficiencies, the economic costs of railway transportation for bulk goods are lower than the costs of road transport, and rail transport helps monitor coffee smuggling.

In the adversarial phase, there are often conflicting social goals. In 1984, managers at Tanzania Railways Corporation were struggling to restructure to meet the needs of diesel technology and to implement internal controls and a marketing orientation demanded by the Ministry of Finance, while still responding to societal pressure for equitable regional service and increased employment, regardless of financial costs. There were internal and external pulls on goal setting, and maintaining internal cohesion was a major managerial challenge.

In the autonomy phase, effectiveness criteria are largely market based. Ethiopian Airlines still performs a service to society but measures that performance largely by its profitability and growth in market share on continental and international routes.

Hypotheses

Linking the Quinn–Rohrbaugh spatial model of effectiveness criteria to the diachronic cultural model leads to three broad hypotheses.

(H1) When societal culture predominates (cooperative phase), effectiveness criteria from the open systems quadrant are most

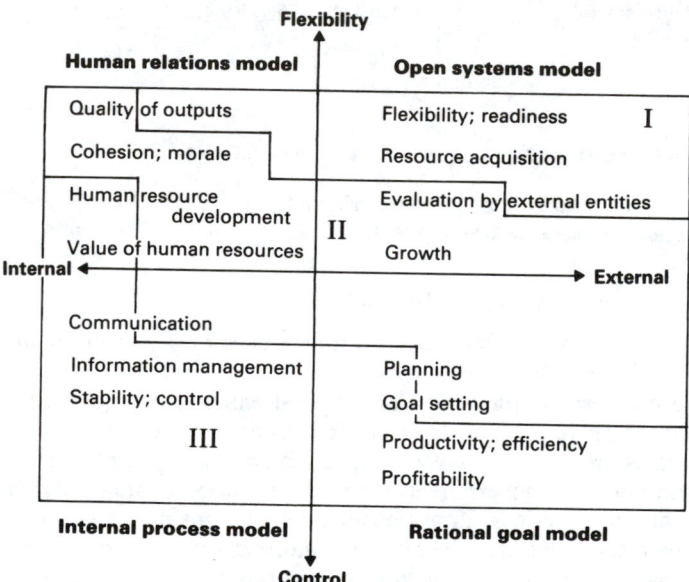

Figure 4.2 Salience of effectiveness criteria over the life-cycle

Note: Circles indicate primary effectiveness criteria for each phase in the SOE–government life-cycle: I, cooperative phase; II, adversarial phase; III, autonomy phase.

Source: Adapted from Quinn and Rohrbaugh 1983

salient: flexibility, readiness, resource acquisition, external evaluation through shared values.

(H2) When societal culture and industry culture vie for dominance over organizational culture (adversarial phase), effectiveness criteria are diverse, drawn from the open systems (formal external evaluation), human relations (cohesion, morale, human resource development, equitable output allocation, formal output quality evaluation), and rational goal models (planning geared to competition for resources, internal–external pulls on goal setting).

(H3) When organizational culture predominates (autonomy phase), effectiveness criteria from the internal process and rational goal models are most salient: stability, control, information management, communication, strategic planning, goal setting, productivity, efficiency, and profitability. The salient effectiveness criteria for each phase in the life-cycle are indicated in Figure 4.2.

Data and methods

In the colonial period Kenya, Tanzania, and Uganda shared common organizations in transport and communications. The forerunner of the East African Posts and Telecommunications was established in 1933. East African Airways was founded in 1946, and the Kenya–Uganda Railway and the Tanzania Railways, each dating to the turn of the century, were merged into East African Railways and Harbours from 1948 to 1967, after which harbours were separated from the railways.

When the East African Community (EAC) collapsed in 1977, its member nations established separate national organizations for air, rail, and posts and telecommunications services (Green 1977, 1979). In most cases the local operations of the former corporation formed the core of the descendant firm.

Because the descendant firms of the EAC shared a common origin, their study offers a quasi-experimental design (Cook 1983) to compare the effects of differences in industry culture (airlines versus railways versus posts and telecommunications) and differences in societal culture ('capitalist' Kenya, 'socialist' Tanzania, and 'fragmented' Uganda) on organizational culture in SOEs. How have these dual pressures influenced organizational culture during and following the break-up?

The following background material was gathered about the descendant firms formed after the break-up: annual reports and

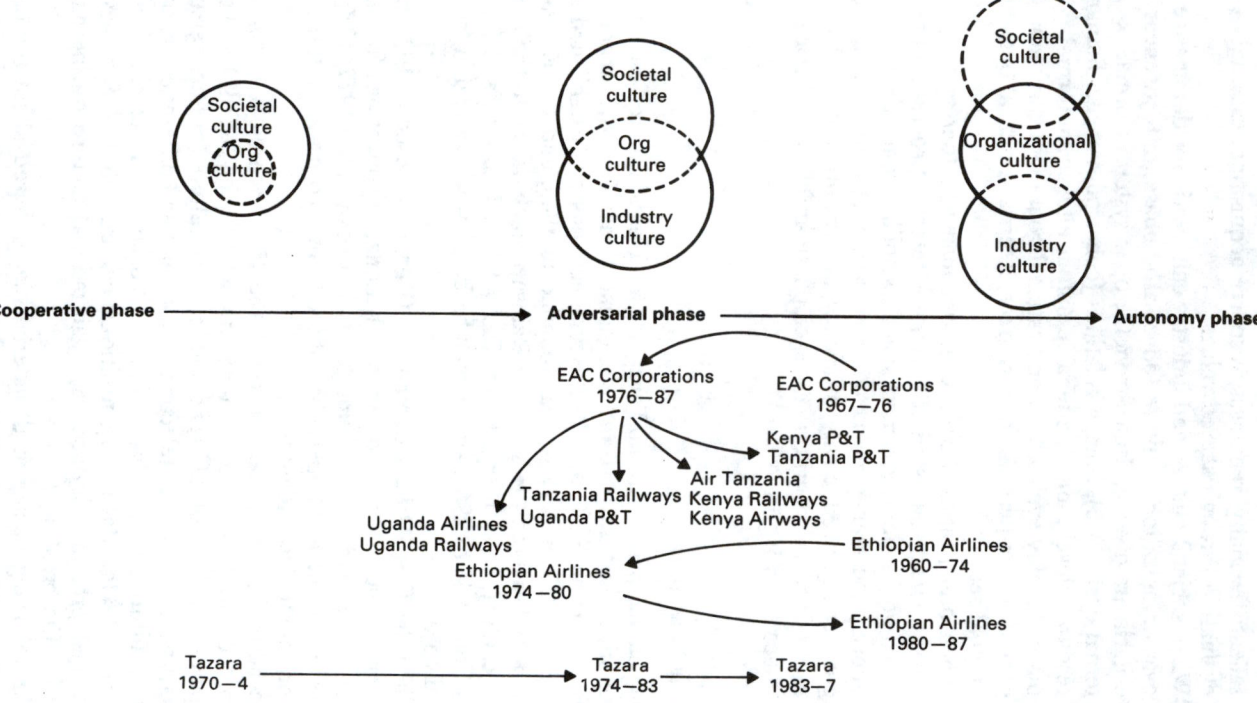

Figure 4.3 State-owned enterprise transitions through the life-cycle in eastern Africa

accounts (when available), budgets, plans, schedules, networks, organizational charts, plus newspaper and magazine articles from East Africa and industry publications. Between 1984 and 1987, ninety-nine interviews were conducted with managers in nine descendant firms of the former EAC. The substantive focus of interviews with these managers (the general manager plus departmental heads) was strategic decision making in functional areas before and after the break-up.

In addition, twenty-eight managers were interviewed at two control firms: the TAZARA railway which was jointly founded by Tanzania and Zambia in the early 1970s; and Ethiopian Airlines, which is a commercially successful state-owned airline operating in a difficult environment.

These interviews allowed the development of a qualitative understanding of differences in societal and industry cultures and their impact on organizational culture. Quantitative and clinical data are also used to examine the relationship between culture and effectiveness criteria.

Qualitative overview

Societal culture's consequences have been studied in the acculturation of the descendant firms of the EAC to their national environments after the 1977 break-up and the acculturation of Ethiopian Airlines to changing societal values following the 1974 revolution (Jørgensen 1989).

At the break-up these SOEs were in transition from the adversarial to the autonomy phase of the life-cycle of SOE–government relations (Figure 4.3). With the break-up, the balance between industry culture and societal culture shifted back toward societal culture as the new national owner took control. This shift was strongest in Uganda, and generally stronger in railways than in airlines and posts and telecommunications firms. In the mid-1980s SOE–government relations in Uganda resembled more the cooperative phase than the adversarial phase, at least in railways and the airline. By contrast, conflict between societal and industry norms was intense within Tanzania Railways (until 1986) and at Uganda Posts and Telecommunications.

The balance between societal and industry culture over the stages in the life-cycle of the SOE–government relationship is shown in Figure 4.3, as well as the transition of the focus of SOEs through these stages. For example, Ethiopian Airlines enjoyed considerable autonomy up to the 1974 revolution. The revolution forced the airline to adapt its culture to the changed societal culture. In the words of one manager,

> In the 1974–80 period, there was chaos in work discipline. People thought it was revolutionary to disobey superiors on all sorts of matters, and there were many attempts by government officials to interfere in the airline.... [The General Manager in that period] was very flexible, attuned to the political winds. He was the best person for the job.

After suffering financial losses in 1979 and 1980, Ethiopian Airlines gradually re-established its autonomy under a new General Manager.

Quantitative data

To test the relationship between changes in effectiveness criteria over phases in the SOE–government life-cycle, data were gathered and indices constructed for six variables: (1) SOE autonomy; (2) internal control capacity; (3) internal planning capacity; (4) profitability; (5) productivity; (6) organizational climate.

Autonomy index

According to the life-cycle model of SOE–government relations, SOE autonomy is linked to the emergence of a strong organizational culture which helps buffer the technical core from the societal culture. Autonomy is used as a proxy variable for the strength of the organizational culture. It is measured by the autonomy index, which is the sum of six components:

(1) the relationship between top management and the board of directors (if professional, then high autonomy – at least one-third of the board consists of members with relevant practical experience, and the board sets broad policy but does not intervene in day-to-day operations; if non-professional, then low autonomy – board membership based solely on political criteria, and the board frequently interferes with day-to-day operations);

(2) foreign exchange autonomy – the degree to which the firm is subject to foreign exchange controls and the difficulty of obtaining foreign exchange;

(3) pricing autonomy – the extent to which the firm controls the pricing of its outputs;

(4) technology sourcing autonomy – the extent to which technology

sourcing is based on the technical/commercial criteria of the firm rather than the political criteria of government;
(5) operational autonomy – the extent to which day-to-day operations of the firm are free from government interference;
(6) strategic autonomy – the extent to which the firm enjoys autonomy in strategy formulation (resource allocation and product market decisions).

Table 4.1 Autonomy index for state-owned enterprises

	Autonomy index (1984–5)						
	A	B	F	P	T	O	S
Ethiopian Airlines	19	1	3	3	4	4	4
TAZARA Railway	17	3	3	2	2	4	3
Kenya Posts and Telecom.	13	1	1	2	3	3	3
Tanzania Posts and Telecom.	13	1	1	2	3	4	2
Air Tanzania Corporation	11	2	1	1	1	3	3
Kenya Railways	9	2	1	0	0	3	3
Uganda Railways	8	1	2	0	0	3	2
Kenya Airways Ltd	8	0	1	1	1	3	2
Uganda Airlines Corporation	7	0	2	1	2	0	2
Uganda Posts and Telecom.	7	0	2	2	1	1	1
Tanzania Railways Corporation	4	1	1	1	0	1	0
Mean	10.5	1.1	1.6	1.4	1.5	2.6	2.3

Note: A, overall autonomy (B + F + P + T + O + S); B, relations with board of directors (5, professional; 0, non-professional); F, foreign exchange autonomy (5, high; 0, low); P, pricing autonomy (tariffs and fares) (5, high; 0, low); T, technology sourcing autonomy (5, high; 0, low); O, operational autonomy (5, high; 0, low); S, strategic autonomy (5, high; 0, low).

The autonomy index and components for the SOEs in 1984–5 are shown in Table 4.1. Although generalizations must be treated cautiously because of the small number of cases, the following patterns are observed: (a) under single-country ownership, overall managerial autonomy tends to be higher in posts and telecommunications and airlines, lower in railways; (b) SOE autonomy tends to be higher in Kenya and Tanzania than in Uganda; (c) based on a single case (TAZARA), multicountry ownership appears to enhance SOE autonomy.

The effect of societal differences on the autonomy of descendant firms was not deterministic: there were wide within-country and even within-industry variations in the degree of autonomy enjoyed by managers. These variations are consistent with the life-cycle model because organizational culture is shaped by internal factors as well as external societal and industry cultures.

Internal control

The life-cycle model hypothesizes that internal control systems are less important in the cooperative phase when societal culture predominates and become very important in the autonomy stage when organizational culture predominates. The timeliness of accounting information is used as a proxy for the importance of internal control systems. It is assumed that an organization with up-to-date accounts (completed within a few months of the close of the financial year) places greater importance on internal control systems than an organization whose accounts are over a year behind.

The timeliness of accounting data varies greatly among these SOEs and has changed over time. For example, Tanzania Railways, which was nearly 2 years late on its 1982 accounts, reduced the gap to 9 months on its 1985 accounts. Kenya Posts and Telecommunications is able to close its accounts 3 months after the financial year ends. In January 1987 some firms still did not know how they performed in 1984. The accounting information delay ranged from 3 months to 26 months for these SOEs.

As hypothesized, there is an inverse relationship between autonomy and accounting information delay. The correlation coefficient between the two variables is -0.32, which increases to -0.54 when the jointly owned TAZARA railway is excluded. Correlation does not establish a causal relationship. However, most firms in the study are in the adversarial phase of the public enterprise–government relationship, where formal controls are important for accountability. One assumes that governments are reluctant to grant much autonomy to firms whose basic internal control systems are in disarray. Moreover, firms with poor accounting information may fare poorly in the political competition for resource allocation. Conversely, for firms closer to the cooperative phase, the government may care more about adequate service than adequate controls, while firms in the autonomy phase need adequate internal controls for their own management.

Internal planning capacity

The internal planning index reflects the planning capacity of the firm. One would expect firms in transportation and telecommunications to have sophisticated planning units. A score of 4 was assigned when the firm developed its own comprehensive strategic plans. A score of 3 signified that the overall plan was largely a collection of plans put forward by operating units. A score of 2 signified that internal planning was geared to operations rather than strategy, and possibly to justify requests for capital allocations from government. A score of 1 signified that all major strategic planning was performed externally by consultants or the government, although there might be internal planning units for operations.

As might be expected, the correlation between internal planning capacity and autonomy was moderately strong: 0.55, increasing to 0.71 with the exclusion of TAZARA. TAZARA here is atypical not only in its joint national ownership but also in that it is a *young* railway, in which basic operating and strategy problems are painfully obvious to all and solutions are sought through problem-solving teamwork as much as by reference to standard operating procedures and plans.

Profitability

Because of internal control problems, it is difficult to obtain standard profitability measures and to obtain figures for the same years for all firms. Profitability was approximated using the most recently available ratio of operating income or loss to total operating revenue. This ranged from 18 to –43 per cent. The correlation between autonomy and profitability was in the expected direction. What proved more interesting was the somewhat higher correlation between planning and profitability: firms with operating losses were subject to external planning, whereas firms with higher operating profits tended to have strategic planning capacity.

Productivity

As in the case of profitability, measuring productivity is difficult, especially across industries or for the same year. As an approximation, one standard employee productivity measure is used to rank firms within each industry. For airlines, the measure is revenue passenger-kilometres per employee (x 1,000 RPK/ employee). For railways, it is tonnes carried per employee. For posts and telecommunications, a standard telecommunications measure was used: the number of employees per main line (x 1,000 employees/line). To make the telecommunications measure comparable with the air and rail measures, the inverse was calculated so that the higher the number the better. The index for each firm was calculated as the ratio of its score to the mean of the three or four firms in each industry.

There are obvious problems with the index. Kenya Railways ends up with the highest overall score simply in comparison with the other railways in the region, even though one senses that on some underlying productivity measure both airlines and telecommunications have higher employee productivity than railways. Also, because of stagnation and sudden layoffs, Uganda's Posts and Telecommunications has a higher productivity score than Kenya's, which has been

Table 4.2 Data on effectiveness criteria for SOEs

	Planning	Autonomy	Accounts delay	Internal planning	Operating profit (%)	Productivity index	Organizational climate
Ethiopian Airlines	High	19	3	4	12.9	1.52	6.0
TAZARA	Low	17	17	2	3.2	1.46	5.5
Tanzania Posts and Telecom.	High	13	5	4	10.7	0.97	4.0
Kenya Posts and Telecom.	Medium	13	3	3	18.0	0.96	4.5
Air Tanzania Corporation	High	11	12	4	6.4	0.68	4.5
Kenya Railways	Low	9	4	2	0.3	1.60	4.5
Kenya Airways	High	8	6	4	10.8	1.32	3.5
Uganda Railways	External	8	26	1	−4.0	0.44	6.0
Uganda Posts and Telecom.	Low	7	17	2	12.9	1.08	2.0
Uganda Airlines	External	7	14	1	−42.8	0.47	2.5
Tanzania Railways	External	4	11	1	−34.0	0.51	3.5

Correlation matrix

	Autonomy	Accounts delay	Internal planning	Profitability	Productivity
Autonomy					
Accounts delay	−0.32				
Internal planning	0.55	−0.63			
Profitability	0.57	−0.31	0.71		
Productivity	0.58	−0.51	0.45	0.59	
Organizational climate	0.65	0.03	0.19	0.33	0.25

Correlation matrix (excluding TAZARA)

	Autonomy	Accounts delay	Internal planning	Profitability	Productivity
Autonomy					
Accounts delay	−0.54				
Internal planning	0.71	−0.62			
Profitability	0.61	−0.34	0.73		
Productivity	0.50	−0.68	0.53	0.61	
Organizational climate	0.60	−0.07	0.25	0.33	0.16

growing very rapidly in both capacity and employees.

Even so, the correlation between productivity and autonomy is in the predicted direction.

Organizational climate

Finally, as a check on autonomy as a proxy variable for organizational culture, an index for organizational climate was developed using qualitative observations of cohesiveness and morale. Cohesion and morale do not in themselves make for an organizational culture. Since they fall within the human relations approach that is salient in the adversarial phase, some low autonomy organizations, notably Uganda Railways, score high on climate. Although the correlation between organizational climate and autonomy is moderately high, the correlation between climate and other variables is low.

The value of each variable for the eleven SOEs and correlations among the variables are shown in Table 4.2.

In summary, although one must treat cautiously correlations based on only ten or eleven SOEs and very simple measures of productivity and profitability, the results suggest that the following relationships merit further study.

(1) SOE autonomy has at least a moderate positive correlation with key performance criteria: formal internal planning, profitability, and productivity (correlations range from 0.71 downward to 0.50).

(2) Despite moderate correlation with autonomy ($r = 0.60$), organizational climate is only weakly correlated with the other performance criteria (highest correlation: 0.33 with profitability).

(3) Weak internal controls (as measured by accounting delays) are associated with low productivity, low planning capacity, low autonomy, and possibly low profitability (correlation with profitability: −0.31).

(4) High operating profitability is associated with strong planning capacity, high productivity, and high autonomy (correlations from 0.71 down to 0.57).

(5) SOEs with large operating losses are likely to have strategic planning performed by external bodies. Not only are losses linked to trusteeship status, but firms with high losses tend to be more concerned with operational and control improvements than with planning and strategy.

Clinical evidence

The life-cycle model helps explain the popularity of performance improvement programmes (PIPs) among these SOEs (East African Community Management Institute 1975; Abramson 1983). In this organizational development intervention, a key task is to identify achievable goals which lie within the domain of the organization's management. This intervention facilitates internal understanding of the conflicting forces and values operating on the SOE and helps to build an effective management team among heads of functional departments who might otherwise be pulled in conflicting directions by external societal forces (Hafsi *et al.* 1987). It is therefore highly appropriate for the adversarial phase of SOE–government relations, which is the phase in which most SOEs in the sample find themselves. PIPs can help avoid what El-Namaki (1979) has coined the 'policy vacuum' of SOEs. The policy vacuum is a situation of inaction: SOE managers fail to take action because they await policy guidance from the ministry; and ministry officials fail to take action because they lack operational expertise. PIPs help SOE managers to understand the SOE's room for manoeuvre and can serve as a tool for building organizational culture.

Discussion and conclusion

The qualitative data lend support to the view that effectiveness criteria from the open systems approach – flexibility, readiness, resource acquisition – are more salient performance criteria for firms in the cooperative phase when SOE autonomy is low and dominated by societal culture.

A wide range of effectiveness criteria from the human relations, internal process, and rational goal approaches appear relevant for firms in the adversarial phase of SOE–government relations. The clinical evidence suggests that PIP-type interventions may facilitate internal communications, cohesion, morale, and goal setting in this phase.

Effectiveness criteria from the rational goal and internal process approaches – strategic planning, productivity, profitability, stability – are most salient for firms with high autonomy and strong organizational culture. Effectiveness criteria from the other two approaches are of secondary importance for SOEs in the autonomy phase. For example, an external orientation is still needed, as posited for planning effectiveness by Ramanujan and Venkatraman (1987), but the locus of the external orientation shifts from government to clients and rivals.

The empirical evidence from eleven state-owned transport and communications firms in eastern Africa lends support to the proposition that effectiveness criteria vary over time depending on the relative strength of three levels of culture in and around the SOE: societal, industry, and organizational. The balance among the three cultures is in turn linked to phases – cooperative, adversarial, and autonomous – in the life-cycle of the SOE–government relationship.

Implications for managers of state-owned enterprises

The life-cycle model suggests which types of effectiveness criteria managers should concentrate on in a particular phase of the SOE–government relationship. For example, the top management at a state-owned railway in the adversarial phase should first devote its efforts to reducing locomotive down-time to ensure the quality of output demanded by external agencies *before* upgrading the internal control system to standards appropriate for the autonomy phase.

Turnover among SOE managers is high in developing countries. Of the eleven SOEs in this study, eight changed leadership between 1984 and 1987. Since governments tend to move top managers from one SOE to another, managers need to be prepared for shifts in effectiveness criteria if they move from an SOE in one phase to an SOE in another phase in the life-cycle.

Because effectiveness criteria shift over phases in the SOE–government relation cycle, the SOE's perceived performance depends on management's ability to recognize where the SOE is in the life-cycle and to act accordingly.

This can be critical in the transition from one phase to another. Managers of SOEs in transition from the cooperative to the adversarial phase need to refocus efforts from flexible adoption of societal norms to identification of the SOEs latitude in setting goals among conflicting societal and industry norms. Since the 'honeymoon' of the cooperative phase is over, they need to undertake planning to justify requests for resources allocated by government. Internal cohesion and morale become important effectiveness criteria in managing the tension between societal and industry cultures in the adversarial phase.

Managers in transition from the adversarial to the autonomy phase need to shift primary attention from formal evaluation by external entities to market-related criteria such as profitability and productivity. The development of appropriate internal control systems constitutes an essential step in this transition.

Implications for policy makers

Government policy makers need to be aware of the need for multiple effectiveness criteria and the appropriateness of various criteria over phases in the SOE–government relations. Specifically the model suggests a sequencing of effectiveness criteria to improve SOE performance. Tackling profitability first may be inappropriate.

For international development policy makers, the three levels of culture approach suggests a new avenue for improving the performance of weak firms: strengthening regional and international industry associations in order to provide credible value models for SOEs in the industry.

Research implications

The life-cycle model clarifies the link between culture and performance by calling attention to differences in effectiveness criteria as the balance of societal, industry, and organizational culture changes.

Longitudinal studies are needed to test the life-cycle model adequately. Additional work is needed to develop cross-industry indices of profitability, productivity, and output quality. Additional research is also needed to determine whether, apart from the SOE–government life-cycle, there are differences between societal cultures or between industry cultures in the emphasis of various effectiveness criteria such as flexibility versus productivity, growth versus stability, or morale versus formal controls.

Finally, this study signals the need for more research on the consequences of industry culture for the operation of the firm.

Notes

1. An earlier version of this chapter was presented to the Symposium on Culture and Effective Management in Developing Countries, Academy of Management Meetings, New Orleans, August 1987. The Social Sciences and Humanities Research Council of Canada provided financial support for this project. Thanks are also due to Karen Indig, Zaheer Khan, Gerald Kibirige, Pamela Mbogo, and Hans Peter Von Sicard for their research assistance and to more than 100 managers in Ethiopia, Kenya, Tanzania, and Uganda for their generous cooperation in interviews for the study.
2. Because of political turmoil, there has been little capital investment by Ugandan SOEs in the 1980s. The SOE share in Uganda's gross capital formation is probably well below 15 per cent. Total government expenditure (recurrent and capital expenditures) equalled only 7 per cent of gross domestic product in 1986–7, the lowest level in Africa (Uganda Economic Study Team 1987).

References

Abramson, R. (1983) 'Organizational development in African public enterprises: with special emphasis on East Africa', *African Administrative Studies* 22: 31–47.

Adler, N. J. and Jelinek, M. (1986) 'Is "organization culture" culture bound?', *Human Resource Management* 25, 1: 73–90.

Allaire, Y. and Firsirotu, M. E. (1984) 'Theories of organizational culture', *Organization Studies* 5, 3: 193–226.

Ayub, M. and Hegstad, S. (1987) 'Determinants of public enterprise performance', *Finance and Development* 24, 4: 26–9.

Child, J. (1981) 'Culture, contingency and capitalism in the cross-national study of organizations', in L. L. Cummings and B. M. Staw (eds) *Research in Organizational Behavior*, vol. 3, pp. 303–56, Greenwich, CT: JAI Press.

Cohen, R. (1981) 'The blessed job in Nigeria', in G. M. Britan and Ronald Cohen (eds) *Hierarchy and Society: Anthropological Perspectives on Bureaucracy*, pp. 73–88, Philadelphia, PA: Institute for the Study of Human Issues.

Cook, T. D. (1983) 'Quasi-experimentation', in Gareth Morgan (ed.) *Beyond Method: Strategies for Social Research*, pp. 74–94, Beverly Hills, CA: Sage.

Deal. T. E. and Kennedy, A. A. (1982) *Corporate Cultures: The Rites and Rituals of Corporate Life*, Reading, MA: Addison-Wesley.

East African Community Management Institute (1975) *Improving the Performance of Public Enterprises in Developing Countries*, Arusha, Tanzania: East African Community Management Institute.

El-Namaki, M. S. S. (1979) *Problems of Management in a Developing Environment*, Amsterdam: North-Holland.

Green, R. H. (1977) 'The east African community: the end of the road', in C. Legum (ed.) *Africa Contemporary Record, 1976–77*, New York: Africana.

Green, R. H. (1979) 'The east African community: death, funeral, inheritance', in C. Legum (ed.) *Africa Contemporary Record, 1977–78*, New York: Africana.

Hafsi, T., Kiggundu, M. N., and Jørgensen, J. J. (1987) 'Strategic apex configurations in state-owned enterprises', *Academy of Management Review* 12, 4: 714–30.

Hofstede, G. (1983) 'The cultural relativity of organizational practices and theories', *Journal of International Business Studies* 14, 2: 75–89.

Jørgensen, J. J. (1989) 'Managing three levels of culture in state-controlled enterprises', in Taieb Hatfsi (ed.) *Strategic Issues in State-controlled Organizations*, London: JAI Press.

Kiggundu, M. N., Jørgensen, J. J., and Hafsi, T. (1983) 'Administrative theory and practice in developing countries: a synthesis', *Administrative Science Quarterly* 28: 66–84.

Klaus, H. G. (1980) 'Analysis and survey of the conference', in H. G. Klaus, and S. E. Migot-Adholla (eds) *The Role of Public Enterprise in*

Development in Eastern Africa; Proceedings of a Workshop, pp. 5–16, Nairobi: Institute of Development Studies, Occasional Paper No. 39.

Moshi, H. P. B. (1980) 'Financial performance of public enterprises in Tanzania', in H. G. Klaus, and S. E. Migot-Adholla (eds) *The Role of Public Enterprise in Development in Eastern Africa; Proceedings of a Workshop,* pp. 91–106, Nairobi: Institute of Development Studies, Occasional Papers No. 39.

Moris, J. R. (1977) 'The transferability of western management concepts and programs: an east African perspective', in L. D. Stifel, J. S. Coleman, and J. E. Black (eds) *Education and Training for Public Sector Management in Developing Countries,* pp. 73–83, New York: Rockefeller Foundation.

Ndegwa, P. (1982) *Report and Recommendations of the Working Party on Government Expenditures,* Nairobi: Government Printer, July.

Nellis, J. R. (1986) 'Public enterprises in Sub-Saharan Africa', World Bank Discussion Paper 1, Washington, DC.

Quinn, R. E. and Cameron, K. (1983) 'Organizational life cycles and shifting criteria of effectiveness: some preliminary evidence', *Management Science* 29, 1: 33–51.

Quinn, R. E. and Rohrbaugh, J. (1983) 'A spatial model of effectiveness criteria: towards a competing values approach to organizational analysis', *Management Science* 29, 3: 363–77.

Ramamurti, R. (1987) 'Performance evaluation of state-owned enterprises in theory and practice', *Management Science* 33, 7: 876–93.

Ramanujan, V. and Venkatraman, N. (1987) 'Planning system characteristics and planning effectiveness', *Strategic Management Journal* 8: 453–68.

Rieger, F. (1986) 'The influence of national culture on organizational structure, process and strategic decision making: a study of international airlines', unpublished Ph.D. thesis, McGill University Faculty of Management, Montreal.

Seers, D. *et al.* (1979) *The Rehabilitation of the Economy of Uganda; A Report by a Commonwealth Team of Experts,* vol. 2, London: Commonwealth Secretariat, June.

Sexty, R. W. (1980) 'Autonomy strategies of government owned business corporations in Canada', *Strategic Management Journal* 1: 371–84.

Shirley, M. M. (1983) 'Managing state-owned enterprises', World Bank Staff Working Paper No. 577, International Bank for Reconstruction and Development, Washington, DC.

Smith, K. G., Mitchell T. R., and Summer, C. E. (1985) 'Top level management priorities in different stages of the organizational life cycle', *Academy of Management Journal* 28: 799–820.

Uganda Economic Study Team (1987) 'Economic adjustment and long-term development in Uganda', Manuscript Report No. 166e, International Development Research Centre, Ottawa.

United Republic of Tanzania (1985) *National Accounts of Tanzania, 1976–1984,* Dar es Salaam: Ministry of Planning and Economic Affairs, Bureau of Statistics, May.

Chapter five

Leadership and strategy making for institution building and innovation: the case of a Brazilian university

Cynthia Hardy

Introduction

Developing countries often face problems that are not encountered to the same degree in developed countries. One such problem concerns high degrees of government centralization and political influence (Kiggundu *et al.* 1983). As a result, organizations are often confronted by a complex web of bureaucratic procedures and political controls placed on them by their governments. A second problem relates to the early stage of economic development, which renders these countries and organizations more vulnerable to cyclical fluctuations, recession, inflation, and external debt.

Brazilian universities face no exception to these constraints. Brazilian higher education began, in 1808, with the creation of two medical schools. The first university did not appear until 1920, however. It was, in reality, a federation of three existing schools (law, medicine, and engineering), and was reportedly created to provide an honorary doctorate for the visiting king of Belgium. The current system dates from 1968, when the then existing system was overhauled by the military government via a series of legislative acts which represented a complex system of controls that determined university structure, the appointment of rectors, the minimum curriculum, salaries, and the various committees that oversee and fund undergraduate studies, graduate programmes, and research. University structures and procedures, as a result, are tightly regulated by government policies and, in the case of public universities, by government funding. Recently, this legislation has been receiving considerable criticism for bringing about excessive levels of bureaucracy and politics and for stifling innovation (see, for example, Fischer 1984; Fracasso 1984). In addition, Brazil has moved from the era of its 'economic miracle' to an era with three-digit inflation and the largest foreign debt in the developing world. Consequently, creating and nurturing high quality research and teaching in the face of such constraints is not easy.

This chapter takes the example of one university – the State University of Campinas (Unicamp) – that, despite these political and economic problems and in the space of only 20 years, has become one of the most renowned universities in Brazil. It illustrates how this success was related to a unique strategy of academic innovation developed by the founder. The analysis explores the critical role of leadership during both the institution building phase and a period of institutional renewal. It demonstrates how the strategy of the original founder has been nurtured after his death through the leadership of successors and organizational structure. Finally, it examines the link between leadership and strategy.

The chapter is organized in four main sections. The first section introduces the reader to Unicamp. The second section describes the strategic phases in its development. The following section defines more clearly the meaning of innovation, leadership, and organizational structure by introducing theory that has been developed from the North American and European literature. The concluding section discusses the relevance and implications of this literature for Unicamp and for universities and public organizations in developing countries in general.

The State University of Campinas

Unicamp was effectively founded in 1965 and is largely the product of one man – Zeferino Vaz. In 1986 the university had 10,000 students, of whom more than 40 per cent were taking graduate programmes. There were 2,000 professors. Unicamp offered fifty-six undergraduate programmes, fifty-eight master programmes, and forty-two doctorates. In 20 years it has achieved a reputation of being one of the top two universities in the country, the other being the much older University of São Paulo (USP, founded in 1935). These two universities offer over half the doctoral programmes in the country.

Unicamp is a state university, which means it is funded by, and responsible to, the government of the state of São Paulo. São Paulo is the richest state in Brazil and its universities therefore have access to resources not always available to federal universities and universities in poorer states. Unicamp is subject to government controls other than funding; for example, the rector of the university is appointed by the state governor, and the statutes of the university, which specify the various committees and administrative posts and their responsibilities, have to be approved by the State Council of Education.

Unicamp differs from many other Brazilian institutions in a number of ways. It was initially created as a university and not, like many older universities, as an amalgamation of pre-existing institutes. Only the medical and dental schools pre-date the university; the remaining faculties were founded as part of the existing institution. Unicamp also has a unique strategy, which it owes largely to Zeferino (as he is called). His intention was to create a research-oriented university. As a result, more than 40 per cent of Unicamp's students are graduate students and half of these are pursuing a doctorate. Second, Unicamp has not followed the traditional lines of other Brazilian universities. So, for example, there is no Faculty of Law and, instead of the more traditional Institute of Languages, there is an Institute for the Study of Language. The third component of Unicamp's strategy was the result of American rather than European influence. Many of Brazil's older universities and institutes were initially created along European lines. Unicamp took the American system as its model, particularly its interaction with society and business. Rather than an ivory tower, Unicamp conceived of itself as a 'modern' university, which was far more open to societal needs and applied research. In summary, Unicamp subscribed to a mission that differentiated it from other Brazilian universities and emphasized research and academic innovation in response to societal needs.

University structure and decision making

The university only recently formalized its statutes – during its formation period, the university did not have its own constitution but used the statutes of USP as a guideline. The current structure was implemented by the current rector (1986–90) following a four-year formulation period initiated by his predecessor (1982–6).

Academic decision making was relatively decentralized. So, for example, a new programme would normally be initiated within the department concerned. It would have to be approved by the departmental committee and passed up to the faculty council. If approved it would eventually go to the central council (much like an academic senate) for formal approval. This University Council was the senior decision-making body in the university. Its members included the rector, the vice rector, five pro rectors, the directors of the eighteen faculties and institutes, fifteen professorial representatives, four representatives of non-academic staff, one-fifth student representation, and six external members representing various community interests. Proposals for new appointments and new departments or faculties took a similar route.

Financial decision making, in contrast, was highly centralized. Until recently, all purchases were made by the central administration. Directors had only recently started to receive their own budgets, and expenditures remained rigidly categorized. The allocation of resources among faculties was determined primarily by the central administration, in consultation with the directors, and was formally approved by the University Council.

Table 5.1 Strategic phases in Unicamp's development

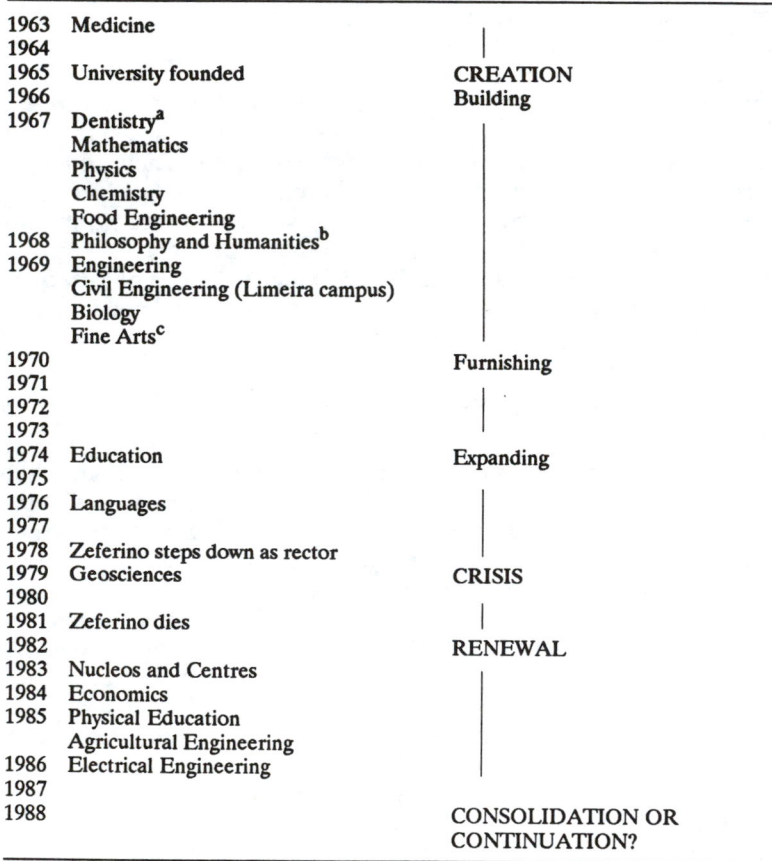

Year	Event	Phase
1963	Medicine	
1964		
1965	University founded	CREATION
1966		Building
1967	Dentistry[a]	
	Mathematics	
	Physics	
	Chemistry	
	Food Engineering	
1968	Philosophy and Humanities[b]	
1969	Engineering	
	Civil Engineering (Limeira campus)	
	Biology	
	Fine Arts[c]	
1970		Furnishing
1971		
1972		
1973		
1974	Education	Expanding
1975		
1976	Languages	
1977		
1978	Zeferino steps down as rector	
1979	Geosciences	CRISIS
1980		
1981	Zeferino dies	
1982		RENEWAL
1983	Nucleos and Centres	
1984	Economics	
1985	Physical Education	
	Agricultural Engineering	
1986	Electrical Engineering	
1987		
1988		CONSOLIDATION OR CONTINUATION?

Notes: [a]Created in 1961 as a separate school; became part of the university in 1967.
[b]Originally Sociology and Economics Institute.
[c]Fine Arts did not offer programmes until the 1980s.

Strategic phases in the development of Unicamp

This section examines the creation of Unicamp and its unique strategy. Its development can be divided into three strategic phases: the creation of Unicamp; a period of crisis; recovery and renewal (Table 5.1).

The creation of Unicamp (1965–79)

The first 15 years of Unicamp's existence represented the period during which both the university and its strategy were created. The origins of the university can be traced back to 1958, when the state made provision for a medical school. The year of inauguration of the university is considered to be 1965, and between then and 1979 Unicamp emerged as a fully functioning integrated university with a clear emphasis on research. It was also the period during which Zeferino was the leader of the institution.

Zeferino was responsible for Unicamp's creation and the development of its research-oriented strategy. He was responsible for all economic, political, and administrative decisions. At that time the university had no formal statutes and so Zeferino had considerable decision-making freedom. His aim was to build a research university and his method was simple – the acquisition of the best qualified researchers he could find, i.e. 'brains'. He found many of these researchers in Brazil, particularly among people experiencing political problems in other universities following the advent of the military dictatorship. Others were lured back to Brazil from the USA and Europe by the idea of this brand new university with its emphasis on research and a non-traditional approach of being open to societal problems. These professors were also attracted by the new facilities – better than those in many American universities, let alone Brazilian ones – and salaries. One professor, for example, found himself earning five times his previous salary at a federal institution.

Zeferino had charisma and external political influence, and was adept at selecting the right people. At first he selected the professors and particularly the directors himself. Later, directors were responsible for recruiting professors, buying equipment, and developing research initiatives, but Zeferino still had ultimate control. He was described as a dictator, an emperor, and a despot but, in all cases, 'a good one'.

This period can be further subdivided into three different stages when the basic infrastructure of the university was built, furnished, and expanded.

Building the infrastructure (1965–9)

The basic faculties of the university were founded between 1965 and 1969. Chemistry, Food Engineering, Philosophy, Social and Human Sciences, Engineering, Mathematics, and Biology were added to Medicine and Dentistry. Provision was also made for arts, although the faculty was not fully developed until much later, and agronomy, which still has not been developed.

During these initial years, the faculties existed very much in name only. Apart from the Faculty of Dentistry which had been offering programmes since the early 1960s, it was not until 1969 that the first programmes were offered. At the institutional level the following 5 years appeared, on the surface, to be a very quiet time for Unicamp, since no new faculties were created. However, the period represented the time when Unicamp became a functioning university.

Furnishing the infrastructure (1969–74)

Having created the basic faculties, Zeferino set about furnishing them with people, equipment, libraries, and other facilities. He personally recruited the directors of these faculties, who were then responsible for making them work. They were told to get the best people and the best equipment. At times, this period was characterized by long and tortuous negotiations during which professors had to be persuaded to give up lucrative appointments in other countries and convinced that Unicamp could provide stability and freedom. At other times, it was characterized by quick and decisive action; for example, the director of Physics was able to buy a complete library from the State University of New York and the director of Mathematics was told to go to the USA and buy the best computer system they had.

It was also during this period that the undergraduate and graduate courses were developed – between 1969 and 1974, thirty programmes were created. So, while the university looked quiet on the surface, there was considerable activity going on within the individual units and, by 1974, the university was clearly a 'going concern'.

Expanding the infrastructure (1974–9)

With the university clearly operational, it became time to develop new initiatives. New faculties were created with the founding of the Faculties of Education and Languages. In addition, fifty-eight new programmes were created during this time in a variety of areas. Prior to 1974, developments had been primarily in the (hard) scientific areas of physics, mathematics, engineering, etc. From 1974 the university started to add the social sciences and humanities to its repertoire, and programmes were created in education, sociology, social sciences, political science, and history.

Thus by 1979 Zeferino had created a fully functioning research university covering the pure, social, and human sciences, which had already achieved the reputation of being one of the best in Brazil. For example, it was categorized as one of only three 'research' universities in which, in 1977, more than 40 per cent of professors had doctoral degrees, and which offered more than ten doctoral programmes (Fracasso 1984).

There are a number of factors that contributed to that development. First there was the role of Zeferino himself. He took personal charge of the university's creation. He was also able to protect it from the external environment and, in particular, the military dictatorship. His external political standing was such that the university encountered few problems from the government unlike, for example, the University of Brasilia which was effectively closed down during the 1960s. Instead of a threat, military rule was transformed into an opportunity for Unicamp and Zeferino – it represented a rich source of highly qualified professors who were experiencing political problems in other universities. The external environment also worked to Unicamp's advantage in another way. It was the time of the economic miracle in Brazil. Between 1968 and 1973, annual growth was 11 per cent. Unicamp is situated in and funded by the richest state in Brazil. As a result, Zeferino was able to raise sufficient funds to attract professors not only from other Brazilian universities but from North America and Europe. Money was also available to build some of the most lavish facilities in the country.

Developments in subsequent years, however, threatened to wreck Zeferino's accomplishments. These years have been described as a period of crisis for the university.

Crisis (1979–82)

In 1978 Zeferino was forced to step down as the rector of Unicamp since he was over the age of 70. In order to retain control over the institution, he took over the directorship of a foundation that administered research grants and contracts for the university and continued to run the university from there. In 1981 Zeferino became ill and suddenly died. His death precipitated a crisis. The university was placed in the position of having to deal with the departure of an absolute monarch without the benefit of a formal constitution. The various internal factions immediately started to compete in the power vacuum created by Zeferino's death. With no formal statutes to constrain them, and without a strong leader, the situation continued to deteriorate into an internal crisis which was impeding the daily functioning of the university, let alone its further development.

External complications had also been brewing since 1979, when a new state government had been appointed. It was led by Paulo Maluf, who was not a strong supporter of higher education. Zeferino's political influence started to dwindle as the university saw its capital and operating expenses curtailed and salaries frozen. With the high rate of inflation, Unicamp's competitive conditions quickly deteriorated.

The increasing internal turmoil prompted the new rector to request the governor's aid. The absence of a formal constitution left considerable ambiguity concerning the roles and responsibilities of university administrators. Consequently there was an attempt by the government, in October 1981, to replace eight directors with professors from other universities and fire fourteen non-academic staff. The response of the university community, however, was immediate and emphatic. A series of strikes, occupations, and demonstrations by students and staff alike physically prevented the new directors from taking up their posts. Eventually, after a series of actions that 'made the campus look like Vietnam', the attempt was withdrawn.

During this period, developments were curtailed and the university at best stagnated and at worst regressed. New construction was abandoned and buildings stood half finished for several years. Some professors left, disillusioned with the political and economic situation. Those who remained found that their energy was devoted to political, rather than academic, issues. New initiatives were not followed up. So, for example, the Faculty of Geosciences, created in 1979, did not mount a programme until 1983, and plans to develop courses in arts had to wait, as did ideas for a centre in biotechnology and genetics. No new programmes were introduced in 1981, for the first year since 1968.

So, in the same way as the creation of Unicamp owed itself to internal (Zeferino) and external (the economic miracle) factors, the period of crisis was marked by internal problems created by the absence of Zeferino and external opposition in the form of the state government. The crisis effectively stopped the development of the university. Despite a new government and an improvement in the economic situation, the new administration faced a difficult task in stimulating Unicamp's recovery.

Renewal (1982–7)

In 1982 a new rector was appointed and the following year a new state government was elected. Relations between the university and the state immediately improved, which helped the new administration in its task. Its strategy involved more than just recovery. During the period following the crisis three initiatives were carried out: fortifying the university against a repetition of the crisis; recovering the lost ground; and recapturing the university's commitment to innovation.

The fortification of the university

The fortification of the university involved the formulation of a 'constitution' – statutes and regulations that clearly defined the roles and responsibilities of the various officers and committees. Unicamp would have had to develop its own constitution in any event – as a fully fledged university it required some formalization of its procedures. Moreover, Unicamp had grown in size since the time when Zeferino was able to run the university almost single handed. The administrative structures which existed were no longer adequate. The attempted intervention of government, however, undoubtedly increased the motivation to formulate the new statutes. It was the ambiguity regarding directorial appointments, caused by the absence of formal statutes, that had rendered the university vulnerable to government intervention.

The previous rector assumed responsibility for formulating the statutes and regulations that underlie the current structure. According to the participants it was a long, hard, and at times tortuous process. It took more than 4 years to formulate the constitution through a process of extensive consultation and amendment. The current structure of the university was not fully implemented until 1986. These changes had become the platform on the basis of which the current rector was elected. Since they had been fully discussed during the term of his predecessor and during his candidacy for rector, he was able to implement them immediately after he took office.

The recovery phase

The recovery phase was designed to enable the university to 'catch up' on ground it had lost during the crisis. It involved, in particular, the physical side of the university. Construction recommenced and physical facilities increased by 140 per cent during this period. Plans were also made to re-equip the university.

Recapturing the mission

Recapturing the mission involved recreating the dynamism that characterized the university's earlier years. The previous rector established a secretariat of university development, headed for 2 years by the current rector. The aim was to explore ways of stimulating innovation by both provoking and nurturing efforts to change.

There was once again a burst of activity in the form of new faculties. Many of these were spin-offs from existing faculties; for example, the Faculty of Economics separated from Philosophy, and Electrical Engineering and Agricultural Engineering both separated from Engineering and were established as separate faculties. These changes were initiated by the professors concerned as departments grew in size and new more specialized programmes were adopted. These proposals progressed through the academic decision-making channels and finally received approval from University Council.

Physical Education was created as a totally new faculty – previously it had not existed, even as a department. In consultation with central administrators, the proposal for a faculty was transformed into the establishment of a faculty designed to offer a 'high level' research-oriented approach to physical education.

The creation of new departmental programmes started to die down during this period and a new structure of centres outside the regular departmental structure was introduced. They were designed to house interdisciplinary activities that could not be accomplished by single departments. They followed a tradition of collaborative research projects at Unicamp, and were designed to be more flexible than the departmental structure. A centre could be created much more easily than a department. It required only that a proposal from an interested researcher be approved by the rector. The centres reported to the rector and received funding directly from him, although many were expected to become self-sufficient in research funding. Over twenty such centres were created between 1983 and 1984..

Thus the period following 1982 was not only a period of recovery for Unicamp but also a period of renewal stimulated by the leadership of the rectors. Innovation thus returned to Unicamp, and it has been occurring at both the institutional level with the formation of new faculties and the micro level with the creation of multidisciplinary centres. Moreover, once again Unicamp confirmed its non-traditional focus, since many of these new developments were occurring outside the formal departmental structure. Recent evaluations show that Unicamp has regained its premier position in research and teaching. In 1986, over 50 per cent of its professors had doctorates and the university offered forty-two doctoral degrees. A 1988 evaluation of the quality of twenty-five undergraduate and twenty-five graduate programmes ranked USP and Unicamp as the top two Brazilian universities (Castilho and de Almeida 1988).

Unicamp provides an example of an institution created by an entrepreneur which successfully carried out a strategy based on innovation and research and attained a position of pre-eminence among Brazilian universities within the first 15 years of its existence. Equally interesting is the fact that after a period of crisis, following the death of the founder, Unicamp has managed to regain its previous position and recapture its mission. The following section examines these issues more closely and discusses some of the lessons that can be learnt from Unicamp's experiences.

The lessons

This section examines the critical role of leadership in Unicamp's success. It then explores Unicamp's emphasis on innovation in more detail. Finally, the link between leadership and strategy is discussed.

The role of leadership

The role of the founder in the institution-building phase of North American and European educational organizations has been well documented (e.g. Clark 1970; Pettigrew 1979). Not only are such individuals important for the hiring of staff and the development of physical facilities, they also create the social fabric of the institution. Clark has argued that excellent institutions often have a saga – a unified set of publicly expressed beliefs which are rooted in history and explain a unique accomplishment (Clark 1970: 178). This saga not only explains institutional excellence, it binds participants together and motivates them to continue to strive towards it. It is often shaped by the founding entrepreneur. In this way, the leader transforms the 'organization' into an 'institution' by infusing it with value, through the creation of a distinctive competence and building commitment among participants (Selznick 1957). The previous analysis has shown the important role that Zeferino played in creating Unicamp and its distinctive strategy. In this respect, Zeferino was an entrepreneur and founded the university in much the same way as a businessman might start up a new business enterprise.

In addition to acting as entrepreneur, Zeferino played another equally important role – as a protector who defended the institution against its environment. Unicamp's development illustrates the close proximity between Brazilian universities and both the larger political system and the economy, and the necessity of some form of protection. Unicamp was created at the same time as the military dictatorship assumed the governance of the country. The political stature of its founder – Zeferino – was a crucial factor in protecting the university from political intervention. In fact, he was able to turn a potential threat into an advantage. While other universities suffered from the repression of the military government and, for example, the University of Brasilia was closed, Zeferino's political standing was sufficient to guarantee academic freedom to prospective professors. He was even able to profit from the problems in other institutions, by appointing professors who had encountered political difficulties elsewhere in Brazil. The risk of ignoring this role is illustrated by the crisis: with the death of Zeferino and the election of a new state government, Unicamp's political protection disappeared, and the university became increasingly vulnerable to state intervention.

The university as an adhocracy

Zeferino was perceived as charismatic and demonstrated many of the characteristics associated with such transformational leaders (see Conger and Kanungo 1987). While the routinization of charismatic leadership has been documented (Trice and Beyer 1986), most research suggests that this form of leadership generally fails to outlive the original leader (see Conger 1988). It has also been argued that charisma is a relational phenomenon, perceived by subordinates only in a particular context; consequently it cannot normally be transferred to another setting. Thus a charismatic leader in one situation may not be charismatic in another (Roberts and Bradley 1988). Such findings highlight the fragility of charisma and the importance of devising ways of enabling organizations to continue to prosper in the event that charismatic leadership dies or fades. Unicamp shows how its original strategy – with its emphasis on innovation – and success was not only maintained after the death of Zeferino but was also recaptured following the political crisis.

Universities typically strive for professional innovation – the continual updating of existing areas of expertise (Savenije and van Rosmalen 1987). In the typical professional bureaucracy, students and professors are slotted into a series of standard programmes or 'pigeon holes' where they receive or carry out a predetermined agenda. So, for example, a medical student receives a clearly defined programme of studies, and the medical professor teaches and researches within clearly and relatively narrowly defined boundaries. Creating new pigeon holes can be difficult, as partitions between departments and faculties often inhibit interdisciplinary initiatives. Innovation does occur, but primarily within the existing pigeon holes, and interdisciplinary activities are usually the result of collaboration between individual researchers, while the formal departmental structure remains the same. Consequently, universities display a remarkable degree of stability in terms of institutional strategy and structure, although continuous change goes on inside the pigeon holes (Mintzberg 1979; Hardy *et al.* 1983).

The key to Unicamp's strategy, however, was a different kind of innovation. The university emphasized the continual development of new courses, programmes, departments, and faculties. This activity has been termed entrepreneurial innovation – the creation of new areas of expertise, which are often multidisciplinary in nature (Savenije and van Rosmalen 1987). It requires a very different type of organizational structure – the adhocracy – which seeks the creation of new pigeon holes. Consequently, it is continually experimenting with new forms of organization as it deals with new problems. Interdepartmental and interdisciplinary initiatives are common as individuals come together and then disband to form new groups and solve new problems. As a result, the institutional profile experiences considerable change. Thus, the adhocracy is directed towards innovation, the professional bureaucracy towards perfection.

> One theater company seeks out new avant garde plays to perform; another perfects its performance of Shakespeare year after year. One engages in divergent thinking aimed at innovation; the other in convergent thinking at perfection.... Both decentralize power to their highly trained specialists but because the Adhocracy seeks to innovate, its specialists must interact informally by mutual adjustment in organically structured product teams; the Professional Bureaucracy, because it standardizes its services, structures itself as a bureaucracy in which each specialist can function on his own, his work automatically coordinated with others by virtue of his standardized knowledge and skills.
>
> (Mintzberg 1979: 436–7)

Unicamp was unlike other Brazilian and Canadian universities (Hardy 1988) in that it was an adhocracy rather than a professional bureaucracy. It made continual changes to its structure. Innovation occurred in multidisciplinary teams – the centres – and by the creation of new departments and programmes. It was a continuous process, clearly illustrated by the following example. The Institute of Philosophy and Humanities was initially created with three departments: Economics; Languages; and Social Sciences, which consisted of Philosophy, History, Anthropology, Political Science, and Sociology. In 1976, Languages became a separate institute. Shortly afterwards, Philosophy separated from Social Sciences to form a department in its own right. In 1978, History followed suit and, in 1984, Economics formed an independent faculty.

This adhocracy enabled Unicamp to recapture its original mission, even though the death of Zeferino ended a period of charismatic leadership, and despite its political crisis. Thus Unicamp's renewal can be attributed not only to Zeferino's original saga, but also to the creation of a structure which played a crucial role in stimulating and enabling innovative changes to promote new pigeon holes.

Leaders and strategy

Unicamp's renewal is not fully understood, however, unless we look at the link between leadership and strategy making. The typical professional bureaucracy is a highly decentralized structure. As a result, change is directed from the bottom up, and administrators have a limited impact on strategy making. Unicamp, in contrast, has been characterized by a relatively high degree of centralization, and rectors have played a key role in directing strategy: first Zeferino, then the previous rector, who spearheaded the renewal of the university's mission, and most recently the current rector, who has been developing priority areas. In fact, the university's greatest problems occurred in the absence of a strong centralizing force – in the vacuum created by the death of Zeferino. In this section the strategic style of Zeferino is examined more closely and is contrasted with the style of his successors.

Clearly, one expects to see strong central direction from a charismatic founder. When Zeferino ran the university, strategy making was entrepreneurial and deliberate (Mintzberg and Waters 1985). Strategies existed as the personal vision of a single leader and the organization was under the personal control of the leader and, at that time, located in a protected niche (by Zeferino) in the environment (Hardy *et al.* 1983; Mintzberg and Waters 1985). As the university grew and the development of the individual faculties was delegated, to a certain extent, to the directors, strategy making changed somewhat. It became ideological in the sense that Zeferino's mission became a collective vision of all the actors. Zeferino began to use process and umbrella strategies when he started to allow the directors to respond to the external environment and determine the specific content of their individual faculty's strategy, while controlling the process through the hiring and committee processes (Hardy *et al.* 1983). In other words, Zeferino hired the directors he wanted and then gave them a mandate to procure staff and equipment.

Zeferino's saga endured, and so strategy making retained its ideological component. The two more recent rectors have also relied on relatively deliberate umbrella strategies and process strategies. Both rectors have specified clearly defined strategic targets, which were then put into practice by the faculty. So, for example, the mandate of the previous rector was the formalization of the statutes. The actual content of the constitution, however, was the result of a 4-year process of negotiation, participation, and consultation. The current leadership has specified a number of priority areas, including biotechnology, computerization, and various administrative changes. Resources are being channelled into these areas to support professorial initiatives. These rectors also used process strategies. For example, the adhocracy provided a system for the creation of new departments, faculties, and centres; the exact nature of these emerged, largely, from the impetus of the professoriate. Thus, while strategy has become less entrepreneurial, leadership nevertheless continues to play a key role in directing and channelling strategic change.

Strategy making at Unicamp has differed from the patterns one would normally expect to find in a university (see Hardy *et al.* 1983). All Unicamp's successful leaders have been relatively interventionist in setting strategic direction. However, they have been able to combine direction with a high degree of academic autonomy. Central figures have imposed fairly deliberate strategies on the university, but only in broad terms. They set the parameters for creating and renewing the university's mission and then used their power as a catalyst – facilitating and provoking innovation. As a result, continuous and unplanned changes occurred as each department and faculty developed the details of a particular strategy.

Conclusions

It has been argued that the rapid innovation associated with many developing countries requires more dynamic models (Thompson 1964; Kiggundu *et al.* 1983). Similarly, arguments have been made that some form of charismatic leadership is particularly crucial in developing countries (see Chapter Sixteen) because of the complex web of bureaucratic procedures and political influence imposed by governments and the impact of precarious economies (Kiggundu *et al.* 1983). The experience of Unicamp offers some insights into these issues.

First, it shows the importance of leadership to the internal setting. In other words, it illustrates the role of the founder in creating an organizational saga that provides the momentum towards innovation and excellence. In this aspect, Unicamp's creation is much like that of many North American and European organizations that owe their existence to a strong entrepreneur (e.g. Clark 1970; Collins and

Moore 1970; Boswell 1972; Pettigrew 1979). Second, Unicamp illustrates the external role of the leader: as institutional protector. This role is probably more important in developing countries, where external political and economic pressures are typically much greater and thus potentially more constraining. Third, innovation at Unicamp was initially achieved through the saga created by the founder. In other words, both the material and the symbolic aspects of the university were geared towards innovation. Fourth, Unicamp indicates how such a strategy can be maintained, even after the demise of the founder, through a fit between leadership, strategy, and the structure, which embodied both centralization and decentralization. Central administrators acted as catalysts – directing and provoking innovation by the use of process, umbrella, and ideological strategies – in a way that balanced central direction with sufficient decentralization to allow experts lower down the hierarchy to carry out innovation.

The lessons derived from Unicamp can be viewed in the light of the administrative theory that has emerged from research in more developed countries. It has been pointed out that such theory often has limited applicability to developing countries. Cases of weak fit between theory and practice have been attributed to three factors: differences in the economic environment; cultural differences; and political differences (Kiggundu *et al.* 1983).

The fact that the theory appears relevant in this case can be attributed to a number of factors. First, publicly funded universities in many developed countries are susceptible to the vagaries of the economic situation and political influence, in much the same way, albeit to a lesser extent, as Brazilian universities are. Second, while specific characteristics have been associated with the Brazilian culture which differentiate it from many Anglo-Saxon countries, there are some similarities with other developed countries such as France. Moreover, Brazil was by no means extreme in holding any of these values (Hofstede 1980). Finally, the university system in Brazil was originally modelled on the US system. Therefore, one might expect Brazilian universities to be structured like and to behave like their US counterparts.

In research on Brazilian companies, it has been found that their structure was more likely to be shaped by technology than by the authoritarian environment (Farris and Butterfield 1972). It is therefore conceivable that in this case the influence of the structure, which is based on the US system, has succeeded in prevailing over cultural and political differences. In other words, it appears from the analysis of this case that Brazil may be different from other more developed countries, but not so different that administrative theories from the developed world do not hold. What differs is not so much the qualitative nature of the relationships between universities and the larger cultural, political, and economic systems, but the degree of influence of the latter on the former. As a result, the lessons learnt from Unicamp may have relevance to institutions in both developed and developing countries.

References

Boswell, J. (1972) *The Rise and Decline of Small Firms*, London: Allen & Unwin.

Castilho, R. and de Almeida, C. (1988) 'As melhores faculdades do Brasil', *Playboy* 13, 3: 127–31, Sao Paulo.

Clark, B. R. (1970) *The Distinctive College: Antioch, Reed and Swarthmore*, Chicago, IL: Aldine.

Collins, O. and Moore, D. (1970) *The Organization Maker*, New York: Meredith.

Conger, J. A. (1988) 'Theoretical foundations of charismatic leadership', in J. A. Conger and R. N. Kanungo (eds) *Charismatic Leadership: The Elusive Factor in Organizational Effectiveness*, San Francisco, CA: Jossey-Bass.

Conger, J. A. and Kanungo, R. N. (1987) 'Toward a behavioral theory of charismatic leadership in organizational settings', *Academy of Management Review* 12, 4: 637–47.

Farris, G. F. and Butterfield, A. D. (1972) 'Control theory in Brazilian organization', *Administrative Science Quarterly* 17: 574–85.

Fischer, T. (1984) 'Departmentos colegiados de curso: dois polos de poder na estrutura universitaria', *Revista Brasileira de Administracao da Educacao* 2, 2: 158–67.

Fracasso, E. M. (1984) *Organizational Planning and Policy Making in Brazil: The Case of the Institutional Program of Faculty Development*, D. Ed. thesis, Harvard University.

Hardy, C. (1988) 'Managing the interest groups in university structures', in F. Hoy (ed.) *Proceedings of the Academy of Management*, 48th Annual Meeting, Anaheim, CA.

Hardy, C., Langley A., Mintzberg H., and Rose, J. (1983) 'Strategy formation in the university setting', *Review of Higher Education* 6, 4: 407–33.

Hofstede, G. (1980) *Culture's Consequences: International Differences in Work Related Values*, Beverly Hills, CA: Sage.

Kiggundu, M. N., Jørgensen, J. J., and Hafsi, T. (1983) 'Administrative theory and practice in developing countries: a synthesis', *Administrative Science Quarterly* 28: 66–84.

Mintzberg, H. (1979) *The Structuring of Organizations*, Englewood Cliffs, NJ: Prentice-Hall.

Mintzberg, H. and Waters, J. A. (1985) 'Of strategies: deliberate and

99

emergent', *Strategic Management Review* 6: 257–72.

Pettigrew, A. M. (1979) 'On studying organizational cultures', *Administrative Science Quarterly* 24: 570–81.

Roberts, N. C. and Bradley, R. T. (1988) 'Limits of charisma', in J. A. Conger and R. N. Kanungo (eds) *Charismatic Leadership: The Elusive Factor in Organizational Effectiveness*, San Francisco, CA: Jossey-Bass.

Savenije, B. and van Rosmalen, K. (1987) *Incentives for Innovation: Purpose and Effect*, presented at the European Forum of the Association for Institutional Research, Enschede, The Netherlands, 24–6 August.

Selznick, P. (1957) *Leadership in Administration*, New York: Harper & Row.

Thompson, V. A. (1964) 'Administrative objectives for development administration', *Administrative Science Quarterly* 9: 91–108.

Trice, H. M. and Beyer, J. M. (1986) 'Charisma and its routinization in two social movement organizations', *Research in Organizational Behaviour* 8: 113–64.

Chapter six

Organization and culture in developing countries: a configurational model

Fritz Rieger and Durhane Wong-Rieger

Introduction

This chapter is organized into three parts. The first part introduces a model of organizational functioning and effectiveness based on cultural characteristics. It describes the dimensions underlying the model and the organizational behaviours typical of each organizational group. The second part describes the field research in which the model was tested: a sample of international airlines in both developed and developing countries. The third section specifically discusses the implications of this model and the research findings for managing organizations in developing countries.

In the cultural configuration model described here it is proposed that the ways in which an organization is structured and behaves are determined, in part, by the culture of the surrounding society. For example, organizations are influenced by elements such as the societal norms regarding the legitimacy of power and status differentials, orientation to time, decision-making style, and preferred work relationships. However, organizations are also technical systems (see Chapter One); hence behaviour is also dictated by the technology needed to produce the goods or deliver the service of the organization. In this sense, organizations are effective to the degree that they can simultaneously meet the constraints imposed by culture and the work technology.

The model described here groups cultural variables into five clusters, each of which defines a unique organizational configuration. A key underlying assumption of these models is that organizations need to function in harmony with their surrounding culture in order to be productive and to satisfy their workers. For example, in Thailand the introduction of an individual merit bonus plan, which runs counter to the societal norm of group cooperation, may result in a decline rather than an increase in productivity from employees who refuse to compete openly with each other. Such a scheme might be successful if it is compatible with existing cultural behaviour (as in the case of Singapore where the Chinese value individual achievement) or the organization is able to modify certain of its members' values, norms, and beliefs that come from the surrounding culture.

The cultural configuration approach is assumed to be universally applicable in that the research on which it is based is from a wide range of cultures, including both developed and developing countries. Field and archival research showed that while two of the five configurations were equally likely in both developed and developing countries, the others were almost exclusively found in one or the other.

In this chapter the need for indigenous management in developing countries will be discussed in the light of this conceptual approach and the findings of a field study comparing management in the international airline companies in eight countries ranging from low to extremely high levels of economic development.

There has been a tendency to presume that the predominant post-bureaucratic form of organization in the Western industrialized countries is the universally optimal form. Indeed, there is ample evidence to the contrary, as witnessed by Japanese, Korean, and other southeast Asian firms. Moreover, even in the Western industrialized nations, there is a range of effective organizational patterns (compare, for example, the Swedish and North American car manufacturers or IBM and Apple Computer). Thus, one of the underlying premises of this chapter is that no single organizational form or management style is most effective for all types of organizations and levels of development.

We suspect that one of the reasons for discounting the indigenous organizational forms of the developing countries has been their perceived similarity (from a Western point of view) to earlier stages of organizational development in the Western countries. Western organizations have evolved, with changes in technology, from simple organic forms, through a period characterized by the bureaucratic form, to the current post-bureaucratic model.

It is important, however, not to confuse 'ontogenetic' changes in one culture with 'phylogenetic' differences across cultures. Rather, as noted in the arguments of Chapter One of this book and Redding (1988), the organizational structure and processes in developing countries are probably more effective when they parallel the features of their societal culture than when they imitate those of the Western industrialized countries.

The purpose of the present chapter is to look more carefully at the role of culture in influencing the management of organizations, especially in developing countries. It will use the findings of the earlier field studies to clarify the differences among the organizational forms most commonly found in developing countries and to suggest effective management behaviour appropriate to each form.

Configuration approach

The conceptual approach used here is based on the insight advanced by Miller and Mintzberg (1983) that it is often more useful to study complex organizations as holistic systems than to analyse the relationships between a limited number of abstract organizational variables. They argue that the more analytical approach, while describing certain relationships in detail, often fails to account for the complexity and variability of relationships among organizational characteristics. A more holistic strategy, termed here the configuration approach, advocates studying the organization in broader terms, simultaneously taking into account many important organizational characteristics, so that a more complete picture of organizational reality can be understood.

Their 'configuration hypothesis' states that the universe of organizations can be represented by a limited number of archetypes. To be viable, organizations (and their representational archetypes) must fit with their external environment and simultaneously maintain consistency among their internal characteristics. Miller and Mintzberg argued that environments cause adaptation over the long run by allowing only a limited number of synergistic and compatible organizational forms to survive. In their terms, organizational configurations are systems of tightly interdependent relationships between environmental forces and organizational characteristics. Therefore, it is both appropriate and useful to take a holistic approach to understanding these organizations as configurations.

The notion of configuration is also useful in understanding the relationship of societal culture to fundamental organization processes. The configuration hypothesis points out that internal organizational characteristics must fit and be in equilibrium with external environmental conditions. For such a situation to occur, the culture of the organization must be more or less congruent with the culture of the society in which it operates. Thus, the societal culture provides the value orientation of its employees and influential managers, and thus helps determine the organizational culture and internal organizational processes (Sathe 1985).

Development of preliminary typology

First we shall briefly review the development of the preliminary typology/framework. Although a few culturally based typologies are widely used in the literature on organizations (e.g. Hofstede 1980), none describes the more macro-organizational processes and structures in great detail. Ideally such a typology would be grounded in whole organization studies which richly describe such processes (Mintzberg 1979a).

In practical terms, construction of the framework involved first reducing the large number of potentially important organizational variables by sorting them according to the most important themes, second, developing a small set of salient cultural dimensions that reflect these themes, and third, using the dimensions to form a framework that distinguishes between the most important archetypes found in the field study literature. These steps will now be described in more detail.

A large number of descriptive studies of organizations in different societies were examined and all elements indicating cultural influences on organizational processes were listed. These are presented in Table 6.1 together with their sources, the countries from which the data were drawn, and whether or not the studies were performed in developed or developing economies.

These elements or 'sub-themes' were then categorized into four principal themes each underlying a principal cultural dimension: (1) *authority distance*, i.e. the structural nature of authority relationships; (2) *power*, i.e. the personal nature of authority relationships; (3) *group orientation*, i.e. the relationship of the individual to the group; (4) *cognitive orientation*, i.e. the cognitive approaches of decision makers. The dimensions were operationally defined as follows.

Authority distance measures the amount and quality of interactions between individuals of unequal status in the organization. Low authority distance is characterized by frequent, direct, and personal contacts and high authority distance by infrequent and/or formal relationships. Overall, authority distance is expected to be higher in industrialized societies than in traditional societies.

Power is defined as the ability of the leader(s) to affect the organization's decisions and influence the actions of its members. Power is expected to be high in developing economies and mixed in developed economies.

Group orientation expresses the extent to which the organization accomplishes its goals within the context of small face-to-face groups, as well as the extent to which the individual identifies with the group. Group orientation is not expected to be related to the

Table 6.1 Themes and cultural dimensions in descriptive studies of organizations

| Related sub-themes | Sources and regions | |
	Developing	Developed

Cultural dimensions and principal themes:
Authority distance and structural nature of authority relationships

Elitism, social stratification	Cochrane 1959, Gillin 1960, Whyte 1969 (Latin America); Fallers 1955, 1964, 1965 (Africa); Geertz 1965; Robinson 1986 (Indonesia)	Hartmann 1959, Lawrence 1980 (Germany); Granick 1962 (Western Europe); Abegglen 1958, Nakane 1970 (Japan)
Personalism/paternalism	Gillin 1960 (Latin America); Davis 1968 (Mexico); Lauter 1969, Kagitcibasi 1970, (Turkey); Kakar 1971 (India)	
Hierarchy, bypassing	Davis 1968 (Mexico); Presthus 1961 (Turkey)	Maurice and Brossard 1976 (France, Germany); Crozier 1964 (France)
Formality norms	Bowden 1976, LeVine 1976 (Africa)	Crozier 1964 (France)

Cultural dimensions and principal themes:
Power and personal nature of authority relationships

Ascription/achievement	Harbison and Meyers 1959 (Latin America); Kapferer 1980 (Africa); Kakar 1971 (India); Nambudiri and Saiyadain 1978 (Nigeria, India); Heller 1969	Hartmann 1959 (Germany)
Ability to command		Crozier 1964, Crozier and Friedburg 1976 (France); Pfeffer 1981 (USA)

Cultural dimensions and principal themes:
Group orientation and relation of individual to group

Individual competitiveness	McClelland 1961, Mead 1962 (Greece); Hsu 1985 (Japan, China, USA); De-Vos 1968, Marsella *et al.* 1985	Crozier 1964 (France)

Continued

Table 6.1 continued

Related sub-themes	Sources and regions	
	Developing	*Developed*
Group identity	Hsu 1985 (Japan, China)	Triandis 1972 (Greece); Vogel 1963, Rohlen 1974, Lebra 1976, Atsumi 1979 (Japan)
Distrust of outsiders	Whyte 1963 (Peru); Triandis 1972 (Greece)	Crozier 1964 (France)
Clientelism	Shor 1960, Deyo 1978 (Thailand)	

Cultural dimensions and principal themes:
Cognitive orientation and how decision maker processes information

Analysis/intuition, universalism/particularism		Enthoven 1969, Leavitt 1975, Mintzberg 1976, Mintzberg *et al.* 1976 (North America)
Holism/time orientation	Redding 1980 (Hong-Kong); Inkeles and Smith 1974	
Subjective probability estimation	Redding 1980 (Hong-Kong); Quinn 1978, Gladwin and Gladwin 1971, Quinn 1978 (West Africa)	
Fatalism	Gillin 1960 (Latin America); Narain 1967 (India)	

level of development of an economy.

Cognitive orientation is a bipolar dimension of information processing. At one extreme it is characterized by the analysis of hard quantitative data, and at the opposite extreme by holistic intuitive judgements of soft qualitative data. Developed countries are expected to be analytical and developing countries are expected to be intuitive in cognitive orientation.

The third step in the development of the typology was to propose culturally based organizational configurations which related the most commonly occurring organizational types to the dimensions. Although the four dimensions taken together yield sixteen (twenty-four) possible combinations, the examination of the field study

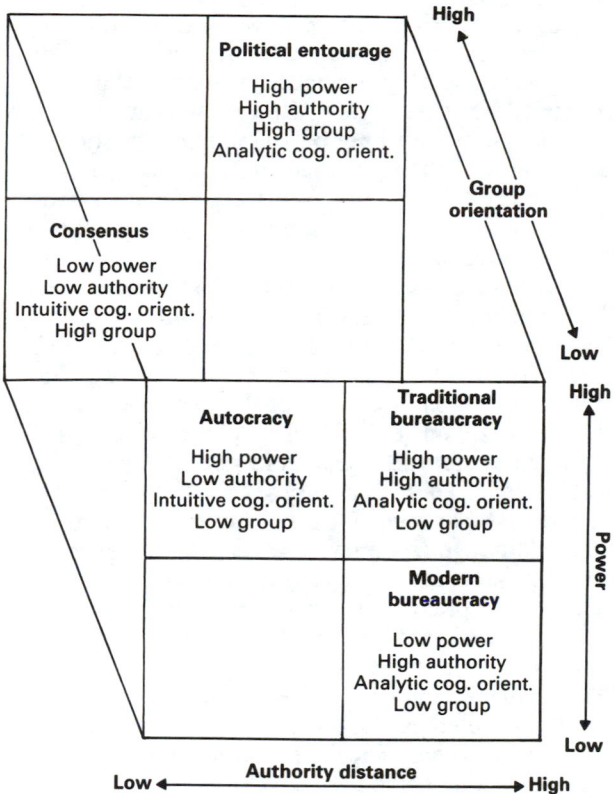

Figure 6.1 Cultural configuration framework

literature revealed only five archetypal configurations. This is consistent with the configuration hypothesis that posits only a limited number of viable organization types. The five types are arrayed on three of the dimensions of the model in Figure 6.1 (the fourth dimension, cognitive orientation, is indicated for each occupied cell). As indicated in the following description, the relationship to the level of development is less equivocal for the configurations than it was for some of the individual dimensions.

(1) The autocracy reflects the presence of a powerful, often entrepreneurial, leader who has the final word on all important issues and often makes unilateral decisions based on personal judgements and intuition. Superior–subordinate communications are informal, reflecting the low authority distance, but

activities, horizontal communication flows, and group orientation are low. The autocracy appears to be incompatible with employees' expectations of participation as may exist in developed countries. Because of its limited horizontal communication, it would also not be suitable for situations of high levels of complexity that characterize technology-based businesses. In contrast, it appears to be the preferred organization type in developing economies that have a background of paternalistic social leadership.

(2) The political entourage is characterized by high group orientation and the proliferation of patron–client relationships within an established bureaucracy. The term 'entourage' refers to the patron–client-based small groups that are the building blocks of the organization. Members of the numerous entourages in these organizations exhibit primary loyalty to their leader and to other entourage members rather than to the organization as a whole. There is significant rivalry among entourages and strategic decisions are the outcomes of negotiation among entourage leaders whose relative influence depends on each entourage's size or the importance of its function. Elements of the political entourage have been described in studies of both developed and developing societies (Shor 1960; Allison 1971). In developed societies, it is often criticized and disdained in favour of less political forms, while it appears to be accepted as an inevitable form in developing societies that share two characteristics: sufficient slack resources to permit competing patrons to develop followings within the organization and sufficient group orientation to foster the formation of an entourage around the patron.

(3) The traditional bureaucracy is a bureaucracy characterized by a rigid adherence to established procedures. Authority distance and power are both high and communication is mechanistic. Strategic decisions are made analytically but are occasionally superseded by the interference of powerful executives. Traditional bureaucracies are found in both the developed and developing world. In the developed economies they often represent the vestiges of mature and sometimes declining institutions while in the developing economies they are often found in state-owned industries, in countries that are former British colonies, or in businesses that were formed as joint ventures with firms from developed countries.

(4) The modern bureaucracy is a bureaucracy characterized by the growing influence of professional staff experts on the strategic decision-making process. Authority distance is generally lower

than in the traditional bureaucracy and cognitive orientation is highly analytical. Power is shared between the executives and staff to a greater extent than in the other types. This type would be expected to be found only in the developed economies.

(5) The consensus configuration is modelled after the Japanese organizational type (Ouchi and Jaeger 1978; Pucik and Hatvany 1983) and is characterized by high group orientation and low authority distance which together facilitate the sharing of decision-making responsibility throughout the organization. Decision making is holistic, combining features of analytical and intuitive modes. This type appears to be found mainly in Japan.

Findings from the field studies

The following discussion is based on field data collected through interviews and unobtrusive observations in international airline companies from eight countries. The data were content analysed for major themes and recurring issues and these results were compared and contrasted to arrive at a holistic picture of each of the airlines within its own cultural and developmental context. Figure 6.2 lists the eight airlines in the sample, their stage of development, and their classification in the typology based on the field study data. Gross national product per capita was used to approximate the level of economic development.

As indicated in Figure 6.2, two of the airlines, one from Singapore and the other from Italy, appeared to be in states of transition. Singapore International Airlines (SIA) is an autocracy which is rapidly moving toward the modern bureaucracy and Alitalia is a traditional bureaucracy that leaned during the period of the study toward autocracy.

Two of the three airlines from the most industrialized/developed countries, Lufthansa and Air Canada, were classified as 'modern bureaucracies'. Compared with all the other airlines in the sample, their most salient characteristics were their technical focus and analytical approach to operational and strategic management, the sharing of power between top executives and staff, and, supporting these, the professional qualification and orientation of their workforces. In Hofstede's (1980) terms, these typified the 'well-oiled machines' of the industry. Both were large, had been founded over 40 years before, and were, at the time of the study, relatively immune from government interference even though they were both state

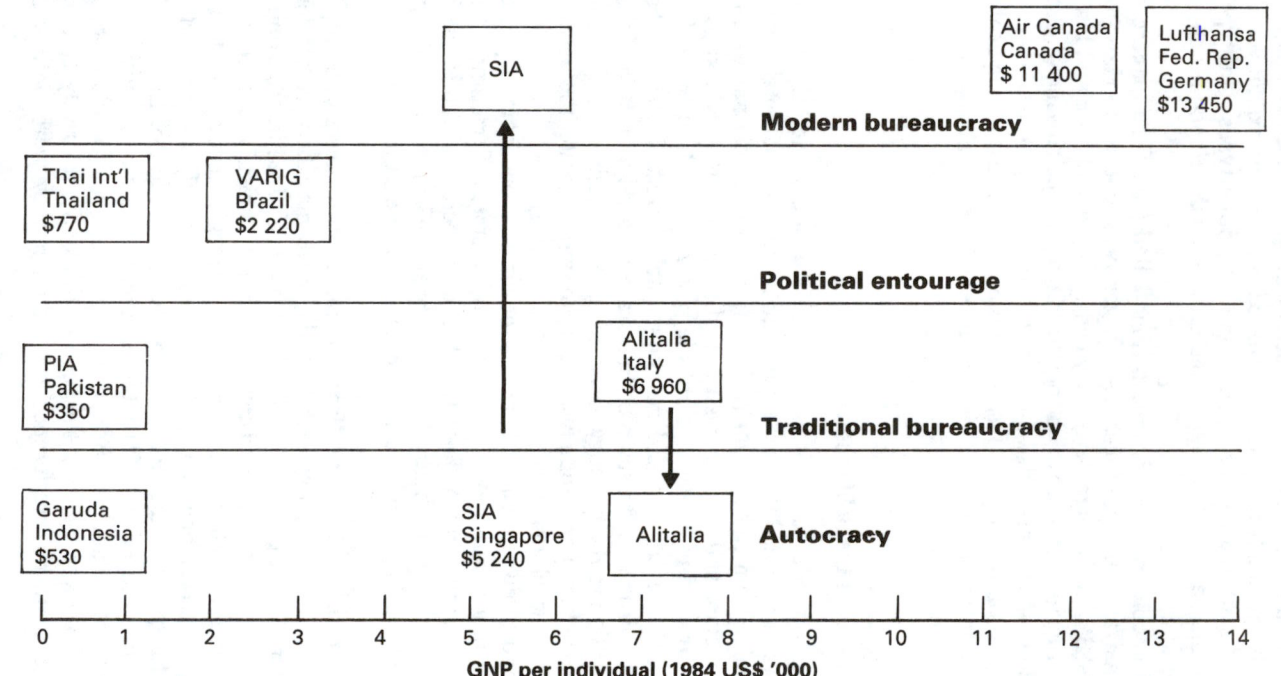

Figure 6.2 Sample of organizations used in field studies, level of economic development, and cultural configuration

owned. Along with Alitalia (Italy) and Varig (Brazil), they will serve primarily as comparison points for the discussion of the companies from the developing world.

The following sections will describe the salient features of the four developing country airlines and discuss the model's implications for effective management in firms in developing countries. Rates of growth and profitability varied considerably among the sample but were positive in all cases. Since these differences in performance can be attributed to a wide variety of factors, the discussion will include anecdotal evidence of managerial effectiveness as well as broad economic measures. The four developing country airlines occupy three cells of the model: the autocracy, the traditional bureaucracy, and the political entourage. They all share one characteristic that also distinguishes them from the modern bureaucracy, namely a much higher degree of personal power.

The autocracy

The highest expression of unfettered personal power was observed in the autocracies, Garuda (Indonesia) and SIA (Singapore). As the term 'autocracy' implies, these companies were dominated by chief executive officers (CEOs) who personally controlled, to the extent that their rapidly growing companies allowed, most aspects of operations and strategic decision making. This could be clearly seen in both companies, although it was perhaps more dramatic in Garuda, the significantly smaller of the two. The Garuda CEO was a former Indonesian war-hero pilot who had been selected by President Suharto to reorganize and manage the airline in 1968. He immediately dismantled the bureaucracy and fired about half its 5,000 employees. Those who survived became the core of an austere company characterized by little slack and no perquisites of office for its few executives.

The CEO established a norm of bypassing the already simplified structure, thus further reducing communications distance between the executive and operations levels. Strategic decisions were made intuitively by the CEO based on his experience and first-hand familiarity with all facets of operations even extending to his piloting the large jets in training flights. Planning, in the sense of detailed programming of future actions, was almost non-existent. Important strategic decisions having long-range implications were decided in accordance with the CEO's personal vision of the future of Indonesia in the world of international aviation.

Related to this intuitive and hands-on approach to decision making were a tinkerer's willingness to innovate in the technical area.

These innovations, which tended to be conceptual rather than detailed, often withered because they ultimately proved impractical. Sometimes, however, they paid off as when Airbus Industrie agreed to his suggestion that it configure a special two-person cockpit version of its popular three crew A-300 aircraft for Garuda.

The question arises whether the autocratic management approach at Garuda is a reflection of cultural norms about authority or a response to deficits in training and technical knowledge of the workforce. The evidence collected in the field study of Garuda seemed to support the cultural explanation. There the CEO seemed to address all areas of management in a similar authoritarian style regardless of the differences in competence that the various functional areas had developed.

By comparison, the autocratic tendency at SIA continued but was tempered by that company's rapid internal commercial and technical development. As the company grew, the SIA CEO, a trained engineer with strong connections with the Republic's finance ministry, no longer immersed himself in the day-to-day management of the company but retained close control over the important decision processes such as aircraft purchases. As indicated earlier and in Figure 6.2, the company appeared to be moving toward the modern bureaucracy model although important elements of the autocratic system remained in both the CEO's influence on decision choices and the overall authoritarian style that pervaded the company.

Control of operations at SIA was achieved through a combination of direct supervision and bureaucratic rules. Intimidation was sometimes used in the supervision of the lower staff and among the cabin crew, where inspections and discipline were very strict. Interviews with younger cabin crew members revealed that younger employees feared their immediate superiors and older colleagues.

The SIA CEO was neither as imaginative nor as flamboyant as his colleague at Garuda, but was nevertheless effective in introducing innovative services or going against the trend in the industry. In contrast with the case of Garuda, which clearly supported the cultural argument, the trend at SIA is less conclusive. On the one hand, the growing technical expertise of the company staff permitted the delegation of routine operational decisions to levels similar to those found in the modern bureaucracies. On the other hand, important strategic decisions were still tightly controlled by the CEO.

The two airlines illustrate variations on the basic theme of autocracy. The centralization of all decision-making processes resulted from both the societies' élitist ideology and the CEOs' distrust of subordinates and competitors. In both cases, the CEOs' effectiveness and power were enhanced by the unstinting support of their respective countries' leaders. This gave them extra leverage over potential resistance which might develop within the organization or in government ministries that had regulatory control over the airline.

Management of both airlines was extremely effective in both economic and anecdotal terms. The Garuda CEO rebuilt an inoperative bureaucracy into a fairly reliable and rapidly growing airline system in a country that lacked a basic aviation infrastructure. In comparison, the SIA CEO is credited with building the fastest growing international system in the world that is additionally renowned for its excellent service.

How then can we account for these impressive successes? What is the contribution of the autocracy configuration? What are the limits of the autocratic form and under what conditions will it be most effective?

In both cases the organizations were immersed in dynamic economic, political, and competitive environments. In the case of Garuda, the CEO could only overcome the entrenched political resistance to change from a position of absolute authority. At SIA, the CEO faced intense competitive manoeuvring in the region that demanded a flexible response and a pre-emptive establishment of lucrative regional routes. Here the required speed and flexibility of response were facilitated by the autocratic nature of the organization. This only worked, however, because of the compliant and diligent nature of the workforce.

The success of both airlines therefore rests on external and internal factors. Internally, the CEOs established and dominated lean organization structures that facilitated the flow of information and directives along vertical channels and permitted rapid response to changing environmental demands. Externally, the powerful CEOs were able to influence the local environment and, through informal coalition formation (particularly deal-making with manufacturers and other airlines), gather strategic information about the environment.

As in the counterpart entrepreneurial organizations in the developed world, the principal strategic strength of the autocracy in the developing world is its ability to respond to the changing environment. A developing country entrepreneur can have considerable external political power which can be used to influence the local environment on behalf of the firm. In the case of the two airlines, power was at first conferred by the country leader but was later developed by the CEOs as their organizations grew. Being the protégé of the government leader makes it easier to establish that power but, even without that initial support, the developing country entrepreneur in such a large organization usually has a sufficiently high profile in society for it to be leveraged into real external political power.

The exercise of that external power also has its limits and risks. In the case of Garuda, the bold strategies of fleet renewal eventually caught the airline in a debt crisis which brought political embarrassment to the government and led to the CEO's dismissal after 16 years of support. Similarly, the Italian government dismissed its autocratic CEO (who presided over a traditional bureaucracy) when consumer complaints about key service caused it intolerable embarrassment.

A similar organizational type, also termed the autocracy, has been described by Mintzberg (1976, 1979b, 1983) in the case of developed countries. An important difference between the two models is the much longer time that this universal form will be tolerated in developing countries. In developed countries, this organic form typically disappears as the firm grows beyond the ability of the manager or the toleration of the workers. In other developed country cases, autocratic managers are brought in for a period to turn a moribund situation around but, once the turnaround takes hold, the demands of the organization for more democratic management typically shorten the manager's stay. These demands are rooted in democratic societal norms. In societies where authoritarian norms exist, these limits can be extended indefinitely, as in the two examples cited here, typically until a truly devastating blunder catches up with the CEO.

From this discussion it is possible to infer some general propositions about the effectiveness of the autocracy in developing countries. First, autocracies will work in a developing country when the cultural norms concerning authority (high power, low authority distance) encourage them. Thus countries such as Singapore whose culture is strongly supportive of a highly autocratic government are prone to having autocratic organizations. State-owned enterprises in these countries will be doubly prone to the autocracy form since their leaders *de facto* have the behind-the-scenes support of the country leadership. Second, autocracies are especially useful in developing countries undergoing dynamic economic change. Third, the success of an autocracy depends not only on the leader's charisma but also on her or his technical competence. Successful developing world leaders of autocracies are usually heavily involved in the production technology of their organization. To summarize, Table 6.2 reviews the application of the autocracy in developing countries and compares it with the other configurations.

Table 6.2 Application of configurations in developing countries

Autocracy	Traditional bureaucracy	Political entourage
Advantages		
Responsive to change in environment	Produces simple products efficiently	Satisfies cultural preference for personalistic relations within large organization context
Effective for introducing new programmes	Produces employment for moderately skilled	
Good for unstable political environment	Fairness – in production and employment	Can effectively defend against threat of external political interference
	Within limits can perform integrated set of tasks	
Disadvantages		
Overloads decision maker – delays	Slow response to environment change	Often exposed to external intervention
Eventually limited in size	Imposes more technology and system on workers than other types; sometimes provokes reaction – mistreatment of clients, strikes, sabotage, sloppy workmanship	Outsiders can penetrate the organization's boundary by seeking sympathetic factions within the organization
Does not prepare for succession		
Stifles employee initiative		Without a technically competent leadership the political entourage will increase in directionless political activity
Plays favourites, internally unfair		
Can rely on fear and coercion	Not adapted to workers' needs	
Not mindful of employee human rights	Similar to classic problems but magnified in developing society	
Favourable circumstances		
Founder-led organizations	Relatively stable environment	Large organizations in societies that react negatively to bureaucratic rigidity, have high group orientation, and have norms against overt conflict
Authoritarian culture – leader as hero	Simple product or service demanded	
Diligent deferential workers	Not a lot of competition – protected	
Workers are low skilled or complacent	Often state ownership or control	
Incompatible with high group orientation	Plentiful literate labour force	Traditions of patron–client relations in society
If government support, must be unequivocal	Workers accept routine work and technology	
Sometimes the only form that works for some very strong leaders	At least minimal analytical orientation	
	Achievement rather than ascriptive culture	
	Managers obsessed with control	
Management skills		
Intuitive approach to problem solving	Analytical approach to problem solving	Leader must simultaneously maintain balance among the factions in the organization
Understanding of technical system	Managers who attend to detail and control	

Table 6.2 continued

Understanding of whole organization Possess skill important to operating core Charismatic or at least people skilled	Requires moderate attention to personal demands – implies balance between mechanistic and personal management approach Managers must control own power needs	Must provide sufficient technical leadership to have a valid, but patient, vision of the organization's future 'muddling through with a purpose' Leader must suppress autocratic tendencies in favour of incremental progress

Traditional bureaucracy

The traditional bureaucracy in general represents a marginally satisfactory solution to the problem of effectively organizing work in the developing world. It combines a norm of personal power with, or more exactly overlays it onto, a basically mechanistic and impersonal bureaucratic structure. The traditional bureaucracy does not by definition suffer from most of the ills attributed in Western literature to Weberian bureaucracy after which it is modelled, but it does appear to be vulnerable to them. Two airlines in the sample were classified as traditional bureaucracies, Alitalia (from Italy, a modern highly industrialized and somewhat politicized country) and PIA (from Pakistan, a developing highly politicized country). It is easy to make the case immediately for some connection between degree of country level politicization and bureaucratization in the case of PIA. CEOs there have historically been moved around with each change of government or hint of government scandal. It is less clear in Italy, where a state-owned holding company operates the airline and acts as a buffer. However, the political instability, or more exactly attempts at political interference in the airline's operations, seems to reinforce the less efficient and less appealing aspects of bureaucracy.

According to the model, the traditional bureaucracy is characterized by high power, high authority distance, low group orientation, and analytical cognitive orientation. The most apparent cultural difference between the traditional bureaucracy and modern bureaucracy is the already mentioned high degree of personal power in the traditional bureaucracy. Almost as important, though less clear, is the degree to which an analytical approach pervades the organization's culture. Both are expected to be high in analysis, but in the modern bureaucracies analytical methods drive the decision-making process, whereas in the traditional bureaucracies analytical methods dominate the management of operations but must compete with personal preferences and can be irrelevant in the process of making important decisions. The more developed countries have more highly qualified analysts to fill key roles, and the greater presence of these professionals with their expectations about sharing power in the organization may also account for lower power measures in the modern bureaucracies. In contrast, fewer analysts are available to work in developing country traditional bureaucracies, and they are relegated to complex operational tasks and seldom share much power with the established hierarchical management.

PIA is a case in point. It is a large airline with historically unstable senior management due to political changes in the country. Most professionally trained analysts work in engineering and the management information system (MIS), but the MIS is used only selectively. MIS analysts recounted cutting off managers' reports to test whether they were being used and discovering that there were no complaints. The internal infrastructure of the airline is weak and is compensated by an excess of underemployed low-paid administrators. Morale at PIA is low, as manifest in sabotage and labour agitation.

In Alitalia, a developed country traditional bureaucracy, there were more qualified technicians and technology, but they were constrained by a rigid system and lack of commitment to analysis, as evidenced by a lack of requisite technological resources for the professionals. Thus a professional culture developed on a departmental basis in Alitalia but did not suffuse the entire airline as it did in the modern bureaucracies at Air Canada and Lufthansa. Indeed, the personal power needs of the Alitalia CEO, exemplified by his statement to the press that he wanted 'to be able to push a button and make things happen', provoked reaction by labour unions and professional staff alike.

Overall, three critical forces drove these two traditional bureaucracies. The first is the strong external control over the airlines exerted by their governments. The second is the management's expressed need for rigidity and control (but not necessarily the analytical approach that logically accompanies them). Both phenomena may have been induced by the perception of a chaotic local environment. Management at both airlines complained about their undisciplined workforce and unreasonable unions to a much greater extent than in any of the other airlines. Whether or not these complaints reflected objective reality, they did reveal the personal biases of the managers toward rigid hierarchical relations which characterize the traditional bureaucracy. The third factor was the administrative subordinates' deference toward authority which was manifest in both Alitalia and PIA by subservience and deference to superiors. It was more pronounced at PIA, where it was observed at all but the highest administrative levels, than at Alitalia, where it was observed mostly among the older middle-level managers.

Overall, in comparing PIA and Alitalia, the same forces and relationships are at work but to a much stronger degree at PIA, reflecting important differences between the developed and developing world. Thus the Italian aviation environment, which is plagued by strong competition, a militant labour movement, and chronic bad winter weather in its most important markets, appears chaotic, especially relative to that faced by other major European carriers. But in Pakistan, the environmental chaos is of a different order of magnitude. Similarly, with regard to the cultural acceptance of strong personal leaders and the propensity of the government to interfere in the management of its enterprises, Pakistan surpasses Italy.

What is the value of the traditional bureaucracy configuration? The traditional bureaucracy seems to be an imposed type in the developing world. It is commonly found in former British colonies such as India, Pakistan, and to a lesser extent East Africa. Other nations such as Thailand or Indonesia maintain bureaucracies that are distinctly different as we shall see in the next section. The traditional bureaucracy is particularly good at two things: dealing with stable business environments where the objective is efficiency and providing employment for large numbers of people. (These activities, it should be noted, may not be entirely contradictory in low wage countries.) However, traditional bureaucracies are poor at dealing with the fluid environments that are typically found in the developing world. Although their leaders may be prepared to make the quick decisions appropriate to the situation, they are constrained in implementing them by a ponderous organizational mechanism.

The traditional bureaucracies are no one's ideal organization type but they will continue to persist for years to come, especially in the developing world. What then are the factors that favour them? These can be framed as a list (albeit shorter) of propositions, as was done previously for the autocracy.

First, the traditional bureaucracies will be most effective when they have a good balance between internal technological resources and professionally qualified analysts. The key term here is 'balance'. In Alitalia there were plenty of qualified analysts but the resources (such as computer time and support personnel) available were inadequate. At PIA, the opposite was often true. In many cases the competence of the workforce lagged the introduced technology and indeed some workers rebelled against it. In other cases (and more probably in the typical developing country situation) the resources were woefully inadequate too. Second, traditional bureaucracies will be more effective, the less outside interference there is. They tend to tighten up already rigid systems when exposed to external criticism and pressure. They also tend to become targets of unscrupulous politicians unless carefully monitored. The task of finding the balance point between insulating the traditional bureaucracy from government interference and control and driving the organization to further rigidity appears to be very difficult. Ideally, efforts should be made on two fronts: increasing the technical competence of the workers at the same time as determining the policy of independence, since the latter is made easier as the workforce develops more competence.

Third, failure in the traditional bureaucracy typically means chronic inefficiency, but not necessarily dissolution of the business, since developing country governments typically support local organizations that are large enough to have the form. On the one hand, this implies significant continuing social and economic costs to societies that can ill afford it. On the other hand, the internal stability of the form means that incremental improvements are possible over the long term.

Political entourage

The feature that distinguishes the political entourage from the traditional bureaucracy is the strong identification of the political entourage members with their group in the organization. However, group orientation is only a necessary but not a sufficient condition of the political entourage, which is clearly a different sort of organization from all the others. First described by Shor (1960) for the government bureaucracy in Thailand, it is distinguished by its continuous internal political activity and a negotiated basis of decision making. Neither of the companies identified as political entourages in this study were pure types; rather, they appeared to be hybrids or transition types that displayed noticeable political characteristics some of the time. After years of stability Varig passed into a period of political activity after the sudden retirement of its CEO for health reasons. Varig had historically accommodated strong loyalties to functional departments which seemed to reflect Brazilians' high group orientation. The sudden leadership vacuum allowed intergroup rivalries to strengthen and be played out in politically negotiated decision making. Nevertheless the company had managed to take advantage of certain functional strengths in operations, marketing, and service to produce a very good product even though it was not strategically strong in all areas. At Thai International, the tradition of political activity was more enduring and was due in part to continuing external political pressures and to the Thais' cultural characteristic of loyalty and deference to superiors and willingness to place traditional relationships above bureaucratic considerations. For example, the chain of command in the airliner cockpit had to be continually reinforced and emphasized through training, since the natural tendency was for chronologically younger crew members to defer to older colleagues regardless of rank.

Thai International had historically been the scene of serious factional confrontations but had stabilized under the influence of a politically astute and capable executive who managed to in Edward Wrapp's (1967) term 'muddle through with a purpose'. As Deyo (1978) notes, the political entourage form can be functional if the political entourages are coextensive with the formal structure of the organization. This was the case in both of the political entourage airlines studied. The question then arises whether the political entourage has any advantage or, like the traditional bureaucracy, is merely a situation out of which one hopes to make the best. The case of Thai International would seem to indicate that in developing countries the political entourage can indeed be functional if managed by a political leader who also possesses sufficient technical skills and a solid strategic agenda.

Unlike the leader of the autocracy who dominates his rivals and builds support through brute strength and charismatic qualities, the entourage leader must work to maintain support of the entourage members and at the same time maintain comfortable relations with his rivals within the company. The game is one not of vanquishing rivals but merely of winning more negotiations than are lost. In Thai International, the most effective and powerful executive was not the CEO, who held most of the formal power, but a subordinate member of the executive committee who was able to structure important decision choices in the proper direction.

To some extent, as implied in the previous section, the political entourage at Thai International represents an escape from an imposed bureaucracy. It accommodates the different cultural antagonisms toward formal organization that exist in Thailand and enables the organization to work from its strengths, which in this case were conscientious service while maintaining the self-respect of the workforce. It requires accommodating personalities within the organization and the astute use of political power to motivate the workforce and build support for organizational programmes.

It is possible to infer a set of propositions concerning the effectiveness of the political entourage in developing countries. First, it represents a viable organizational form for large organizations in societies that react negatively to bureaucratic rigidity and have high group orientation. The political entourage form partially solves the problem of societal-culture-based reaction against bureaucratic rigidity by setting up a parallel informal organization that resolves conflict by means that are acceptable in the societal culture, in particular by means that value the individual's identification with a clientelist-based in-group. It is therefore better suited for a society such as the Thais' than for that of the more individualistic and mechanistic Singaporeans.

Second, the political entourage form can provide an effective organizational defence against outside interference in societies that have intense political activity external to the organization. Whereas the autocrat thrives with the support of the strong and stable government leader and is at the mercy of shifting power in the government, the skilled leader of the political entourage can extend internal coalitions beyond the limits of the organization to react to changes in external power.

Third, the political entourage can be managed as a positive organization form by a skilled leader who is sensitive to the needs to maintain balance among the factions in the organization and possesses sufficient technical knowledge to have a valid, but patient, vision of the organization's future. Without a knowledgeable leader, the political entourage will increase its directionless political activity that will eventually lead to crisis or external political intervention.

Fourth, in even the best of circumstances, the political entourage is exposed to external intervention since outsiders can penetrate the organization's boundary by looking for sympathetic factions within the organization (Mintzberg 1983). However, the political entourage leader also has a better chance to manage external influencers than do the leaders of traditional bureaucracies or autocracies.

Fifth, in addition to the dangers of external intervention, the political entourage is also vulnerable to an additional internal danger. Political entourages fail when the internal entourages do not align with the formal structure (e.g. when rival entourages extend across departmental boundaries).

Summary and conclusions

We have presented three culture-based organization configurations commonly found in developing countries. Each reflects a unique combination of cultural dimensions, each has particular advantages and disadvantages, each requires particular management skills, and each fits a particular set of environmental demands and circumstances (Table 6.2). The autocracy appears to be best suited for a dynamic environment and entrepreneurial activities. The traditional bureaucracy can work well where efficient larger-scale operations are called for, particularly in the case of state-owned enterprises. The political entourage offers one solution to the bureaucratic dilemma between mechanistic efficiency and personalistic loyalty and needs, but requires particularly tolerant societal norms.

Each type reflects the need to maintain a 'fit' between organization form, local culture, and the demands of the task environment that premises this approach to understanding organizations. How then can an organization in a developing country respond to changing demands in its task environment? Does the hypothesized need for cultural fit unduly constrain its responses?

Three alternative approaches that allow some flexibility in this regard are available to the developing country organization. First, the organization may look for ways to adapt an imported organization form to local culture. Second, it may consider how to change an existing culturally compatible form to meet technological or environmental needs. Third, it may consider developing a whole new organizational form reflecting an as yet unobserved synthesis of the cultural elements.

The three cases which follow will illustrate examples of the first two strategies. In the first case, Thai International successfully adapted an imported form to the local culture. In the second, Garuda unsuccessfully attempted to adapt an imported form, and instead rejected it in favour of an indigenous organizational form which it then modified slightly to meet its task demands. In the third case SIA avoided trying to adapt an imported form, but instead extensively modified an existing culturally compatible form to build a distinct advantage.

Adapting an imported organization form to the local culture may be the most common but also the most difficult strategy to pursue successfully. Thai International provides a successful example from our own field work. As a joint venture between the state-owned Thai Airways and SAS, the organization imported the well-established bureaucratic form from Scandinavia and then modified it to suit the local cultural norms of group orientation, deference based on age, avoidance of conflict, and interpersonal formality. The Thais, who grew to dominate the relationship and ultimately to eliminate their dependence on SAS, managed to borrow the most useful organizational systems from the Scandinavians and adapt them for their own use. This could not have worked without the guidance and cooperation of a few key bridging people. These were SAS employees on secondment to Thai International whose sensitivity to cultural issues enabled the smooth transition to Thai control and Thai organizational principles.

A less successful example of adaptation comes from Indonesia where Garuda was not able to modify an imported Dutch bureaucratic form successfully to suit its needs. The airline had been jointly owned and operated by KLM and the Indonesian government. After the joint venture dissolved and most Dutch expatriates left the airline, the company slumped into an almost inoperative state before it was finally reorganized as an autocracy, keeping few remnants of the imported form.

The parallels between the two cases are striking. Both airlines had been joint ventures with major European airlines that introduced organizational forms that were less than compatible with local cultural norms. Both host country airlines dissolved their joint ventures and eventually dismissed almost all expatriate managers. The Thais, perhaps more comfortable with the non-colonial Scandinavians, were able to modify the imported bureaucracy into their more traditional political entourage form. The Indonesians, in contrast, limped along with the imported bureaucracy until a dynamic leader dramatically replaced the collapsing structure with an indigenous form of autocracy. This new form, slightly modified to accommodate advancing technology and rapid growth, enabled Garuda to develop its domestic system rapidly and to begin to compete in the cut-rate international market.

SIA, unlike Garuda, did not attempt to adapt an imported form but rather modified an indigenous autocratic structure to meet technological and competitive needs. In this case, SIA took advantage of its individualistic yet deferential cultural norms to deliver a conspicuously high level of service to its passengers that far surpassed that of its competitors. As the company grew rapidly, it selectively added certain Western organizational features such as strategic planning without reducing the prerogatives of its CEO. Indeed, SIA grafted useful features from its world-class European competitors onto its own structure without adopting the Europeans' modern bureaucratic form. The core values and structure of SIA remain rooted in the local culture.

An even more well-known example of the second alternative is of course exemplified by the Japanese. There a distinct organizational form based on high group orientation and consensual decision making has been finely modified to meet various technical and competitive requirements.

The third strategy, developing a whole new organizational form based on a synthesis of the cultural elements, was not directly observed in these field studies although there was evidence in Thai International that it might develop presently. In terms of the model, such a strategy would mean new combinations of cultural dimensions, in effect shifting the organization to an as yet unoccupied cell. It appears that the well-functioning political entourage of Thai International, under the influence of key executives, is slowly reducing personal power while still maintaining the formal authority distance that is required in the Thai culture. Indeed, the individual political entourages would seem to constitute power-reducing mechanisms in their own right. Additional reduction of power amounts to a shift to the unoccupied cell below the present political entourage and next to the consensus configuration. To the extent that conflict among the entourages could be reduced, this new type might herald the displacement of political activity in favour of more consensual approaches to decisions.

Earlier, we noted that the configuration theory hypothesized only a limited number of stable organization types. Whether such a new synthesized type will ever exist as a stable type or will merely constitute a transitional type in a political entourage's transition to the consensus form is unclear. Given the model, the same question must be asked regarding any newly synthesized or hybridized organization form. Nevertheless, as cultures change, the viable combinations of dimensions will change, thus inducing new stable configurations. Indeed, as both cultures and our knowledge of them change, the current dimensions will be replaced by more salient dimensions and entirely new models will be necessary. For the time being, the proposed model offers a useful organizing system for understanding the influence of culture on organizations in developing countries.

References

Abegglen, J. (1958) *The Japanese Factory: Aspects of its Social Organization*, New York: Free Press.
Allison, G. T. (1971) *Essence of Decision*, Boston, MA: Little, Brown.
Atsumi, R. (1979) 'Tsukiai – obligatory personal relationships of Japanese white collar employees', *Human Organization* 38: 63–70.
Bowden, E. (1976) 'Maladministration: a thematic analysis of Nigerian case studies in the context of administrative initiative', *Human Organization* 35: 391–4.
Cochrane, T. (1959) *The Puerto Rican Businessman*, Philadelphia, PA: University of Pennsylvania.
Crozier, M. (1964) *The Bureaucratic Phenomenon*, Chicago, IL: University of Chicago Press.
Crozier, M. and Friedburg, E. (1976) *Actors and Systems*, Chicago, IL: University of Chicago Press.
Davis, S. (1968) 'Managerial resource development in Mexico', in R. Rehder (ed.) *Latin American Management: Development and*

Performance, pp. 166–79, Reading, MA: Addison-Wesley.

DeVos, G. A. (1968) 'Achievement and innovation in culture and personality', in E. Norbeck *et al.* (eds) *The Study of Personality: an Interdisciplinary Appraisal*, pp. 220–77, New York: Holt, Rinehart & Winston.

Deyo, F. (1978) 'The cultural patterning of organizational development: a comparative case study of Thai and Chinese industrial enterprise', *Human Organization* 37: 68–73.

Enthoven, A. C. (1969) 'Analysis, judgement and computers: their use in complex problems', *Business Horizons* 12: 29–36.

Fallers, L. (1955) 'The predicament of the modern African chief: an instance from Uganda', *American Anthropologist* 57: 290–305.

Fallers, L. (1964) 'Social stratification and economic processes in Africa', in M. Herskovits and M. Harwitz (eds) *Economic Transition in Africa*, pp. 113–30, Evanston, IL: Northwestern University Press.

Fallers, L. (1965) *Bantu Bureaucracy, a Century of Political Evolution Among the Busoga of Uganda*, Chicago, IL: University of Chicago Press.

Geertz, C. (1965) *The Social History of an Indonesian Town*, Cambridge, MA: MIT Press.

Gillin, J. (1960) 'The middle segments and their values', in R. Adams *et al.* (eds) *Social Change in Latin America Today*, New York: Vintage.

Gladwin, H. and Gladwin, C. (1971) 'Estimating market conditions and profit expectations of fish sellers at Cape Coast, Ghana', in G. Dalton (ed.) *Studies in Economic Anthropology, Anthropological Studies*, vol. 7, pp. 122–42, Washington, DC: American Anthropological Association.

Granick, J. (1962) *The European Executive*, New York: Doubleday.

Harbison, F. and Meyers, C. (1959) *Management in the Industrial World*, New York: McGraw-Hill.

Hartmann, H. (1959) *Authority and Organization in German Management*, Princeton, NJ: Princeton University Press.

Heller, F. (1969) 'The role of business management in relation to economic development', *International Journal of Comparative Sociology* 10: 292–9.

Hofstede, G. (1980) *Culture's Consequences*, Beverly Hills, CA: Sage.

Hsu, F. (1985) 'The self in cross-cultural perspective', in A. Marsella, G. DeVos, and F. Hsu (eds) *Culture and Self*, pp. 24–56, New York: Tavistock.

Inkeles, A. and Smith D. (1974) *Becoming Modern: Individual Change in Six Developing Countries*, Cambridge, MA: Harvard University Press.

Kagitcibasi, C. (1970) 'Social norms and authoritarianism: a Turkish–American comparison', *Journal of Personality and Social Psychology* 16: 444–51.

Kakar, S. (1971) 'Authority patterns and subordinate behavior in Indian organizations', *Administrative Science Quarterly* 16: 298–307.

Kapferer, B. (1980) 'The colonialism of management and the management of colonialism: the cultural and structural constitution of power in an industrial organization under colonial rule', presented at Burg Wartenstein Symposium no. 84, New York: Wenner-Gren

Foundation for Anthropological Research.

Lauter, G. (1969) 'Sociological–cultural and legal factors impeding decentralization of authority in developing countries', *Academy of Management Journal* 12: 367–78.

Lawrence, P. (1980) *Managers and Management in West Germany*, New York: St Martin's Press.

Leavitt, H. J. (1975) 'Beyond the analytic manager', *California Management Review* 18: 5–12.

Lebra, T. S. (1976) *Japanese Patterns of Behavior*, Honolulu, HI: University of Hawaii Press.

LeVine, R. (1976) 'Patterns of personality in Africa', in G. DeVos (ed.) *Responses to Change*, pp. 81–97, New York: Van Nostrand.

McClelland D. (1961) *The Achieving Society*, New York: Van Nostrand.

Marsella, A., DeVos, G., and Hsu, F. (1985) *Culture and Self*, New York: Tavistock.

Maurice M. and Brossard, M. (1976) 'Is there a universal model of organization structure?', *International Studies of Management and Organization* 6: 11–45.

Mead, M. (1962) 'Studies of whole cultures: Greece', in *Cultural Patterns and Technical Change*, Paris: UNESCO.

Miller, D. and Mintzberg, H. (1983) 'The case for configuration', in G. Morgan (ed.) *Beyond Method: Strategies for Social Research*, pp. 57–73, Beverly Hills, CA: Sage.

Mintzberg, H. (1976) 'Planning on the left side and managing on the right', *Harvard Business Review* 54, 4: 49–58.

Mintzberg, H. (1979a) 'An emerging strategy of direct research', *Administrative Science Quarterly* 24: 582–9.

Mintzberg, H. (1979b) *The Structuring of Organizations*, Englewood Cliffs, NJ: Prentice-Hall.

Mintzberg, H. (1983) *Power In and Around Organizations*, Englewood Cliffs, NJ: Prentice-Hall.

Mintzberg, H., Raisinghani, D., and Theoret, A. (1976) 'The structuring of unstructured decision processes', *Administrative Science Quarterly* 21: 245–75.

Nakane, C. (1970) *Japanese Society*, Berkeley, CA: University of California Press.

Nambudiri, C. and Saiyadain, M. (1978) 'Management problems and practices – India and Nigeria', *Columbia Journal of World Business* 13, 2: 62–9.

Narain, D. (1967) 'Indian national character in the twentieth century', *Annals*: 124–32.

Ouchi, W. and Jaeger, A. (1978) 'Type Z organization: stability in the midst of mobility', *Academy of Management Review* 3: 305–14.

Pfeffer, J. (1981) *Power in Organizations*, Marshfield, MA: Pittman.

Presthus, R. (1961) 'Weberian vs. welfare bureaucracy in traditional society', *Administrative Science Quarterly* 6: 1–24.

Pucik, V. and Hatvany, N. (1983) 'Management practices in Japan, an integrated system focussing on human resources', in R. Lamb. (ed.)

Advances in Strategic Management, vol. 1, pp. 103–32, Greenwich, CT: JAI Press.

Quinn, N. (1978) 'Do Mfanste fishsellers estimate probabilities in their heads?', *American Ethnologist* 5, 206–26.

Redding, S. G. (1980) 'Cognition as an aspect of culture and its relation to management processes: an exploratory view of the Chinese case', *Journal of Management Studies* 17: 127–48.

Redding, S. G. (1988) 'Beyond bureaucracy: towards a comparative analysis of forms of economic resource co-ordination and control', presented at the Workshop on Relevance in International Management Research, Windsor, Ontario.

Robinson, R. (1986) *Indonesia: The Rise of Capital*, North Sydney: Allen & Unwin.

Rohlen, T. (1974) *For Harmony and Strength: Japanese White Collar Organization in Anthropological Perspective*, Berkeley, CA: University of California Press.

Sathe, V. (1985) *Culture and Related Corporate Realities*, Homewood, IL: Irwin.

Shor, E. (1960) 'The Thai bureaucracy', *Administrative Science Quarterly* 5: 66–86.

Triandis, H. (1972) *The Analysis of Subjective Culture*, New York: Wiley.

Vogel, E. (1963) *Japan's New Middle Class*, Berkeley, CA: University of California Press.

Whyte, W. F. (1963) 'Culture, industrial relations and economic development: the case of Peru', *Industrial and Labor Relations Review* 16: 583–94.

Whyte, W. F. (1969) 'Culture and work', in R. A. Webber (ed.) *Culture and Management*, pp. 30–9, Homewood, IL: Irwin.

Wrapp, H. E. (1967) 'Good managers don't make policy decisions', *Harvard Business Review* 55, September–October: 91–9.

Part two

Limitations of Western techniques in the management of organizations in developing countries

Chapter seven

The applicability of Western management techniques in developing countries: a cultural perspective

Alfred M. Jaeger

Introduction

Modern management theories and techniques have generally taken their roots in the developed countries, most notably the USA. These theories and practices have been imported by the developing countries to speed up their industrial development. However, as was pointed out in Chapter One, many organizational practices and management training programmes in the developing countries are based on an uncritical adoption of the experiences of the economic growth model in vogue in the USA, without any consideration of the fundamental differences in socio-cultural constraints and local environmental conditions and circumstances. This uncritical use of Western management theories and techniques has contributed not only to organizational inefficiency and ineffectiveness in the developing countries but to the resentment and other negative feelings associated with the perception of being subject to 'cultural imperialism', i.e. being forced to adopt and accept practices which run counter to deeply held values and assumptions of the local culture.

This chapter takes a cultural perspective for looking at the differences between developed and developing countries in a managerial context. Utilizing the framework of socio-cultural and work culture dimensions set forth in Chapter One (Table 1.1), we shall identify several management behaviours which would be inappropriate in developing countries compared with developed countries. This will be done by examining some common American management practices and analysing them in cultural terms. Within the context of our framework, the basic assumptions and values underlying these management practices will be identified. This will enable us to look for a match between the practices which have been so analysed and the value configurations found in developing countries. As a result of this analysis, we shall be able to identify management practices which would be culturally inappropriate in developing countries, as well as begin to gain some insight into the cultural aspects of appropriate indigenous management techniques. This analysis will follow an approach similar to that taken by several other scholars (e.g. Hofstede 1980a; Jaeger 1986) who have analysed the 'fit' of management practices and cultural dimensions.

Culture and management

The concept of culture and dimensions of culture were introduced in Chapter One. There culture was described as a set of ideas shared by members of a group (e.g. Allaire and Firsirotu 1984). The definition of culture from this perspective which we shall use is the following: 'an individual's theory of what his fellows know, believe and mean, his theory of the code being followed, the game being played' (Keesing 1974). Culture is therefore not an individual characteristic but rather denotes a set of common theories of behaviour or mental programmes that are shared by a group of individuals. This is an 'ideational' definition, as culture is seen as being a set of ideas. Furthermore, culture thus 'resides' in the minds of the members of a cultural group.

With the foregoing perspective, one can also look at culture in terms of Schein's (1985) three levels: basic assumptions and premises; values and ideology; and artifacts and creations. Basic assumptions and premises refer to preconscious and taken-for-granted assumptions about such things as the relationship of man to nature, time, and space, and beliefs about human potential and social nature. These taken-for-granted assumptions determine values and ideologies defining ideals and goals as well as means for achieving them. These two levels are in a sense the ideational base of culture. They are reflected in the components of the third level, cultural artifacts and creations (such as manifest behaviour, language, technology, and social organization). It is the third level that is observable and that is the first arena in which management is played out.

The basic assumptions and values are the foundation on which actual values rest. They are also generally held subconsciously, meaning that if a person were asked what their assumptions were about, say, man's malleability or creative potential they might find it difficult to articulate a response. In contrast, if they were asked whether it would be appropriate to send a clerk to a management training programme, they would be able to tell you and could explain their reasons for it.

People's assumptions, beliefs, and values are shaped by the culture to which they belong. Basic assumptions and premises are fairly deeply rooted in an individual and one must therefore assume, at least in the short run, that culture cannot be changed to meet the demands of management. In the case of national or ethnic cultures, they are also usually supported by a complex and long-established social system which has a vibrant existence outside the context of a business organization. Thus we must take the position here that individuals' behaviour in an organization will in the main be guided by the outside culture from which they come. Members of an organization in a given cultural environment therefore would share a common set of assumptions, beliefs, and values which originate from the local environment. One assumption implicit in most work in the area of comparative or cross-cultural management, and one shared by the author, is that the organization is indeed an 'open system'. These cultural values from the environment are brought into the work place and have a very strong impact on the behaviour of persons within the organization.

To understand better how culture can impact on management behaviour in a practical sense, we can review how culture affects the interaction of individuals. On the one hand, culture *facilitates* certain behaviours. Members of a cultural group share complementary behavioural programmes which regulate their interaction. Associated with these programmes are values and ideology which provide a guide and a meaning to what they are doing. Implicit in this view is the fact that a culture also *inhibits* other behaviours, behaviours which run counter to the values or practices of the culture. A culture also provides a guide for perception and attribution of others' behaviour. Thus, within a cultural group, certain behaviours will generate a feeling and response that is positive while others will generate a negative feeling and response.

The practical impact of culture on management practices will therefore be twofold. First, it will influence management behaviour which might be said to be occurring 'naturally'. Thus, management behaviour will reflect the values of the local culture. It will not include behaviour which runs counter to the culture. Second, culture will influence the perceptions which individuals in organizations have of the world around them. This will include their perceptions of both the internal and external organizational environments (Negandhi 1975), i.e. what is happening in the organization as well as what is happening outside it. Culture will influence what *is* perceived and what is *not* perceived or noted. It will also affect the evaluation of what is perceived. With respect to the external environment, culture will have the greatest influence on where and to what the greatest attention is paid. With respect to the internal environment, culture will affect the perception and evaluation of behaviours of individuals in the system. It is this process that will result in resistance to counter-cultural management behaviour.

Characteristics of developing country cultures

In Chapter One, one senses the contrast between the developing countries and developed countries on the characteristics of their socio-cultural environment. One notes that the developing countries can be characterized as generally higher on uncertainty avoidance, higher on collectivism (i.e. lower on individualism), higher on power distance, higher on feminine orientation (i.e. lower on masculine orientation), and relatively lower on abstractive thinking (i.e. higher on associative thinking). It should be pointed out that these characterizations represent overall trends and may not hold for every developing country on every dimension. Nevertheless, they reflect a perceived mean or norm for the two groups and are presented as a broad framework for the purposes of analysis and discussion. The reader will be left to judge whether or not they are appropriate for the particular country or situation which may be of interest and should modify the conclusions arrived at accordingly.

Comparing the cultures of developed and developing countries, one notes that they differ with respect to the assumptions regarding the nature of causation and control over outcomes (pleasant and unpleasant) that one experiences in life. Can people be dominant over their environment or are they subjugated by it? Most Western industrialized societies generally see themselves as being in control of nature and of events. In contrast, developing societies see themselves more as being at the mercy of events in the environment. Thus, in developing countries, the notion of context dependence will be more likely to guide behaviour in organizations.

Another difference in cultural assumptions which affects behaviour in work organizations concerns beliefs about human potential and malleability. Within organizations in developing countries, human capabilities are often viewed as more or less fixed with limited potential. In developed countries it is believed that individuals are malleable and have unlimited creative potential. Thus one expects more attention to be paid to training in developed country organizations.

The temporal focus of life is one of the major assumptions along which cultures can be differentiated (Kluckhohn and Strodtbeck 1961). Societies can be classified as being oriented to the *past*, the *present*, or the *future*. Developed countries tend to have more of a future orientation. Future-oriented cultures have relatively less regard for past social or organizational customs and traditions and base their decisions on their possible implications for the future. Developing countries tend to be more present or past oriented. Past-oriented cultures believe that life should be guided by the customs and traditions of the society. Past experience should be the guide to any change. Present-oriented cultures tend not to be guided by tradition or to plan for the future but live for the moment (Adler 1986). In an organizational context, this results in a more short-term orientation to activities.

Furthermore, activity or task orientation ranges from doing or *action* to *being* (Kluckhohn and Strodtbeck 1961). Cultures which are action oriented, such as those of the developed countries, stress measurable accomplishments and encourage a proactive stance in dealing with a given task. People in action-oriented cultures are doers and they live to work. For people in being-oriented cultures such as can be found in many developing countries, the focus is on experiencing life and on the quality of their life experience. They work to live. This leads to comparatively more passive or reactive responses to tasks in organizational situations.

The success of people is often judged in developed countries using pragmatic results of their endeavours. In the developing countries success has more to do with the maintenance of the well-being of the group.

Finally, in developed countries one is more likely to find an abstractive mode of thinking, resulting in the use of abstract principles, rules, and procedures that are considered absolutes and override contextual forces in guiding behaviour. In developing countries, in contrast, the influence of contextual forces may often negate principles in determining individual or organizational behaviour when the two are in conflict.

Culture's effect on management behaviours in developing countries

In order to understand the influence of the cultural values of developing countries on management behaviour, we can start with the work of Lane and DiStefano (1988). In a very systematic fashion they have postulated the effect of the basic assumptions or value orientations of Kluckhohn and Strodtbeck on management behaviour. In developing countries, therefore, as a result of the assumption of being subjugated to nature, Lane and DiStefano argue that goal setting would tend to be 'qualified, hesitant and vague', and that budget systems would be futile with predetermined outcomes. The feeling of being subjugated to nature and context dependent would, in effect, make specific planning and budgeting seem pointless, as events could alter their expected outcomes. A past time orientation would result in planning indicating an extention of past behaviour, decision criteria emphasizing precedence, and reward systems being historically determined. A being activity orientation would influence decision criteria to be emotional, reward systems to be feelings based, and information and measurement systems to be 'vague, feeling based and intuitive'. This is also congruent with a more 'feminine' value orientation. A collective orientation and high power distance would, not surprisingly, result in a status-based reward system, authority-based communication and influence patterns, attention paid to vertical differentiation in the organizational structure, and teamwork which is regulated and more formal. Anyone familiar with Western management practices can see that the foregoing behaviours are very different from what one normally would expect in developed countries.

An example that illustrates one of the above conclusions is the behaviour of 'bypassing', a subordinate making direct contact with a superior of his boss. In a situation of low power distance, this behaviour will be more likely to occur and will not be viewed very negatively. In a situation of high power distance, this behaviour will be less likely to occur and, if it does, it will be viewed very negatively. Thus, in the latter situation, bypassing behaviour not only will be inhibited but will in effect be punished and thus unlikely to recur.

To examine the applicability of Western management concepts in developing countries from a cultural perspective more specifically we must first look at what is meant by 'Western management concepts'. These have been mentioned earlier and they are usually either spoken of very highly as being responsible for the high standard of living in the developed countries, particularly the USA, or referred to contemptuously as a set of culturally inappropriate practices which are forced on developing countries by multinational companies or misguided locals who 'worship' foreign ways. Despite being revered or condemned, these famous or infamous practices are rarely spoken of in more than generalities.

In order to examine this 'beast' more closely, we must make an attempt to specify what we are actually discussing. To this end, we can turn to one of the more popular American management textbooks, *Management* (4th edn) by D. Hellriegel and D. Slocum (1986). They describe a well-known model of management which delineates management in terms of managerial functions. These functions are planning, organizing, leading, and controlling. According to this model, if a manager carries out these functions effectively, it leads to success.

To carry out our examination of management here, we shall utilize this framework as a guide and add one other category, making changes. As management is not always successful, major problems sometimes arise which call for making changes and require direct interventions for this purpose. To proceed with our analysis, we have gleaned from the text by Hellriegel and Slocum, *Management*, a set of well-known practices and terminology with behavioural implications which could be analysed within the cultural framework that has been presented here. These are listed in Table 7.1 and categorized according to the framework of managerial functions just described. We shall discuss them in turn with respect to their underlying values and see whether they indeed fit with the predominant value structure which has been presented here as characteristic of developing countries.

Listed first in Table 7.1 is the category of planning. As was pointed out earlier, the developing country environment with its short-term time and activity orientation is less conducive to planning than is the developed world. One form of planning which is often mentioned as being an important part of human resource management is career planning. Career planning is said to benefit both the organization and the employee. For the organization, a systematic and widespread career planning programme for its employees provides it with a vehicle for making an inventory of its human resources, knowing what

Table 7.1 Some common American management terminology and practices

---

Planning activities
    Career planning
    Strategic planning
    Management by objectives (MBO)

Leadership and decision making
    Leadership models
    Theory X, theory Y
    Brainstorming
    Decision-making models

Organizing and controlling
    Decentralization, delegation
    Bureaucracy
    Adhocracy
    Matrix structure

Organizational change
    Organization development

Source: Derived from Hellriegel and Slocum 1986

will be available in the future, and deciding where to invest in training if skill deficiencies are seen from an organizational perspective. For the employee, career planning can give him or her an opportunity to participate in the direction which their work life will take, including possibilities of further skill training. It will also generate a greater commitment to the company which is of benefit to both parties. Career planning would thus be inhibited not only by a short-term time orientation but also by a belief in the limited changeability and creative potential of individuals.

Strategic planning is advocated by many management theorists, although it has recently come into question in some circles (e.g. Mintzberg 1976). Beyond formal strategic planning, a large body of knowledge exists concerning strategy making. It is argued that strategy making, be it strategic planning or some other process, is a crucial element for the survival and success of a business enterprise. Engaging in this activity is hindered in developing countries not only by the present and past orientation of the culture but also by the relative unpredictability of events in the environment.

Another example of a future-oriented management technique which fits with the values of the developed world is management by objectives (MBO). MBO is a process by which managers and their subordinates jointly set goals and action plans for individuals and departments. These are then used as the basis for the management of the organization. Hofstede (1980b) describes MBO as 'perhaps the single most popular management technique "made in USA"'. He states that MBO presupposes the following underlying value orientations:

(1) that subordinates are sufficiently independent to negotiate meaningfully with the boss (not-too-large power distance);
(2) that both are willing to take risks (weak uncertainty avoidance);
(3) that performance is seen as important by both (high masculinity).

These values are in line with those found in North America, but are clearly incompatible with what is often the case in developing countries. As a result, one would expect any attempts at using MBO there to be less than successful. In fact, one could imagine a situation where the use of MBO would be clearly dysfunctional, ultimately causing mistrust and suspicion between a superior and his subordinates, the former essentially trying to force the latter to interact in a manner distinctly foreign to the local culture, while at the same time not really willing to accept that type of behaviour.

The next category in Table 7.1 is leadership and decision making.

Leadership is a topic central to management. We cannot address all the issues associated with leadership here but we can make some observations with respect to key issues of leadership behaviour. First of all, we can note that the values which have been presented do address two dimensions which directly affect leadership (and followership) behaviour, namely power distance and people orientation. The relatively high power distance and the authoritarian/paternalistic people orientation of developing countries imply a certain type of leadership behaviour and leader–follower relationship. It can be characterized as being more congruent with Theory X (McGregor 1960) leadership, which also presupposes limited and fixed human potential. In contrast, Theory Y leadership, a participative approach which believes that individuals must be given the opportunity to unlock their creative potential, for their own good as well as that of the organization, will be more favoured in developed countries.

An example of an indigenous approach to leadership has been reported from India by Sinha (1980): the nurturant task leader. A nurturant leader 'cares for his subordinates, shows affection, (and) takes personal interest in their well-being' (1980: 55). The effective leader, however, makes nurturance contingent on the subordinate's task accomplishment. This model incorporates an authoritarian/paternalistic leadership style which allows for a high power distance.

Related to leadership is the area of decision making. Listed here is a technique called brainstorming. It is advocated for use when creativity is called for in the solving of difficult problems, in making difficult or complex decisions, or when one is in need of new creative ideas for some aspect of the business. Brainstorming is carried out in a group where the participants essentially share ideas concerning the issue in question as they come to them. There is an explicit norm that people should be allowed to share their ideas without being criticized, so that creative and divergent views are not suppressed and will come out for the benefit of the organization.

Looking at the cultural dimensions of developed and developing countries, one notes that this technique generally fits with the ratings assigned to developed countries. One could argue that this technique is used in order to circumvent a predominant abstractive mode of thinking when a non-obvious or more intuitive solution is called for. Nevertheless, one notes that it is in conflict with many of the values of the developing countries. If one wanted to use this technique, one would note that it clashes with a passive–reactive task orientation, with a context-dependent environment orientation, with a perception of an external locus of causality, and with a view of human nature as having limited creative potential. The *process* might also be in conflict with an authoritarian/paternalistic people orientation and a high power distance if people from differing hierarchical levels need to be present to address a problem properly.

Representative of the area of decision making is the normative model of Vroom and Yetton (1973) for choosing a decision-making process. Its prescriptions reflect most of the results of American research on effective decision-making styles. Depending on the characteristics of the decision to be made, the model recommends either an autocratic, consultative, or participative decision-making approach. Here again we note that participative decision making is recommended to increase the input of information into the decision process. As this approach is often not feasible in a developing country context, indigenous management techniques must seek to provide information to the locus of decisions by alternative methods.

Turning to the more 'macro', i.e. organizational, level management concepts, we come to the category of organizing and controlling. This category comprises structural arrangements for the distribution of tasks, the coordination of tasks, and making sure that tasks have been performed. Listed first here is decentralization and delegation. Delegation is the 'process of distributing and entrusting work to others. It involves assigning a person a duty to perform and giving that person adequate authority and responsibility to do the assigned work effectively' (Hellriegel and Slocum 1986: 350). Decentralization is a concept applied to formal organizations. It is the opposite of centralization, which means that the responsibility and authority for making decisions is maintained at the highest hierarchical levels. Decentralization means formally and institutionally delegating decision-making authority to lower levels in the hierarchy. Both delegation and decentralization are based on assumptions which are often not present in developing countries: an unlimited creative potential in individuals, a lower power distance, and a participative people orientation.

A number of organizational types with relevance to developing countries are also found in the management literature. Bureaucracy is a type of organization first described by the German sociologist Weber (translation, 1947). It is the most formal of organization forms, based on a strict definition of positions and their responsibilities within a well-defined hierarchy. Bureaucracies usually operate according to well-established rules or standard operating procedures and have well-defined formal control mechanisms. This type of organization actually fits well with the value configurations found in developing countries. Some adjustments to the bureaucratic form are made to accommodate the values of developing countries, as described by Rieger and Wong-Rieger in Chapter Six.

Value conflicts would come into play in developing countries if it were decided to adopt a matrix structure or utilize the adhocracy form of organization (Mintzberg 1983). A matrix structure is one which embodies a 'multiple command system' (Davis and Lawrence 1977), i.e. subordinates report to multiple bosses. This type of structure originated in the American aerospace industry and has proved to be useful in managing very complex projects which required a high degree of coordination. The multiple boss system inherent in the matrix structure sets up dual (or multiple) lines of communication which aid in coordinating activities across functions. A relatively low power distance as well as a collegial atmosphere is required for a matrix structure to work, as it is the subordinate who must 'manage' the potentially conflicting demands of the two or more superiors.

Similar problems may exist with the adhocracy form of organization. First identified by Mintzberg (1983), the adhocracy is a flexible organizational form where coordination is based on mutual adjustment (as opposed to the bureaucracy where coordination is accomplished through rules and regulations). It can also be characterized as a relatively decentralized collegial organization of trained specialists who tend to be grouped in teams. Because of its flexibility and ability to respond to uncertain environments, the adhocracy would in many cases be ideally suited to operate in the environments of developing countries. In fact, in Chapter Five, Hardy describes a successful university adhocracy in Brazil. Nevertheless, the cultural barriers of high power distance and authoritarian people orientation have to be overcome for adhocracy to function in the cultural environment characteristic of developing countries.

The final category in Table 7.1 is 'Making Changes'. Here we have listed organization development (OD). This is a term applied to a collection of organizational interventions which are utilized with the goal of improving organizational functioning. There are many definitions of OD and many are 'broad enough to include almost any technique, policy or managerial practice used in a deliberate attempt to change the individuals in an organization or the organization itself to accomplish organizational objectives' (Huse 1980: 23). In practice, however, any planned behavioural intervention for the improvement of organizational functioning is usually considered to be OD.

The origins of OD are in the USA and thus it can be expected to reflect American cultural values. Nevertheless, Jaeger (1986) has shown that this is not necessarily the case. Analysing the underlying values of the original OD values in terms of Hofstede's (1980a) cultural dimensions, he found them to reflect a low power distance, a low uncertainty avoidance, low masculinity, and medium individualism. The only countries in Hofstede's sample which had this value configuration were three Scandinavian countries: Denmark, Norway, and Sweden. Only somewhat different from OD values (on one dimension) were Finland, Ireland, Israel, and the Netherlands. All the aforementioned could be considered to be developed countries.

The developing countries in general differed from OD values on the dimensions of uncertainty avoidance and power distance. These two values are often crucial for OD interventions, as many interventions focus on groups and require open face-to-face interaction (and sometimes confrontation) across hierarchical levels. The process as well as the outcome of these interventions is often unpredictable and therefore their acceptance would be facilitated by a low uncertainty avoidance. Nevertheless, several cases of successful OD in developing countries using indigenous approaches have been reported. For example, Bourgeois and Boltvinik (1981) found that, in Latin America, OD has sometimes consciously incorporated a process of building awareness of Latin Americans' tendency to please others and smooth conflict and thus avoid it. Only in this way can problems be brought to light and thus ultimately dealt with appropriately.

Discussion and conclusions

We have reviewed the value configurations of developing countries and looked at their implications for management practice. The value configuration of the developing countries is clearly very different from that of the developed countries. Based on the analysis of Lane and DiStefano (1988), these values generally result in behaviours very different from what can be characterized in Western terms as 'modern management practice'. Planning is non-existent or based simply on precedence, organizational structures are very rigid, hierarchical, and status oriented, decisions are made on 'non-rational' criteria, and rewards are based not on performance but on other criteria. All this runs counter to what can be termed, albeit somewhat paradoxically, 'traditional' modern management practice.

This combination of values, however, does fit to a certain extent with an emerging more radical literature on management (e.g. Mintzberg 1976). This perspective considers intuitive processes to be very important for making management decisions, particularly when facing uncertain environments. When environments are uncertain, rational planning and abstract reasoning may be of little use and may in fact be counter-productive. Uncertain environments are usually very complex and do not behave in the 'linear' fashion which most 'rational' planning models would predict. Intuitive processes are ultimately able to factor in more complexity and non-linear reasoning and thus might be more appropriate and effective for analysing the uncertain and unpredictable environments confronting organizations in developing countries.

As part of our analysis we have also identified a set of American management practices and techniques and compared them with the value configuration which we postulate as existing in developing countries. Here again, we note that the value configuration of developing countries is in most cases in conflict with the values which we see as underlying the American management practices that we have identified. Thus, brainstorming may encounter difficulties in developing countries. 'Preferred' management styles, such as Theory Y or other participative approaches to management, are inappropriate. Decision-making models are of limited usefulness as they call for counter-cultural behaviours. Goal setting or MBO also runs counter to a number of the values in the cultures of developing countries. An analysis of the basic values of OD showed them to be in conflict with the values of developing countries on most of Hofstede's (1980a) dimensions of culture. On the organizational level, we noted that delegation and decentralization may be inhibited by a number of value orientations in developing countries. Furthermore, the more 'avant-garde' organizational forms, such as the matrix structure and adhocracy, may also run into cultural difficulties.

In spite of the general mismatch of the values of developing countries and those underlying American management techniques, there were a few instances where this was not the case. For example, there are some situations identified by Vroom and Yetton (1973) where autocratic decisions would be appropriate. Furthermore, in most cases where a group decision is called for, this is indicated not just so that the maximum information can be input into the decision, but also to ensure acceptance of the decision by subordinates where this acceptance is critical. Thus, in a situation of high power distance where subordinates would be willing to accept autocratic decisions, a consultative process could gather the requisite information to make an informed decision. One can therefore see that it is possible to make modifications to the model of Vroom and Yetton, or the questions asked in it, to make it fit better with developing country values.

One fairly good fit of developing country values with Western management concepts occurs in the case of bureaucracy. The hierarchical well-defined nature of relationships in a bureaucracy is highly congruent with the values found in traditional societies. Bureaucracies are found in the public sector in all countries. In developing countries they are either a legacy of a colonial past or they are of the 'home grown' variety. Their 'fit' with the value configuration of developing countries may help explain their apparent pervasiveness, which is recounted by any person from a developing country or one who has lived in or even visited such a country for any period of time. Bureaucracies in developing countries are not immune to the 'dysfunctions' of this organizational form which were described by Merton (1940). This problem was officially recognized by the Brazilian government which established a ministry of 'debureaucratization' in the 1980s. Its experiences and the less than successful outcomes are described in a book by Araujo e Oliveira (1984).

The overall picture which has been presented by the foregoing analysis indicates that there is a wide gap between the cultural values of developing countries and the values underlying most American management techniques and practices. Thus, one should not be surprised if these techniques and practices are not well received and if they do not work. From the perspective of those who have been looking to the developed countries for all the solutions to the management problems of the developing world, this is a dismal picture indeed. This conclusion highlights the need for the development and identification of indigenous management techniques. Some have been alluded to or mentioned in this chapter, others are described in other chapters, and many others still need to be developed, described, and promulgated.

References

Adler, N. J. (1986) *International Dimensions of Organizational Behavior*, Boston, MA: Kent.

Allaire, Y. and Firsirotu, M. E. (1984) 'Theories of organizational culture', *Organization Studies* 5: 193–226.

Araujo e Oliveira, J. B. (1984) *Desburocratizacao e Democracia*, Campinas, SP: Papirus.

Bourgeois III, L. J. and Boltvinik M. (1981) 'OD in cross-cultural settings: Latin America' *California Management Review* 23, 3: 75–81.

Davis, S. M. and Lawrence, P. (1977) *Matrix*, Reading, MA: Addison-Wesley.

Hellriegel, D. and Slocum, J. (1986) *Management* (4th edn), Reading, MA: Addison-Wesley.

Hofstede, G. (1980a) *Culture's Consequences*, Beverly Hills, CA: Sage.

Hofstede, G. (1980b) 'Motivation, leadership, and organization: do American theories apply abroad?', *Organizational Dynamics* 9, 1: 42–62.

Huse, E. F. (1980) *Organization Development and Change* (2nd edn), St Paul, MN: West.

Jaeger, A. M. (1986) 'Organization development and national culture: where's the fit?', *Academy of Management Review* 11, 1: 178–90.

Keesing, R. (1974) 'Theories of culture', *Annual Review in Anthropology* 3, 73–97.

Kluckhohn F. R. and Strodtbeck F. L. (1961) *Variations in Value Orientations*, New York: Harper & Row.

Lane, H. W. and DiStefano, J. J. (1988) *International Management Behavior*, Toronto: Methuen.

McGregor, D. (1960) *The Human Side of Enterprise*, New York: McGraw-Hill.

Merton, R. K. (1940) 'Bureaucratic structure and personality', *Social Forces* 18: 560–8.

Mintzberg, H. (1976) 'Planning on the left side and managing on the right', *Harvard Business Review* 54, 4: 49–58.

Mintzberg, H. (1983) *Structure in Fives: Designing Effective Organizations*, Englewood Cliffs, NJ: Prentice-Hall.

Negandhi, A. (1975) 'Comparative management and organization theory: a marriage needed', *Academy of Management Journal* 18, 334–44.

Schein, E. H. (1985) *Organization Culture and Leadership*, San Francisco, CA: Jossey-Bass.

Sinha, J. B. P. (1980) *The Nurturant Task Leader*, New Delhi: Concept.

Vroom, V. and Yetton, P. (1973) *Leadership and Decision Making*, Pittsburgh, PA: University of Pittsburgh Press.

Weber, M. (1947) *The Theory of Social and Economic Organization* (trans. A. M. Henderson and T. Parsons), New York: Oxford University Press; originally published 1924.

Chapter eight

Limitations to the application of socio-technical systems in developing countries

Moses N. Kiggundu

Since its early development and applications in the English coal-mining industry during the early 1950s, socio-technical systems (STS) theory has been applied throughout the world in various organizational, industrial, and community settings. Some unsuccessful STS experiments (Goodman 1979; Cunningham and White 1984) and critical reviews (Kelly 1978) have been reported in the literature, but most STS interventions have been associated with the development of high-performing organizational systems and with improved employee morale and quality of working life. A recent discussion of the evolution of STS theory (Trist 1981) indicates that successful interventions have taken place in England (Trist *et al.* 1963; Hill 1971), Western Europe (Emery and Thorsrud 1964; Englestad 1972), the USA (Davis and Cherns 1975; Trist *et al.* 1977; Cummings 1978; Pasmore *et al.* 1982), Canada (Kolodny and Kiggundu 1980; Trist and Westley 1981; Cunningham and White 1984), Israel (Golomb 1981), and Australia (Emery 1976, 1978). In this chapter my investigation of the extent to which STS interventions have been undertaken in developing countries and have achieved similarly positive results is reported.

The study

Initially, a systematic structured computer search of the literature was conducted using several management data bases. This search showed that the applications of STS in developing countries have been spotty and limited in scope. For example, for the 25-year period beginning in 1953, documented evidence was available for only twenty-five STS case studies from only three developing countries – India (Rice 1958; Miller 1975; Nitish 1979; Kanawaty *et al.* 1981), the Sudan (Kidwell *et al.* 1981), and Tanzania (Kanawaty *et al.* 1981) – and included a reference to Peru (Trist 1975). Detailed discussions of this search of the literature and the results of the review appear in works by Kiggundu *et al.* (1983) and Kiggundu (1986).

These surprising findings led me to abandon the original plans for making a comprehensive review of STS interventions in developing countries. Instead, I sought to determine the reasons why applications of STS theory in these countries had been limited. This investigation led me to establish three broad categories of limiting factors: (1) prevailing conditions, tenets, and practices in developing countries and the extent to which these conflict with STS principles and assumptions; (2) the extent to which the conduct, values, beliefs, and assumptions of Western change agents hinder or facilitate the development and longevity of interventions; and (3) the limitations of indigenous managers and change agents in developing countries. For most developing countries, the success of the applications of interventions based on imported theories such as STS depends on the nature of the organization, the environment in which it operates, the quality of the partnership or working relationship between the Western change agents and their counterparts in the developing country, and the degree to which the indigenous managers and powerful local stakeholders facilitate or resist the intervention.

Part of the development efforts of such countries requires them to import various forms of technology in massive amounts. This causes them to create industrial and organizational conditions requiring different models of organization and management. In general, the social, technical, and environmental context within which organizations in developing countries operate change constantly. STS theory is rather weak with respect to cultural adaptation, so I sought to review and identify the conditions in which it may be successfully applied in organizations in developing countries.

Prevailing conditions in developing countries

Prevailing conditions in most developing countries make it difficult for STS to gain wide acceptance and application. These conditions include (1) management and organization practices that conflict with STS principles and design, (2) different legal, social, political, and cultural systems, (3) different economic and technical realities, and (4) individual and systemic powerlessness.

STS theory is based on principles favouring open systems in organizations, democratic values, beliefs, and practices in society and the work place, the availability of options, and minimal critical specifications (Cherns 1976). The dominant management and organization practices in most developing countries, however, are

147

hierarchical, mechanistic, autocratic, and based on Theory X assumptions. For example, little autonomy and decision-making power is delegated down the chain of leadership. Employees are subjected to excessive division of labour and close supervision, partly because managers believe in the myth of worker indolence (Myers 1959; Blunt 1983; Dasah and Kiggundu 1985). Management tends to be paternalistic rather than participative and expects absolute obedience and loyalty from the workers.

The recent literature has focused on the importance of culture in the management and organization of work in developing countries (Riggs 1960; Hofstede 1980; Bourgeois and Boltvinik 1981; Faucheux *et al.* 1982; Kiggundu *et al.* 1983). The discussions lead to the conclusion that one faces difficulty applying STS theory in settings in developing countries. The reasons for such difficulty can be summarized as the following.

• Organizations in developing countries are managed as closed systems that are barely responsive to environmental changes, whereas they actually exist in complex divided dualistic socio-cultural environments with multiple constituencies (Hafsi *et al.* 1985; Kiggundu 1985).
• Government plays a dominant and pervasive role and government bureaucrats are averse to taking risks (Tandon 1982; Ramamurti in press).
• Organizations in developing countries display little structure, a low tolerance for ambiguity, and great uncertainty (Faucheux *et al.* 1982).
• Motivation to work stems from different sources, including the need for individual rather than group recognition by one's superior (Miller 1975; Hofstede 1981; Kanawaty *et al.* 1981; Kanungo 1982).
• Organizations in developing countries exhibit dysfunctional modes of conflict management, closer social and emotional interactions, intergroup rivalry, little capacity for openness, trust, and the rational expression of feelings, and well-established hierarchical and social status barriers (Bourgeois and Boltvinik 1981; Faucheux *et al.* 1982).
• Inadequate physical, managerial, and institutional frameworks exist for effective use of technological innovations (Wallender 1979).
• American theories of management do not apply abroad (Goodstein 1981; Hofstede 1981; Hunt 1981).
• Organizations employ ambiguous, ill-defined, abstract, and symbolic measurements of performance and organizational goals (Kiggundu *et al.* 1983).

148

In discussing the limits to the application of organization development (OD), Faucheux *et al.* (1982) make the following observations, which appear valid for STS as well:

the tremendous centralization of business, the marked intervention of the state, ideological splits, the preeminence of the external processes of change over internal processes, the importance of law, the representative structure needed for every change, and the distributive model of power, constitute many elements likely to jeopardize what is often called the true-love–trust models of OD.

(p. 355)

Organizations in developing countries also operate under different business, economic, and technical realities, and often operate under conditions of organizational and managerial scarcity with insufficient resources, weak or insufficient physical and institutional support systems, and inadequate management and technical personnel. This is particularly the case for the less-developed countries of the Third World (Blunt 1984; Kerrigan and Luke 1985; National Association of Schools of Public Affairs and Administration 1985).

The more advanced developing countries, including those becoming newly industrialized, have different economic agenda that, instead of emphasizing the provision of basic needs, focus on rapid industrialization based on mass production of a single product, extreme rationalization of the production processes, and low labour costs. Under such conditions, technical imperatives are deliberate and STS design is not especially suitable.

Among the limits to STS in developing countries is a pervasive persistent sense of powerlessness or helplessness at the individual, group, organization, and community levels. The literature on helplessness (Seligman 1975) and powerlessness (in terms of empowerment) (Bryant and White 1982; Murrell 1984; Brown and Covey 1985) clearly shows that these are debilitating conditions for individuals and their social work organizations. STS design, however, presupposes high levels of power, control, and influence by individuals, groups, and organizations. Such a design requires taking initiatives from all levels of management and labour, including the learning of new behaviours and participative skills, experimentation, group dynamics, and a high level of tolerance for ambiguity as the organization's design remains incomplete and in a constant state of change. Creating such conditions in organizations in developing countries is difficult if their employees feel powerless or helpless.

The failures of programmes promoting decentralization and popular participation in various parts of the developing world, including Africa (Muwanga-Barlow 1978; Blunt 1984), South America (Toth 1971), and Asia (Szal 1979), may well result from a widespread sense of powerlessness and helplessness. According to this argument, problems associated with applications of STS to developing countries may not result as much from a concentration of power at the top as from feelings of powerlessness at all levels of the organization. In many instances, this may indicate absolute powerlessness corrupting absolutely.

Effective management of organizations in developing countries, as in organizations elsewhere, stems from effective management and delineation of tasks related both to strategic management and to critical operating tasks. Strategic tasks, often associated with top management, concentrate on the long-term aspects of the organization, deal with relationships between the organization and its environment, and include formulating and implementing strategy, managing contextual interdependences, and developing a clear organizational philosophy and 'nichemanship'. Critical operating tasks, however, focus on internal management, processes of production and transformation of the organization, and such technical and administrative support functions as keeping inventory, maintaining the system, and supervision. Unlike strategic tasks – which are mostly unstructured, ambiguous, and highly dynamic – operating tasks are often performed according to well-established standard operating procedures.

Evidence from organizations in developing countries indicates that they pay little or no attention to strategic management tasks (Paul 1983), while in many cases sustaining high-performing operating systems is equally problematic. Recent studies of strategic management tasks performed in developing countries have found that such tasks are characterized by dualities (Kiggundu 1985), divisions (Hafsi *et al.* 1985), and multiple conflicting systems (Brown and Covey 1985). The responsibility for managing some of these tasks may fall on individuals or groups outside the boundaries of the particular organization or country. Moreover, some of the tasks commonly regarded as procedural may, in certain circumstances, assume strategic significance. For example, under conditions of scarce resources, tasks related to inventory and technical support (e.g. performing repairs and maintenance during periods of unfavourable foreign exchange) become strategic management tasks under the direct control and responsibility of those occupying the strategic apex.

Organizations and institutions in developing countries experience serious difficulties designing and diffusing high performance systems. This stems, at least in part, from limits to the organization and to effective management of both the strategic and operating tasks of some of these systems. A relationship exists between experienced powerlessness and the inability to manage strategic tasks. Effective strategic management requires, among other things, the capacity to manipulate and exploit environmental symbols and cues to one's advantage and to acquire and organize internal resources for effective implementation. Consequently, change agents of developing countries and their Western counterparts find empowerment of vital importance to the development of strategies for creating sustainable high performance systems.

STS theory and its associated diagnostic and intervention tools and methods can provide information as to the extent to which strategic and operational tasks are effectively managed. For example, applications of environmental scanning and variance control analysis (Kiggundu 1981) can provide the basis for developing high performance strategic and operating systems for organizations in developing countries.

Western action researchers in developing countries

The extent to which action researchers and change agents from the West facilitate or hinder effective applications of STS in organizations in developing countries is an important subject of study. Other factors being equal, what these people do or fail to do, the methods used (e.g. scouting, diagnosis, interventions, evaluation, and the like), their motives, commitment, ideological values, and beliefs, their cross-cultural training, experience, and sensitivity, their ethnocentrism, and their linguistic and cross-cultural translation skills (Adler and Kiggundu 1983) all have profound effects on the immediate and long-term applicability of STS in developing countries.

Successful foreign change agents must be sensitive to indigenous characteristics. Among other things, this requires introspection into one's own values and assumptions and those of the proposed intervention's theory and methods. These should not conflict with the values and ideology of the client organization and its constituencies (Brown and Covey 1985). Quite often, the foreign change agent lacks the time, incentive, mandate, or training for assessing whether or not a fit exists between the agent, the intended intervention(s), and the client system(s). The change agent should take care to avoid inconsistencies between the agent's espoused theories – such as mutual trust, democratic values, and fairness – and the theories in use, such as extractive diagnosis without meaningful feedback to the clients. Shepard's (1983) rules of thumb for the change agent performing domestic consulting (e.g. build local support systems, encourage empathy, and the like) must be observed even more strictly when fulfilling assignments in developing countries.

The training, experience, and general professional acumen of the foreign change agent is extremely important, for in most developing countries the agent assumes the role of an expert rather than that of a facilitator. Most STS change agents are trained in the social and behavioural sciences as they are developed, taught, and practised in North America through such organizations as NTL Institute for Applied Behavioral Science. Few of these agents are trained in economic development, development administration, the transfer of technology, social and economic history, colonial administration, international relations, cross-cultural dynamics, or the management of cultural differences (Harris and Moran 1979). Yet all these fields affect the management of operations in developing countries. The dilemma is that it may be impossible for any one person to claim expertise in all these areas, yet multidisciplinary teams do not work well in one's own nation, let alone on foreign assignments.

The foreign change agent must also determine exactly who the client is. Hafsi *et al.* (1985) and Kiggundu (1985) point out that most organizations in developing countries have divided multiple constituencies, which are often in conflict with one another. These divisions may stem from political, economic, social (e.g. cast or tribal), religious, or regional differences. In determining whose interests are being addressed, the Western change agent faces ideological and moral dilemmas that are not easily escapable. Moreover, consulting abroad often leads to much stress resulting from working in unfamiliar conditions away from one's home, from pressures to meet various schedules and deadlines related to travel, project achievements and 'deliverables', social functions, and the like, and from the client's unrealistically high expectations that the consultant should provide magical solutions to the organization's long-standing complex problems. These conditions give the change agent little opportunity to reflect on the broader moral issues of the assignment.

Consequently, the short-term foreign assignment – common for most Western change agents working in developing countries – is not conducive to the effective transfer of STS or similar interventions, even for those agents with the best intentions. These assignments are often more complex than the change agents first realize. Moreover, the client's problems may not be easily managed by Western methods of diagnosis, analysis, or intervention. Western change agents need to spend considerably more time living, studying, and working within the system before making prescriptive statements or designing interventions for change. Minimal residential requirements of 6–12 months for Western change agents should be given serious consideration.

Managers and change agents in developing countries

Managers and change agents in developing countries are the most important facilitators or gatekeepers for any organizational innovation. For this reason, their roles, personal values, motives, collective interests, and behaviour – and the context in which they work as potential change masters – must be examined (Kanter 1983).

Good managers and change agents in developing countries are in short supply (National Association of Schools of Public Affairs and Administration 1985). The few available ones are spread thin in multiple, often conflicting roles cutting across organizations. Shortly after returning home, students from developing countries who have studied abroad often complain of excessive workloads resulting in part from multiple conflicting roles that hinder their engaging in creative work. Such persons spend most of their working time managing conflicts and crises instead of planning for organizational change and development such as STS. They are often too busy to learn – even from their own mistakes.

Moreover, most managers of developing countries are not entrepreneurial and do not readily take risks. Some of the reasons for this aversion to risk include the following.

- Their positions already involve too many extra-organizational risks.
- The organization's incentive system does not reward risk taking, for compensation is based on an individual's rank, tenure, seniority, or age rather than performance (Tandon 1982).
- Organizations have multiple constituencies, all of whom cannot agree on a single strategy of innovation and commit the necessary resources (Hafsi *et al.* 1985).
- Most of these managers work for the government or for government agencies, and so are not entrepreneurs but bureaucrats (Tandon 1982).
- They operate in inappropriate organization forms, personnel systems, and management and administrative cultures that discourage initiative and risk taking, but the managers are powerless to change this (Kanawaty *et al.* 1981).
- They lack intimate understanding of the internal operations of their organizations and the organizations' social, cultural, and political environments, and therefore are not equipped to choose the most appropriate change strategies.
- They work for organizations characterized by conditions of imperfect competition, elaborate and tedious forms of inter-organizational relationships, and lack of management depth.

- The managers' interests are served by maintaining the status quo.

This analysis leads one to conclude that these persons are not yet ready to act as effective change masters for their organizations. According to Kanter (1983), change masters are

> the right people in the right place at the right time. The right people are the ones with ideas that move beyond the organization's established practice, ideas they can form into vision. The right places are the interactive environments that support innovation, encourage the building of coalitions and teams to support and implement vision. The right times are those moments in the flow of organizational history when it is possible to construct reality on the basis of accumulated innovations to shape a more productive and successful future.
>
> (Kanter 1983: 306)

Most organizations in developing countries urgently need change masters, not only for STS applications but also for other innovations in management and technology.

Suggestions for future applications

The suggestions offered in this chapter are based on four premises. The first is that the theoretical framework of STS and its associated diagnostic and intervention tools and methods are intrinsically sound and, with appropriate adjustments, can significantly aid the advancement of organizational development and change in developing countries. This conclusion stems from my personal experiences with the STS framework in the West, personal knowledge of organizations and environments within developing countries, and the limited empirical evidence of the twenty-five case studies reviewed for this study.

The second premise is that one cannot take short-cuts to progress. The limitations discussed in this chapter cannot be overcome overnight. Rather, even under ideal conditions, progress requires hard work, experimentation, perseverance, and extraordinary good will on the part of all stakeholders – including management, labour, unions, change agents, civil servants, politicians, and aid agencies – to accept the necessary structural and behavioural changes supporting STS interventions.

The third premise is that one cannot use a single prescriptive evolutionary path. A comparative analysis of the applications of STS and organization development paradigms in North America and Europe

(Mills 1978; Trist 1981; Faucheux *et al.* 1982) shows that their epistemological basis is potentially robust enough to allow for different implementation strategies and processes to emerge to meet local needs and circumstances. Therefore, STS applications could evolve along alternative strategies and paths that are not only different from those in Europe and North America, but also unique for different regions, countries, sectors, or communities within the developing world.

In North America, OD and STS interventions have had different degrees of success in different sectors or types of industries (Weisbord 1976; Pava 1983; Kolodny and Armstrong 1985). Similarly, STS applications are more likely to succeed in some sectors of developing countries than in others. In the future, efforts should be directed at investigating and specifying the organizational and environmental conditions in those countries most likely to respond positively to STS interventions.

The fourth premise is that the successful application of STS in developing countries, as is the case with any management or technological innovation, depends on the quality of the partnership between the major actors of the specific organization in the developing country and the Western change agents. Therefore, any suggestions for future applications must be directed toward both parties to the partnership. Developing countries cannot make these applications alone, just as Western change agents cannot spur progress without the support and active involvement of local interests (Kanawaty *et al.* 1981; Kiggundu *et al.* 1983).

The review of STS case studies in developing countries and the discussion in this chapter of the limitations to STS interventions inspire several suggestions for future applications. Such limitations in developing countries and the West can easily be translated into action plans. This chapter presents only those suggestions most likely to improve the chances for successful applications of STS in developing countries.

The first suggestion is that fundamental structural changes take place with respect to both the change agents and their clients. The primary objective of these changes should be facilitation of a gradual but steady movement toward a more optimal combination of the social, technical, and economic subsystems of the organizations in developing countries. Recent research by Jørgensen *et al.* (in press) shows that, for example, market imperfections in the economy distort managerial and organizational behaviour along with the design and structure of work in these organizations.

Developing countries must also determine their own most appropriate sector(s) for STS. Such sectors usually consist of the areas or industries in which improvements in performance have a high organizational and societal pay-off. For example, in post-World War II England, productivity in coal mining was an important national goal because coal was badly needed for rebuilding the war-torn industries. This sector provided the basis for the first STS studies. In Norway, the most appropriate sector for STS consisted of the declining pulp and paper mills in isolated small towns or communities (Trist 1981). According to Kolodny and Armstrong (1985), in the USA this sector currently consists of those industries using automated manufacturing technology. For the more advanced developing countries, export-based industries would be appropriate for STS, whereas the less-developed countries unable to feed themselves would find agriculture, food production, and other industries serving basic needs – such as water and security – prime candidates for STS. The creation of high-performing systems in these sectors is crucial to the survival and development of the countries.

The third suggestion is that more attention be paid to improving the understanding and diagnosis of the environments within which organizations in developing countries operate. STS has been accused of being 'soft' on the environment, yet, as Faucheux *et al.* (1982) and others have found in these countries, 'societies pervade organizations'. One cannot realistically analyse strategies for organization development and change without properly understanding and diagnosing the socio-cultural and socio-economic environments of multiple constituencies. Available STS methods of diagnosis (e.g. environmental scanning) and intervention (e.g. team building) must be refined to capture the unique societal, economic, political, and technological context of each planned organization change.

The spheres of work and life outside work are highly interrelated in developing countries. Therefore STS interventions should aim not only to develop high performance in work organization, but also to improve the general quality of life. As both Hofstede (1984) and I (Kiggundu 1982) have argued, this requires moving beyond the STS model as applied in the West and giving up Western ethnocentric concepts. For example, interventions should be designed not only for organizations but also for different levels of analysis, including the community, family, and individuals living in both rural and urban areas.

Western change agents should also be encouraged to support and play a significant role in bringing about the changes discussed above and to examine their roles, motives, and conduct as consultants to organizations in developing countries. For each foreign consulting assignment they should determine whether they have enough information about the potential client system(s) to make professional judgements as to whether they are part of the problem or part of the potential solution(s). A simple force field analysis might prove quite revealing in such situations.

The final suggestion deals with empowerment. With STS or any other change strategy, the persons responsible for implementing it must feel that they have enough control or mastery of their lives and environment to make a difference. The most effective precondition for self-generated self-directed changes such as STS is empowerment. Change agents in developing countries (e.g. employees, work groups, managers, community leaders, and the like) must be empowered before they can participate meaningfully in planned change strategies.

At this time, most developing countries lack the necessary physical and institutional infrastructure to support these suggestions. Many of them experience economic, technological, and socio-political constraints that severely limit their ability to initiate and sustain system-wide interventions. Even those countries that are relatively better off than most cannot make major structural adjustments, partly because of problems of scarcity, inequality, and instability. Therefore, those advocating the STS framework may have to wait some time before conditions in developing countries are conducive to its widespread application.

Summary and conclusion

A review of twenty-five studies found that the applications of STS theory in developing countries have been spotty and limited in scope. This chapter discusses some of the limiting factors, focusing on the theory itself, the conditions prevailing in developing countries, and the roles and quality of the partnerships between Western change agents and managers in developing countries as potential facilitators of organization development and change.

To improve the chances for the success of future applications of STS theory in developing countries, several suggestions have been made that call for fundamental structural, institutional, and behavioural changes, both within the developing countries themselves and for Western change agents. Because of the differences among organizations in developing countries and the environments within which they operate, applying the theory requires different evolutionary paths within each country, region, or community so that they may make their own adjustments to the theory consistent with their own organizational, national, or local needs and circumstances. The agenda for developing countries is varied and complex. With varying degrees of emphasis, this agenda includes the following: the provision of basic human needs, rights, and freedoms; strengthening physical, institutional, and managerial capacity; rehabilitating institutions; managing small and island states; and managing the selection and transfer of technology, knowledge, and skills (Stobaugh and Wells 1984). Whatever the needs of any particular organization in a developing country, future applications of STS – or of any other innovative organization development and change intervention – should be directed at both the operational and strategic key variances. Focusing on one at the expense of the other is unlikely to lead to effective lasting solutions. This is the context in which this chapter's suggestions and action plans for the potential use of STS theory and methods for the development of high-performing systems in developing countries should be read and understood.

Note

Reprinted from *The Journal of Applied Behavioral Science* 23, 3 (1986): 341–53, with permission.

References

Adler, N. J. and Kiggundu, M. N. (1983) 'Awareness at the crossroads: designing translator based training programs', in D. Landis and R. Brislin (eds) *Handbook of Intercultural Training*, vol. 2, pp. 124–52, New York: Pergamon.

Blunt, P. (1983) *Organizational Theory and Behavior: An African Perspective*, London: Longman.

Blunt, P. (1984) 'Conditions for basic needs satisfaction in Africa through decentralized forms of decision making', *Journal of Applied Behavioral Science* 20, 4: 403–21.

Bourgeois III, L. G. and Boltvinik, M. (1981) 'OD in cross-cultural settings: Latin America', *California Management Review* 22, 3: 75–81.

Brown, D. L. and Covey, J. G. (1985) 'Development organizations and organization development: implications for the organization development paradigm', presented at the National Meetings of the Academy of Management, San Diego, CA.

Bryant, C. and White, L. (1982) *Management Development in the Third World*, Boulder, CO: Westview.

Cherns, A. B. (1976) 'The principles of sociotechnical design', *Human Relations* 29, 5: 19–23.

Cummings, T. G. (1978) 'Sociotechnical experimentation: a review of sixteen studies', in W. A. Pasmore and J. J. Sherwood (eds) *Sociotechnical Systems: A Sourcebook*, pp. 259–70, La Jolla, CA: University Associates.

Cunningham, J. B. and White, T. H. (eds) (1984) *Quality of Working Life: Contemporary Cases*, Ottawa: Government of Canada.

Dasah, B. Z. and Kiggundu, M. N. (1985) 'Report on the debriefing of the Canada–Kenya business forum', Toronto: Canadian International Development Agency, Briefing Centre.

Davis, L. E. and Cherns, A. B. (eds) (1975) *The Quality of Working Life*, vol. 2, New York: Free Press.

Emery, F. E. (1976) *Futures We Are In*, Leiden: Martinus Nijhoff.

Emery, F. E. (1978) *The Emergence of a New Paradigm of Work*, Canberra: Centre for Continuing Education, Australian National University.

Emery, F. E. and Thorsrud, E. (1964) *Form and Content in Industrial Democracy*, Oslo: Oslo University Press.

Englestad, P. H. (1972) 'Socio-technical approach to problems of process control', in L. E. Davis and J. C. Taylor (eds) *Design of Jobs*, pp. 328–56, New York: Penguin.

Faucheux, C., Amado, G., and Laurent, A. (1982) 'Organizational development and change', *Annual Review of Psychology* 33: 343–70.

Golomb, N. (1981) 'Socio-technical strategy for improving the effectiveness and Q.W.L. of three kibbutz plants and one government institute', Ruppin Institute, Kibbutz Management Centre, Israel.

Goodman, P. S. (1979) *Assessing Organizational Change: The Rushton Quality of Working Life Experiment*, New York: Wiley.

Goodstein, L. D. (1981) 'American business values and cultural imperialism', *Organizational Dynamics* 9, 1: 49–54.

Hafsi, T., Kiggundu, M. N., and Jørgensen, J. J. (1985) 'Structural configurations in the strategic apex of state-owned enterprises', Working Paper No. 85-07, Ecole des Hautes Etudes Commerciales, Université de Montréal, September.

Harris, P. R. and Moran, R. T. (1979) *Managing Cultural Differences*, Houston, TX: Gulf.

Hill, P. (1971) *Towards a New Philosophy of Management*, London: Gower.

Hofstede, G. (1980) *Culture's Consequences: International Differences in Work-related Values*, Beverly Hills, CA: Sage.

Hofstede, G. (1981, Summer) 'Motivation, leadership and organization: do American theories apply abroad?', *Organizational Dynamics* 9, 1: 63–8.

Hofstede, G. (1984) 'The cultural relativity of the quality of working life concept', *Academy of Management Review* 9, 3: 389–98.

Hunt, J. W. (1981, Summer) 'Applying American behavioral science: some cross-cultural problems', *Organizational Dynamics* 9, 1: 55–62.

Jørgensen, J. J., Hafsi, T., and Kiggundu, M. N. (in press) 'Towards a market imperfections theory of organizational structure in developing countries', *Journal of Management Studies*.

Kanawaty, G., Thorsrud, E., Semiono, J. P., and Singh, J. P. (1981) 'Field experiences with new forms of work organization', *International Labour Review* 120, 3: 263–77.

Kanter, R. M. (1983) *The Change Masters: Innovation for Productivity in the American Corporation*, New York: Simon & Schuster.

Kanungo, R. N. (1982) *Work Alienation: An Integrative Approach*, New York: Praeger.

Kelly, J. E. (1978) 'A reappraisal of sociotechnical systems theory', *Human Relations* 31, 1069–99.

Kerrigan, J. E. and Luke, J. S. (1985) 'Management training strategies for less developed countries', unpublished manuscript, United States Agency for International Development, Bureau of Science and Technology, Washington, DC.

Kidwell, J., El, J. A., and Ketchum, L. (1981) *Sociotechnical Study for Locomotive Maintenance Workshop at Sennai, Sudan*, McLean, VA: Parsons Brinckerhoff (CENTEC International).

Kiggundu, M. N. (1981) 'Variance control analysis: a diagnostic and intervention strategy', *Academy of Management Proceedings*, 122–6, San Diego.

Kiggundu, M. N. (1982) 'The quality of working life in developing countries: beyond the sociotechnical systems model', presented at the 20th International Congress of Applied Psychology, Edinburgh.

Kiggundu, M. N. (1985) 'Africa in crisis: can organization theory help?', presented at the National Meetings of the Academy of Management, San Diego, CA, August.

Kiggundu, M. N. (1986) 'Sociotechnical systems in developing countries: a review and directions for future research', Working Paper No. WPS-86-01, School of Business, Carleton University, Ottawa, Ontario.

Kiggundu, M. N., Jørgensen, J. J., and Hafsi, T. (1983) 'Administrative theory and practice in developing countries: a synthesis', *Administrative Science Quarterly* 28, 1: 66–84.

Kolodny, H. F. and Armstrong, A. (1985) 'Three bases for QWL improvements: structure, technology, and philosophy', presented at the National Meetings of the Academy of Management, San Diego, CA, August.

Kolodny, H. F. and Kiggundu, M. N. (1980) 'Towards the development of a sociotechnical systems model in Woodlands Mechanical Harvesting', *Human Relations* 37, 9: 623–45.

Miller, E. J. (1975) 'Socio-technical systems in weaving, 1953–1970: a follow-up study', *Human Relations* 28: 349–86.

Mills, T. (1978) 'Europe's industrial democracy: an American response', *Harvard Business Review*, November–December: 143–52.

Murrell, K. L. (1984) 'Empowerment: new concepts and new thinking about power', unpublished manuscript, University of West Florida.

Muwanga-Barlow, C. H. (1978) 'The development of administrative sciences in English speaking Africa', *International Review of Administrative Sciences* 44: 93–105.

Myers, C. A. (1959) 'Management in India', in F. Harbison and C. A. Myers (eds) *Management in the Industrial World*, pp. 137–53, New York: McGraw-Hill.

National Association of Schools of Public Affairs and Administration

(1985) 'Improving management in Southern Africa', Final Report to the Regional Training Council of the Southern African Development Co-Ordination Conference, Washington, DC, July.

Nitish, R. D. (1979) 'India', in *New Forms of Work Organization*, No. 2, Geneva: International Labour Office.

Pasmore, W., Francis, C., Haldeman, J., and Shani, A. (1982) 'Sociotechnical systems: a North American reflection on empirical studies of the seventies', *Human Relations* 35, 12: 1179–204.

Paul, S. (1983) *Strategic Management Development Programmes*, Geneva: International Labour Organization.

Pava, C. (1983) *Managing New Office Technology: An Organizational Strategy*, New York: Free Press.

Ramamurti, R. (in press) 'Public entrepreneurs: who they are and how they operate', *California Management Review*.

Rice, A. K. (1958) *Productivity and Social Organization: The Ahmedabad Experiment*, London: Tavistock Institute.

Riggs, F. W. (1960) 'Prismatic society and financial administration', *Administrative Science Quarterly* 5: 1–46.

Seligman, M. E. P. (1975) *Helplessness: On Depression, Development and Death*, San Francisco, CA: W. H. Freeman.

Shepard, H. A. (1983) 'Rules of thumb for change agents', in W. L. French, C. H. Bell, and R. A. Zawacki (eds) *Organization Development, Theory, Practice and Research*, pp. 422–6, Plano, TX: Business Publications.

Stobaugh, R. and Wells, L. T. (eds) (1984) *Technology Crossing Borders: The Choice, Transfer, and Management of International Technology Flows*, Boston, MA: Harvard Business School Press.

Szal, R. J. (1979) 'Popular participation: employment and the fulfillment of basic needs', *International Labour Review* 118, 1: 27–38.

Tandon, P. (1982) 'Hierarchical structure and attitudes toward risk in state-owned enterprises', in L. P. Jones (ed.) *Public Enterprises in Less-Developed Countries*, Cambridge: Cambridge University Press.

Toth, S. (1971) 'A comment on the poder project', *International Development Review* 13, 4: 18–20.

Trist, E. (1975) 'Planning the first steps toward quality of working life in a developing country', in L. E. Davis and A. B. Cherns (eds) *Quality of Working Life: Problems, Prospects and the State of the Art*, vol. 1, pp. 78–85, New York: Free Press.

Trist, E. L. (1981) 'The evolution of sociotechnical systems: a conceptual framework and an action research program', Occasional Paper No. 2, Ontario Quality of Working Life Centre, Ontario Ministry of Labour, Toronto, June.

Trist, E. L. and Westley, W. A. (1981) *OWL in the Federal Public Service*, Ottawa: Government of Canada.

Trist, E. L., Higgin, G. W., Murray, H., and Pollock, A. B. (1963) *Organizational Choice*, London: Tavistock Institute.

Trist E. L., Susman, G. I., and Brown, G. R. (1977) 'An experiment in autonomous working in an American underground coal mine', *Human*

Relations 30, 3: 201–36.

Wallender, H. W. (1979) *Technology Transfer and Management in the Developing Countries*, Cambridge: Ballinger.

Weisbord, M. (1976) 'Why organization development hasn't worked [so far] in medical centers', *Health Care Management Review* 1, Spring: 17–38.

Chapter nine

Will China adopt Western management practices?

Shirley C. Zhuang and Arthur M. Whitehill

China may be modernizing its economy, but it is still communist and Eastern in outlook. So do not expect Western management practices to surface there very soon.

The People's Republic of China today seems to be entering the modern world, coming out of the shadow of the warlords, the 20-year struggle between communism and nationalism, and the Cultural Revolution. Moves are afoot to shift the Chinese economy more toward the market-oriented end of the spectrum. Some even insist that the Chinese are using capitalistic practices to run private companies in this new era of freedom. But appearances can be deceiving; in this chapter we discuss whether this is the case in the People's Republic of China.

In all cultures, management practices must reflect a society's social, political, and economic systems. Although these elements can be analysed separately, they all play an important role in determining management practices. In this chapter, three aspects of the Chinese economy are discussed: the nature of ownership; the prevailing planning system; and the relative importance of production and profit.

The economic environment of management

State ownership versus private ownership

One reason to assume that China is becoming capitalist might be the recent reports concerning the opening of private enterprises. A brief analysis of ownership structure can help us understand the true impact of this phenomenon on the Chinese economy.

In the major cities, three ownership categories exist: state, collective, and private (individual). According to 1981 data (Engle 1985), the total urban labour force was 117.4 million, of which 75 per cent worked for the state-owned enterprises, 23 per cent for collectively owned enterprises, and only 2 per cent for privately owned enterprises.

State enterprises have played a consistently dominant role in China's economy. The number of state-owned enterprises in the early 1980s was more than 80,000, and output of the state-owned sector was 420 billion yuan (US$113.51 billion), 81 per cent of total industry output. Furthermore, the fixed assets of these enterprises were around 346.52 billion yuan (US$93.65 billion), three-quarters of the total fixed assets of all industries ('China industrial economics and management' 1983).

Most state enterprises are large or medium sized. It is clear that they have been and still are the backbone of the nation's economy. These enterprises possess relatively modern technology and exercise control over industries in the collective and private sectors with a few exceptions, such as fast-food services. State-owned enterprises usually provide machinery, raw materials, fuels, and energy sources to other industries. At the same time, they produce the majority of consumer goods. Such enterprises also enjoy the privilege of receiving government grants or loans for their expansion. And they have guaranteed markets for their products, as well as ready access to raw materials.

Therefore the dominant role of state enterprises is unquestionable. A great deal of evidence indicates that this is unlikely to change dramatically in the near future.

The second category, collectively owned enterprises in the cities and townships, are mostly small- to medium-sized service and manufacturing firms. The number of employees varies from about twenty to as many as several hundred. Many of them have contracts with state-owned enterprises to provide parts for machinery. Some develop their own products, mainly to meet consumer needs such as garments or food services. The output value in this section of the economy is about 15 per cent of total industrial output.

Like state enterprises, collective enterprises offer their employees a standard wage system that depends largely upon seniority. Employee wages tend to be about 20 per cent lower than those paid in state enterprises, although their bonuses may be higher if they enjoy large profits. These companies have lower priority for access to raw materials and grants from the government. Managers of collectives are allowed to exercise more autonomy than those in state-owned enterprises but less than the owner–managers of private firms.

The third category, private enterprises managed by the owner perhaps with a few hired employees, are commonly known as 'individual enterprises' in China. Such entities play an insignificant role in China's economy, in both the number of people employed and the volume of output. Their output represents less than 4 per cent of the total value of industrial production.

Although these enterprises are labelled 'private', it should be stressed that they differ from the Westerner's usual perception of private enterprise. First, they are complementary elements serving the main frame of the economy – state-owned enterprises. As such, they are unlikely to become a dominant element in the economy in the near future. Second, most owners of these enterprises are also employees in their daily operations, and over 90 per cent are family businesses. Third, most are not concerned with mass production, but are concentrated in the service sectors. Quite often it is economically impractical for a state enterprise to meet demand in such segments of the economy, especially in consumer services. Therefore private enterprises play a necessary role in filling these gaps. Finally, their expansion is restricted by limited financing and government regulations.

Central planning versus market planning

In a centrally planned economy, all major decisions – including strategic planning, allocation of resources, pricing, and distribution – are top-down decisions. This means that the central government makes decisions and the local government agencies implement them. Currently, market planning plays a negligible role in China's economy. The central government designs a 5-year plan for economic development. Then a yearly target for each industry is set.

The central government of the People's Republic of China directly controls the local governments of twenty-nine provinces and three cities (Beijing, Shanghai, and Tianjing). In addition, there are five minority regions that have more autonomy but are still under the supervision of the central government. The State Council directly controls eleven ministries covering major industries. Each has several smaller branches at the provincial level. These branches are then subdivided into bureaus at the city level. The subdivisions under the bureaus assign quotas to factories. Usually, these quotas are based upon the previous year's data plus a certain percentage increase. A vertical relationship between these administrative entities represents a communication and control channel through which the higher level gives instructions and the lower level submits requests for approval of various activities.

There are two main types of quotas: compulsory and general guidelines. At the beginning of each year, a state-run enterprise receives quotas from its bureau or ministry if it is directly under the control of the central government, or from subdivisions if it is locally controlled.

165

Either each month or each quarter the enterprise is required to report to the next higher level on its performance. These reports, for most industrial enterprises, are focused on eight major areas: output value, output quantity, product quality (reject rate), sales, cost reduction, production efficiency, profits, and innovation. This type of enterprise has little autonomy, either in the type of product to produce or on the optimal output level to achieve.

The overall economic system thus clearly depends on central planning. It ignores the market functions of demand and supply in guiding economic growth.

Production versus profits

The centrally planned economy forces state enterprises to focus on their quotas rather than other indicators of success in their operation. The measurement of an enterprise's performance is largely based upon the assigned production goals. Therefore, how to fulfil – or more than fulfil – its quotas becomes the enterprise's first priority. Profits earned by enterprises are appropriated by the government and used to reimburse those units that suffer losses. Therefore state enterprises have little real incentive to achieve substantial profits.

A key question is whether the quotas alone are sufficient incentives for efficient production. Among the eight inputs mentioned above, quantity of output carries the heaviest weight. This may well lead to low quality products. Another problem is that profits are arbitrarily set and based on the assumption that all products can be sold. This is a dangerous assumption without market research assessing demand and supply. In the past, certain products have been left sitting in the warehouse for years. Yet the enterprise that produced them was still designated as a highly profitable organization.

Furthermore, the cost of a product does not truly tell the nature of all expenditures made in producing it. For example, because the allocation of resources is controlled by the central government, it is impossible to balance allocations to all enterprises perfectly. Because of the shortage of supplies, some factories may receive raw materials while others may not. Those that are not in key industries or priority economic sectors may have to spend extra resources on travel and transportation to obtain sufficient materials to produce the required output. One enterprise may receive a government grant for expansion while another may not. Therefore, cost estimation and accounting procedures do not have the same meaning as in the Western world.

In addition, a fixed-price system leaves enterprises little product price control to use to achieve cost effectiveness and profit targeting.

An enterprise usually does not perform marketing functions such as advertising, consumer surveying, and selling on its own. Instead, over 90 per cent of commodities are priced and distributed through channels set by the central planning system. Industrial goods are usually reallocated to producers of final products. The majority of consumer goods are sold in state-owned department stores, where the price is fixed. Under this kind of system, there is not much a supplier can do to control profitability.

In summary, it is clear that Chinese managers face a number of variables beyond their control. Therefore, it seems that to fulfil one's quota is the only meaningful evidence of managerial achievement.

Management in China since 1949

Since the state-run enterprises account for over 80 per cent of industrial output and three-quarters of the urban labour force, the Chinese management practices discussed in this section reflect these operations.

Stages in the development of China's management system

It is useful to focus upon the four stages in the development of China's management system: 1949–56; 1957–66; 1967–79; 1980–6.

1949–56

This early stage saw a transformation from a semi-feudal, semi-capitalist China to a socialist China. After the Communist Party took over the control of major industries, administrative personnel were either appointed from within or transferred to state-owned enterprises.

At the beginning of this period quite a few manufacturing and service enterprises were still privately owned and run by capitalistic owner–managers, but by 1956 all such enterprises, except small businesses operated by the self-employed, were merged into state and private cooperatives and then transformed into state-run enterprises. The transition was handled smoothly and peacefully. The former capitalist managers lost their power and independence, although most of them still remained in these enterprises to perform technical consulting functions.

1957–66

The second stage featured overall implementation of the Soviet model of 'one-man management', which implied rigid central control and left little autonomy for local enterprises. Most important operational decisions were made by the central ministries and their departments. The centralization of production control was accompanied by a simultaneous attempt to strengthen financial control. Enterprise managers had virtually no direct voice in the economic, social, humanistic, or political goals of their enterprises. Within an enterprise, all decisions were made at the top level of management. Little autonomy was assigned to lower levels of management and participative management was not encouraged.

However, by the early 1960s enterprises were allowed more independence. During this period planning was decentralized to allow economic recovery to occur. This recovery was crucial after the losses the economy suffered during the 'Big Leap Forward', natural disasters, and the Soviet withdrawal of technical assistance during the previous period.

1967–79

The third stage in Chinese management was the Cultural Revolution. Enterprise management was again centralized; many managers were replaced by radical revolutionaries. Operational efficiency was neglected, and profits suffered dramatically. Criticism was directed at those who remained in privately owned enterprises and were 'going capitalist'. Their numbers were reduced to the lowest level since 1949.

Between 1976 and 1979, the economy of China experienced some recovery and development. However, since the economic reforms started in rural areas, changes in enterprise management were not yet considered a high priority target for the government.

1980–6

The fourth stage brought management reforms, which were instituted to cope with the economic reforms that had at last spread to urban areas. Decentralization was once again emphasized, and more autonomy was granted to enterprises and their managers. A new phenomenon seemed to emerge: managers of both state and collective enterprises were younger and better educated. At the same time, individual enterprise was officially sanctioned and encouraged.

Organizational structure of state-owned enterprises

In most state enterprises there are three levels in the vertical structure: the overall factory, or enterprise level; production workshops; and production groups. The leaders at these levels are the director of the factory, the directors of the workshops, and the group leaders. Parallel to this administrative structure is the party organization within the enterprise: the party secretary and committee of the factory; the party secretaries of the workshops; and the party group leaders. The director of a factory is usually a member of the party committee at the top enterprise level. Therefore any major decisions made by the director will be discussed with party officials at the committee meetings.

Collective enterprises have an organizational structure similar to the state-owned enterprises. However, the party control may be less stringent. At the private enterprise (individual enterprise) level there is little extensive formal organization, and party control is not an important factor.

Recent management reform

According to the *World Economic Herald*'s year-end report on China's economic reform, ten tasks were achieved in 1986:

(1) horizontal cooperation was developed across industries;
(2) the marketing function was expanded;
(3) enterprise autonomy was increased;
(4) promising managers were developed;
(5) a responsibility system for factory directors was initiated;
(6) financial reform was started;
(7) labour laws and a labour contracting system were established;
(8) economic zones were formed in urban areas;
(9) second-step reform was started in rural areas; and
(10) state planning and control were improved (Wu *et al.* 1986).

We do not wish to understate the scope and importance of recent changes in the ownership and operation of the Chinese economy. But the changes thus far have been uniquely Chinese and do not indicate a rush to adopt Western values or practices. The following sections examine the role of private enterprise and explain some of the reasons for this reluctance to emulate the West.

The role of private enterprises

In recent economic reforms, private enterprises have been encouraged to organize and grow. A total of 600,000 Chinese started their own businesses in 1983, most of them in catering and other commercial and service trades. Stories of some pioneering individuals have been published in both domestic and foreign newspapers and magazines. These probably give Westerners the impression that the Chinese are on the way toward imitating Western practices.

However, if one takes a closer look at what is really happening in

China, no simple conclusion can be reached. The term 'private enterprise' is well known as *Getihu* in China. The literal meaning of *Geti* is individual and *hu* is family. The term itself has some implications. First, it shows that it is still not comfortable to advocate the concept of strictly private ownership. 'Getting rich is glorious' somehow conflicts with the ideology of 'Everything belongs to the state; everybody works for the public welfare'. The latter belief has been planted in people's minds for 30 years.

Second, the government does not want to leave the socialist track completely by pushing the private sector too much. People in China are still not quite sure whether this reform will continue. If they think it will continue, they do not know how far it will go.

Third, *Getihu* indicates the scope of operation – essentially a family business although in recent years it has no longer been strictly limited to family members. Some farmers started to sell chickens and flowers; urban residents opened restaurants or became tailors. Then they started to hire employees. Until 1983 the number of employees was limited to fewer than seven, but this restriction has been loosened; some now have as many as twenty or more employees.

People engaged in *Getihu* operations are totally responsible for their profit or loss. They are required to pay taxes to the state on their earnings. It should be pointed out that the tax system in China is still in transition. In contrast with treatment of *Getihu*, for example, there is no income tax for people who work for state-owned or collectively owned enterprises.

Reasons for the lack of Western-style management

The political system and ideology in China since 1949 have emphasized that a socialist country is not supposed to adopt any Western values or practices. Socialism and capitalism are viewed as two opposite ends of a continuum. Government officials have this firmly set in their minds, and they have led the people to accept this dichotomy.

Based on socialist ideology, and reflecting the development of China's management system described above, the criterion for a manager has been loyalty to the party, not knowledge or skills as seen from a Western viewpoint. In the past, special Cadres Training Programmes were organized in which administrators were trained mainly in ideology. With this emphasis, it is obvious that Chinese managers were not trained by Western standards. Furthermore, most factory administrators did not have a college degree, and the majority tended to be followers rather than effective business leaders.

This lack of trained managers has been perpetuated in a sense by the type of education available in China since 1949. Universities and colleges have produced highly qualified personnel in science and technology. Yet there have been few business schools, and a broad business education was not given a high priority either by the government or by students until about 2 years ago. Most of the earlier courses offered were limited to accounting, political economics, and foreign languages.

In recent years more colleges have expanded their curricula, yet business courses are still very limited and unsophisticated relative to the needs of present-day economic development. With the development of economic reform, a critical challenge has been to educate and train a large group of qualified managerial personnel who would be able to achieve economic efficiency with limited resources. Moreover, the fast growth of joint ventures with foreign companies requires Chinese managers to be able to understand Western business practices and behaviour.

It is also true that the central government has recently realized the importance of investment in human resources. Students and scholars have been sent to the USA and other countries. At home, new business schools and programmes have been planned to offer Western-style courses to high school graduates.

In addition, management training centres have been established to help factory managers, government officials, and university educators understand Western-style management. A centre in Dalian staffed by American professors and another in Chengdu sponsored by the Canadian International Development Agency are two examples of this new phenomenon in China.

Zhao Ziyang, the premier of the State Council, reported to the Fifth Session of the Sixth National People's Congress (which opened on 25 March 1987) that the State Council has decided to invigorate enterprises further, especially large and medium-sized state ones. The aim is to make enterprises relatively independent economic entities that enjoy full authority for management and full responsibility for their profits and losses.

Problems in management reform

China has made progress in its management reform, but still faces some problems with the existing system. The China Academy of Social Science recently conducted a survey in forty large and medium-sized enterprises in Beijing and Tianjin. The majority of respondents reported that they still have many difficulties managing their company effectively.

American investors have been paying close attention to political trends in China, especially to criticism of the so-called 'bourgeois liberalization' launched after the first university students' uprising. A paradox remains unresolved: can the Chinese government continue its attack on 'bourgeois liberalization' without interfering with the pace and direction of economic reforms? If such an attack continues, how much room is left for the practice of Western-style management in enterprises? Conservatives within the Communist Party would prefer to strengthen the Soviet model of central planning; they strongly oppose the danger of all-out Westernization. It has to be stressed that China is still a socialist country with communist leadership. Even reformers within the party persist in using socialism rather than capitalism as the framework for China's political and economic system.

A recent visitor from the Economic Planning Committee commented that some Western management practices have been discussed but implementation has scarcely begun. Especially in this period of ideological uncertainty, everybody takes the attitude of 'wait and see'. His comments reflect the thinking of a majority of Chinese middle-level leaders, who are very cautious about the long-term future of liberalization.

If a Westerner concludes on the basis of only a few isolated cases of American-style management that China is adopting capitalism, he may have neglected some of the important underlying factors in the system. The persistent centralized political system, combined with the ambitious plans for economic reform, leave the Chinese with a serious dilemma.

A new development at the Thirteenth Congress

The Chinese Communist Party concluded its Thirteenth Congress in November 1987. Zhao Ziyang, the Party General Secretary, made it clear in his report to the Congress that China is at its primary stage of socialism. A principal guideline should be the continuation and development of socialism with Chinese characteristics during this primary stage. Political reforms were also discussed at the Congress, and many government offices will be reorganized to give more autonomy to enterprises.

At a news conference during the Thirteenth Congress, Gao Shangquan, the vice director of the State Economic System Reform Commission, released three important messages. First, China should develop a new economic system in which the state makes adjustments to the market and the market provides directions to the enterprises. Second, China allows the existence of private enterprises. Regarding the numbers of employees, it is suggested that under eight employees would be considered as an individual enterprise and over eight would be a private enterprise. Third, there has been heated debate as to whether China should allow the issuing of stocks and bonds. The Chinese leaders are very cautious about this and will not make further comments until more experimentation can show the benefits of doing so.

Will China adopt Western management practices? We feel that this is unlikely, at least in the near future. China is a country of over 1 billion people. No Western economic system has yet been found that could support this huge population. The Chinese leaders have made great efforts to formulate economic reforms, yet the process is quite often hindered by the reluctance of middle-level officials in both rural and urban areas to make fundamental changes in the existing system. If the environment remains basically unchanged, the management style, structured upon the existing economic and political systems, will also not be likely to change.

The opening of China to the Western world has enabled the Chinese to study management systems outside their own country. However, to adopt Western management patterns totally would clearly be unsuitable for most Chinese enterprises. It is not surprising to learn that some recent MBA graduates from American universities are not able to teach what they have learned when they return to China. They could not practise their book knowledge in finance, for example, since there is no public stock exchange in China. And the management training programmes sponsored by Western firms and universities in both China and the USA are reconsidering their strategies. The critical question is how much the Chinese will be able to utilize Western practices in their operations. This process may take 10 years or more before a comfortable and effective management style can be developed.

Furthermore, the fact that Chinese are learning Western management practices does not imply that China will ever completely adopt these practices. Zhao Ziyang, China's then premier and acting general secretary of the Chinese Communist Party, commented in his report to the Fifth Session of the Sixth National People's Congress on 25 March 1987, 'We are now making thorough and systematic investigations and studies and will, on this basis, formulate a feasible reform scheme that is *suited to China's circumstances*' (Ma and Guo 1987, italics added). Seven months later, Zhao was elected General Secretary of the Party at the Thirteenth Congress. He concluded that China is still at the primary stage of socialism and should continue with socialism with Chinese characteristics.

The Thirteenth Congress showed the determination of the Chinese top officials to continue the reforms. The state and local governments will give more power to enterprises. A *Changzhang* (similar to a general manager in the USA) is expected to exercise full responsibility in managing an enterprise. Chinese business leaders, like those in all newly industrializing Asian nations, must develop their own policies and practices to solve management problems in ways most appropriate to the prevailing social, political, and economic environment within which they live and work. For the People's Republic of China, such solutions will be uniquely Chinese in nature and not a diluted version of Western management systems.

Note

© 1989 *Business Horizons* 32, 2, March–April 1989: 58–64; reprinted by permission.

References

'China industrial economics and management' (1983) Beijing: China Social Science Press, 110.

Engle, T. (1985) 'Reforming the labor system?', *The China Business Review*, March–April: 41.

Ma, L. and Guo, Z. (1987) 'China will pursue its reforms – Zhao outlines key tasks for country', *China Daily*, 26 March: 1.

Wu, J., Liu, J., Li, J., and Zhang, J. (1988) 'Modernization needs entrepreneurship and entrepreneurs need reforms', *World Economic Herald* 1, 22 December: 13–15.

Chapter ten

Indian organizations: value dilemmas in managerial roles

Indira J. Parikh and Pulin K. Garg

Introduction

Indian society today holds two distinct ethos. One comes from the traditional culture of India and the other comes from the West. The first is deeply rooted in the emotional experiences of growth during childhood and operates in an all-pervasive subconscious manner. The second is an acquired rational knowledge and operates from a logical base. The choices of action and the quality of relatedness with situations and other persons are invariably influenced by these two ethos. Depending on one's involvement with a given situation, either of them can become the major determinant of choices. For example, the greater the separation between the self and the situation, the greater is the possibility of the individual making a 'rational' choice. On the other hand, the smaller the separation, the greater is the possibility of the individual making a choice from the emotive ethos. Cognitively, most managers utilize the abstract logic and rationality of the Western ethos. However, when it comes to translating those beliefs into action choices in real social settings, their responses are based on the emotive maps anchored in the traditional culture. This is the crux of the value dilemmas inherent in managerial roles and in this chapter we discuss the universe of these value dilemmas encountered by Indian managers.

Indian organizations reflect a scenario of juxtaposition of divergent multiple heterogeneous elements of two diverse cultures. In India one can find organizations which operate with technologies of the 1890s side by side with very modern organizations. Similarly, Indian organizations have a managerial population which is diverse and heterogeneous as well as highly parochial. There are organizations which are assemblages of small units as well as organizations which are mammoth in size, in the amount of technology employed, and in the workforce. Indian corporations range from private to public, and national to international. Sometimes the same organizations display different structural forms, a variety of management systems, and variations in leadership styles and managerial roles. In a way each Indian organization is a micro-unit but its organizational phenomenology reflects and represents a macro-cosmic aspect of Indian society today.

The Indian organizational scenario can provide a rich and fertile context in which to engage in deciphering issues such as the following: What constitutes an Indian organization? What are its unique characteristics and how is such a vast divergence managed for results? Is there a coherent pattern of assumptions, values, and processes which operates behind the manifest diversity of forms?

In order to understand Indian organizations, a historical perspective of shifts in Indian culture and society during the twentieth century is necessary. There are four basic shifts: (1) a shift in agrarian relatedness from the self to a system; (2) a shift in role locations; (3) a shift in technology; and (4) a shift in the size and the processes of relatedness. These shifts are the results of the adoption and enforced implementation of organization structures, management systems, and managerial role definitions derived from Western models. The interplay of these shifts creates some major value, role, and structural dilemmas in Indian organizations.

Shift in agrarian relatedness

For centuries Indian society was primarily agrarian and had an integrative design of social and work components woven into a relatively fluid dynamic system. It gave a sense of meaning and belonging to the individual. The design promoted continuity between processes of primary family systems and secondary work systems.

The introduction of industrialization in India created a large population of wage earners. Secondary systems, as distinct from the primary agrarian systems, were introduced. The goals and objectives of the secondary systems were quite different from those of the primary systems: in work organizations people had to respond to highly structured, organized, and routine expectations of their tasks. Faced with the two systems, individuals experienced value dilemmas relating to the nature of relationships.

Indian agrarian society was basically a producer trading society, where traditional structures, systems, and relationships worked effectively. The introduction of medium and large manufacturing units led to the borrowing of structures and systems from the early industrial era of the West. This created a movement towards a wage-earning society, and led to two major discontinuities in relatedness as it had existed in agrarian society.

First, work became separated from the socio-cultural identity of the individual and became a matter of economic exchange. This caused distress for the individual. He felt shame, because of the traditional value that 'serving as an employee is menial' whether employment was white or blue collar.

Second, a discontinuity of membership between the primary and secondary systems occurred. In the traditional society, the family, neighbourhood, village community, caste, and even the region were related through common role processes, attitudes, and relational modes. Here everybody was a relative, with a predictable and ensured quality of emotional cathexis and expectations. In the Western style work systems, however, the structures created a different kind of hierarchy with seniority and subordinacy based on different criteria. The framework of expectations was thus changed. As a result of this shift, employers today demand loyalty, commitment, and hard work from the employees, and in return they are willing to offer patronage or punishment. However, the mutuality or the reciprocity of the agrarian society has disappeared. This most intriguing paradox is a major source of value and role dilemmas for both individuals and systems.

Shifts in role locations

In the agrarian society the roles were highly bounded and well defined. Each individual knew the location of his role and of those with whom he interacted. He had a clear idea of role expectations and counter expectations. To a large extent, these were available to him through convention and the ingrained *samskars* (conventions). Furthermore, there was a clear distinction in role locations of men and women and children and adults. To a large extent the world view, the nature of aspirations, and expected consequences were also clearly articulated. Individuals' mobility – geographical, social, and psychological – was also heavily bounded and as such limited.

The introduction of newer work systems designed around Western technology and organization structures created major upheaval. It separated the individual from the social role structures, role processes, and activities of the primary system and demanded from him action which was in harmony with the structure, processes, and action expectations of the new secondary system. The individual was also detached from the goals traditionally defined by the primary systems based on class, caste, and community and introduced to the goals of formal work and profession. Over the last 80 years, this upheaval has affected all areas of interaction in work organizations and can be characterized by three major shifts.

First, an individual in the new organization is required to make his role and not merely play his role. This creates uncertainties, ambiguities, and diffidence. He is called upon to be assertive and functional and to disown his traditional ethos of interpersonal relationships and his geographical location. He acquires a status analogous to that of a migrant, a transient, or an exile. He becomes the representative of his family responsible for generating a cash flow.

Many individuals in Indian industries and cities, even after four generations, exhibit this pattern. Their entry and membership as full individuals in work systems is still dubious. They remain in the employee status but do not claim membership either in the organization or in the community and neighbourhood.

The second shift is in the location of men's and women's roles. In agrarian society, women lived and worked in groups. Men worked in isolation and very often lived in public places. The emergence of employment as a way of life led to a shift of people into towns and cities. It has created a pattern where men work in groups and women live in isolation. The deeply embedded role pattern for men to work in isolation and live in public places has led them to recreate a life style of over-engagement with the work details and of spending a large part of their time at the work place or with people at work. Women, on the other hand, are left bereft and have no place to feel that they are members of a community. They feel uncertain, rootless, and transient. This pattern has created many dilemmas centring around integrating work and home for both men and women. Men, despite being forced to work together, continue to cherish the lone performer's role. This has created a major dilemma in organizations in terms of a lack of lateral cooperation, negotiation, and collaboration and a neglect of task interdependencies. This has also loaded the organizational hierarchy with the task of constant arbitration rather than delegation.

The third shift concerns parent–child relations. As a result of the above-mentioned role shifts, traditional family role obligations for bringing up children to become mature adults have been undermined. Children in urban settings are either pushed into becoming self-centred achievers or left on their own without proper guidance. They lose the opportunity of maturing emotionally. Their relationships with adults and institutions remain uncertain and nebulous.

In essence, these shifts have created value dilemmas both in organizations and in individuals. They have de-emphasized the significance of the primary social system and have highlighted the secondary systems. Individuals began to encounter dilemmas in prior relationships and in their expectations in both the primary and secondary systems. Faced with such dilemmas, individuals demanded from organizations sentient role support, role processes, and social interdependences which could provide them with a sense of meaning and belonging. Organizations, however, were designed only to provide formal work structures, task space, formal relationships, and task interdependencies. They have failed to provide sentient interdependencies. This has led to the breakdown of systems of relationships and individuals are left without any feelings of enduring systemic belonging.

Shift in technology

A large part of the agrarian society depended upon the energy of men and animals to carry out work. The shift to the new work systems replaced men and animals with machines. The shift also created a strong sense of invalidation. That is, it imposed limitations on a person's skills and made him resistant to learning new skills. It also created an attitude where new knowledge or skills were seen as a threat. 'Sticking with the old and well tested' became a motto for many. This shift created two attitudes in Indian managers: (a) a sense of invalidation when confronted with new technology and new knowledge, leading to resistance and regression to older traditional styles of management, and (b) an inability to feel competent.

The progress of technology in terms of continued innovations leading to growth and complexity creates a process lag. By the time Indian organizations and managers adapt and settle down with one kind of technology and begin to feel secure, the next onslaught hits the markets with greater momentum. The existing structures and managerial role processes become inadequate for the new wave that comes along. Some organizations redesign their structures; others continue with the old ones. Managerial designations and role contents are often defined and redefined but the actual role behaviour and relatedness to the systems remains entrenched in older modalities.

The environmental conditions of business keep pushing the organizations to adopt newer and newer technology. The resultant phenomenon is the emergence of the culture of transience which initiates the managers into a cognitive understanding of the role structures and processes of secondary systems. However, the role processes of the primary system determine the nature of role taking and relatedness to systems.

The primary dilemma that has existed for the last 50 years is how to generate role-taking processes which are a good fit with the structures and systems that have been technologically determined as the best for achieving results.

Shift in size and processes of relatedness

Traditionally, in the agrarian society all production systems were small and revolved around persons rather than technology. There was interchangeability of roles in those systems. Different functions could be performed at different times by the same individual. A primary feature of this system was that the individual simultaneously belonged to both social and work systems. There was visibility of operations, exchange of skills, and an interface across ranks so that direct and immediate interventions could be made more easily.

As organizations initially grew from small to medium size, some of these traditional patterns of role taking remained operative. Once the organizations became very large, the quality of relatedness with the system and its significant people underwent major changes. Social as well as psychological role distances increased. All the potential of direct, immediate, and face-to-face transactions which ensured involvement and security was eroded. The sense of insecurity and uncertainty about individuals' own role locations and their links with other people and systems increased. Formalization, which is the hallmark of Western models, became difficult to tolerate. Organization processes based on new modes of structures and systems became a constraint.

Individuals sought to reduce this uncertainty and insecurity by resorting to personalization and familiarization of relationships in large organizations. This process gave rise to cliques which governed themselves by affiliative interdependencies rather than by task interdependencies. The politics of the organization were thus retranslated to affiliative politics rather than the politics of task, performance, and merit. It seems then that the introduction of business organizations, especially the manufacturing systems anchored around the borrowed technology, structures, and management systems of the West, added and speeded forces of movement away from the agrarian social design. This introduction had an impact on the quality of social relatedness, role locations, the quality of technology, and the size of work organizations.

In order to understand how value dilemmas finally crystallized in Indian organizations, we need to look at another historical process. Business organizations engaged in manufacturing emerged in India through the initiative of two groups. The first group was the European investors who had already come as traders to India. They brought two basic orientations. The first was related to the process of organizing work and designing structures and role allocations. They introduced result-focused and finance-dominated orientations into organizations. They were also concerned with mechanisms of control and coordination. To them every person in the organization other than their own class was an employee, a serf, a hand. The local employees were excluded from policy formulation. They could be trusted for implementation but needed vigilant supervision and monitoring.

The second orientation was related to their own role location in a colonial country and economy. Independent of the level in the social hierarchy in the society to which they belonged, they put themselves in India as the class of nobles or feudal lords. As such they acted from patronage and the compulsions of what is termed *noblesse oblige*. This mode of relating to the employees reinforced some of the processes of agrarian relatedness in Indian organizations. Thus no clean break between the newer organizations and their processes and the culturally pre-existing processes was ever made in Indian society.

The second group was the Indian entrepreneurs who were traders themselves initially. When they entered the business of manufacturing, they borrowed the structural forms from Western models. However, they continued to operate with cultural roles. This also did not provide a clean break from the traditional social agrarian ethos.

For a long time, therefore, the cognitively determined and understood forms of organization structure and role allocations from the West continued to be reproduced in the design of organizations. But behind these forms, the essential processes such as decision making, exercise of authority, communication, evaluation, reward, and punishment continued to remain anchored in the emotive map of the agrarian culture.

It is obvious that these two sets of value parameters belong to two distinct universes. It is also clear that they cannot be integrated in their totality. They therefore lead to value dilemmas in Indian organizations in various managerial roles which will be examined next.

Value dilemmas in managerial roles: taking on job responsibilities

In the traditional agrarian society of India, the role of the individual was located in the network of social relations and had certain well-defined expectations and modes of conduct associated with it. While there was a hierarchy of elders and juniors, the system provided opportunities, through work, for experiencing a psychological closeness with elders. These opportunities reinforced the sense of being a central member of the system, and not just a dependent or an obedient junior on the periphery. The role was also associated with a unilateral commitment to carrying out one's duties. Evaluation of the individual's actions generally included the context of his membership, his actions and intentions, and resources available to him. Such a role construct in a sense united the individual's responsibility to task commitment with his self-identity.

As Indian organizations grew towards large complex structures, managers experienced difficulties in defining roles. They started to feel a lack of the support on the job that was available to them in the traditional social system. As such, in the formal business organization the individual found his role to be very constrained. He became a performer only. He experienced loss of psychological membership, which affected his social identity. For example, individuals experienced value dilemmas when they had to report to superiors who were either juniors in age or came from a much lower position in the social hierarchy than their own. The loss of the traditional contextual support system for the role made it difficult for the managers to locate themselves in the organization as members. A quality of relatedness determined by the rules and regulations, job description, and reporting relationships did not provide a sense of trust in one's location. Thus managers found it difficult to act from their convictions.

This problem can also be illustrated by examining an individual's entry into the formal business organization. It begins with an induction process in which the entire language reflects the logic of a formal role construct which defines his being an employee, a performer, and a receiver of compensation. His job responsibilities and performance criteria are laid down. Rules and regulations are explained. He is entering a contract. As the individual begins working, he experiences organization processes where Western models operate along with deeply embedded cultural modes of relatedness. This juxtaposition of formal and psychological expectations leading to contradictions in what is expected and given makes the individual confused. He then takes a defensive stance by searching for psychological and social relatedness that can provide him with a sense of belonging and membership. The value dilemma faced by the individual is in terms of his inability to reconcile his role as a member in a formal organization while being emotionally rooted in a traditional social system.

Faced by the value dilemma, the individual addresses himself only to the prescribed job responsibilities and finds it difficult to accept the responsibilities for lateral linkages as well as contextual corporate responsibilities. For example, the largest part of organizational conflict in the current Indian context revolves around the interpretation of how the job has been described. Workers and staff constantly seem to be refusing many role actions which were once taken for granted as an implicit part of the job. There is a strong demand for role clarity and the laying down of detailed job charts. The slogans 'This is not my job', 'This is not my work', have become increasingly loud. Refusal to take corporate responsibility can be illustrated by the general proneness of Indian managers not to train and develop their juniors. A manager only invests in his subordinates as long as he can ensure loyalty and commitment to himself. He personally believes in making himself indispensable to the system, and treats all developmental efforts of the organization, such as being sent for training, either as a punishment or as a legitimized holiday type of reward.

The logic of modern organizations, as reflected in the designs of performance appraisal systems, seeks evidence of initiative, creativity, interpersonal relations, and many other kinds of behaviour which are an integral part of a manager's expected role. However, the operational process discourages the manager from mobilizing himself to produce this evidence. In India today, performance appraisal processes either have become a matter of mockery or are seriously contested. A large number of managers do not trust the appraisal processes. Not only have they become sceptical but they use the appraisal processes to bargain and undermine many other organizational processes. At the time of yearly promotions, for example, the talk in the corridors is always about individuals' relationships with power élites rather than about merit. There is a general belief in Indian organizations that only good manipulators of the politics of relationships in the organization get promotions, rather than more competent but politically less adept employees.

In summary, the value dilemmas in the managerial role of taking on responsibilities on the job are expressed in several ways. They determine the quality of commitment, sense of membership, feelings of self-worth, and the overall attitude towards responsibility. Most often, managers tend to be either reactive or defensive or actively aggressive in registering personal victories at the cost of sacrificing task objectives. At another level, the value dilemmas often create inertia, disengagement from the system, disenchantment, and partly disaffiliation. Many Indian organizations hire highly talented people with initiative, creativity, a need for achievement and independence, a spirit of challenge, a high degree of self-acceptance, and an ability to deploy their resources for purposive action. But over a short period of time, these people succumb to value conformity, withhold initiative, show low responsiveness to people and task challenges, and display little tolerance for differences with colleagues and increased deference to authority. This transformation of once vibrant managers into 'tamed ones' is telling evidence of how Indian organizations are caught in the flux of two distinct cultures.

Value dilemmas in managerial roles: taking on position authority

An individual in the agrarian society grows up internalizing a number of beliefs. First, he believes that membership in the system provides both task and sentient interdependence. The second belief he grows up with is about resource location. He learns that there are a number of resource holders and controllers in the system including himself. He can use his own resources and/or can claim resources from others. The third belief is that the authority in the system manifestly rests with the elders but can be moderated through the available consensus-making processes. As such, he also holds a certain amount of authority as an individual. Despite many transformations over hundreds of years, these beliefs about the authority and location of resources in the system are still deeply embedded in Indian managers. However, the formal business organization confronts him with a different scenario.

Within the organization, a manager sees himself as a resource with membership, authority, and power. But he also sees himself as a performer, an implementer of policies and tasks laid down by his superiors. He is supposed to do the assigned task (often as desired by his boss) and to keep the boss pleased. The manager's concept of authority is further confused when he brings his training and professional skills to the job, as he is expected directly and indirectly to leave his training and knowledge behind. He is expected largely to learn from the experiences of his superiors and not to depend on his own resources. In effect, he is expected to bring only his performance, devoid of functional and professional authority, and to give up any possibility of feeling equally competent to his superiors. In this process, his potential contribution to the system is denied, and he experiences a sense of marginality.

Furthermore, the manager often receives another message – 'all resources of the organization are controlled by one or a very few people, and all the resources he receives from others are gifts of patronage'. He finds his personal psychological resources are the only ones that belong to him, and he is constantly under scrutiny and subject to evaluation. The manager then learns to use his personal resources for engaging in politics rather than the task at hand, to control the system's resources for keeping good relations with those in authority. His goal is to seek and establish centrality in the system. Behaviourally, this creates various kinds of value dilemmas for the manager. One of the central dilemmas is whether the individual can be himself or must be a proxy, an echo, or a shadow of somebody else in the system. This conflict is compounded by his restrictive role as a performer for economic exchange. It also creates an ever-present anxiety and insecurity about the quality of the individual's membership and relatedness in the organization. The manager either conforms or rebels but finds it difficult to assert. Many managers turn the conformist face to superiors and the aggressor face to subordinates and colleagues in the organization. Thus the whole organization gets infected with a sense of isolation and lack of communication. Thus most managers learn to operate on the basis of a principle of half disclosure.

Another value dilemma that managers encounter relates to the difficulty of separating the systemic from the personal processes. In the agrarian society the simultaneity of task and sentient interdependence allowed individuals to operate with both these processes. In Indian organizations today, however, the systemic processes are neither trusted nor followed seriously. Individuals, while operating with systemic processes (functional relatedness), tend to seek personalization in a very acute and intense manner.

The focus on personalization creates an interesting but dysfunctional process. Operationally, a practice emerges whereby all rules and regulations are manipulated for the benefit of people with whom the individual has built up personal relations. However, rules and regulations are strictly adhered to when the individuals concerned do not have a personal relationship. One of the most glaring manifestations of this process is reflected in performance delays by employees in a role network, which in turn necessitates follow-up actions by managers. A large part of the time and energy of Indian managers is spent in the game of 'follow-up' within the role network in organizations. Employees resist this game by being lone performers and restricting themselves to a limited interpretation of job responsibility. When the follow-up fails, most managers turn to authority figures for intervention.

Value dilemmas in managerial roles: taking one's place in the system

The agrarian ethos encouraged the simultaneity of task and sentient interdependences. This created institutions, locations, and occasions where the individuals could express their pent-up emotions, i.e. have catharsis, absolve themselves from the shame of their acts of omission and commission, reinforce their emotional sense of belonging through joint rejoicing and reviving and fostering hopes for a new ambience in the organization. In the adopted Western models of organizations, the designers either exclude these institutions or recommend Western forms such as picnics, clubs, cocktail parties, and joint lunch rooms. These, however, have failed to evoke the same ambience and response as the institutions of agrarian society did. Very often these new introductions remain formal occasions in which participation does not lead to unfolding of personal psychological processes. They have become more of a forum for formal membership rather than builders of psychological membership in the organization.

Behaviourally, this has created the problem of integration of membership and mobilization of work ethics in the organization. In the traditional agrarian society there were community and family spaces where both men and women in their respective groups could share the stress of the system and pains of relationships. In today's formal organization such spaces are not available. Thus the stress accumulates and the individual ends up responding in the following three ways.

(1) *Abdication of role*: most individuals become apathetic to the routine tasks. They feel demotivated and do not engage in their role transactions with enthusiasm and initiative. They disengage psychologically from the system. They then seek further monetary incentives to cathect with the organization.

(2) *Fragmentation of role space*: individuals learn to keep silent in formal situations and then create 'organizational galleries or corridors' where they can express their grumblings and dissatisfactions with superiors, subordinates, and coworkers, and with organizational policies. This allows the managers to keep themselves and their experiences of people and the system in separate boxes.

(3) As job stress accumulates, the manager becomes entrenched in three kinds of *reactive feelings*: feelings of being discriminated against, deprived, and denied. He gets caught in a comparative frame, and struggles to seek a fair, equitable, and fail-safe system. He searches for objectivity and elimination of so-called personal and subjective elements of evaluation. However, when every manager feels this way, it becomes difficult to satisfy them all by system changes. Any change becomes a matter of further contests and grumblings. When organizations and managers remain caught in this entrenchment, the rank and

file workers then become a party to it, and industrial strikes and labour unrest become more pronounced.

The imposition of Western organization structures and systems, however, have created a new setting where individuals can aspire to move beyond their original level in the traditional social hierarchy. They can also change their life style and create new opportunities for their children. Behind the creation of these opportunities is the message that by hard work, application, and deployment of effort and commitment an individual can improve his location, status, and quality of life. However, the juxtaposition of the two ethos reflected in organizational processes has created unrealistic expectations in the individuals. Today, the individuals expect organizations to promote them, give increments, and take them to the highest levels with the assumption that their performance is as good as that of any other person. They expect bestowal of these prizes without too much investment. When these expectations do not come through, feelings of discrimination, deprivation, and denial get reactivated and the whole cycle is repeated.

Value dilemmas in managerial roles: exercising authority and leadership

In Indian agrarian society, leaders were those who held the ethos with a certain degree of clarity and applied it in day-to-day transactions. The leaders emerged through a social process of convergence and consensus on the basis of experience, knowledge, and practice of the *samskars* and of appropriate modes of behaviour in conflict and crisis situations. In a way they were recognized for their social and psychological wisdom. The leaders did not have to give evidence of either generating wealth or being better in economic activities. As such the leaders held a social authority which provided their leadership with the quality of being a sustainer and regulator of transactions. This construct of leadership did not include the element of monitoring, scanning, directing, and ensuring performance through assuming the position of resource controller on the one hand and dispenser of reward and punishment on the other.

The introduction of formal business organization modalities necessitated a formal task leadership role. But the individuals who were designated as functional task leaders in organizations were also expected to maintain a harmonious ambience and social climate as demanded by traditional norms. As long as this aspect was fulfilled, employees responded to their leadership in functional tasks. However, whenever the leaders displayed an inability to provide fulfilment of such expectations, tensions and sometimes open conflict surfaced in the transactions between the leaders and their followers.

The interplay of the cognitive demands of the task systems and the emotive demands of the cultural system leave the following options for the leaders: (a) to become a task owner and act as the master of a group of serfs; (b) to become a benign master who by ensuring patronage and personalized relationships creates commitment and loyalty; and (c) to become the so-called charismatic leader who inspires and evokes on the one hand and controls and hounds on the other.

The last 40 years reflect an increasing demand on all leaders to become charismatic. These leaders are then put on a pedestal and are distanced from the collegial framework. The entire burden of holding the vision of task, direction, and achievement is put on their shoulders. The followers then enact the very deep-seated existential drama of sibling rivalry between themselves in order to claim the closeness and exclusive patronage of the charismatic leader. These leaders, then, become the proverbial monkey who sits with a weighing scale to weigh out the bread between two fighting cats but finally eats all of it himself. The leaders become the sole holder of power and the system becomes mortgaged to their maturity or immaturity.

Value dilemmas in managerial roles: dealing with technology

With the adoption of Western technology, a major shift occurred in the kind of energy used in production. In agrarian society, the technology had been kept at a simple and minimum level. Modern technology is more complex. This has changed the role relatedness of workers with the technology. Due to the persistence of task and sentient interdependence in the agrarian society, work was a part of one's social identity and not just an input in the economic transaction. Hence workers did not experience alienation.

The introduction of Western technology, however, led to a number of interesting consequences for managerial roles in India. The technology in India became personified. Instead of technology being an extension of the self, the personification triggered a concept of the machine as having its own motivation and self-renewal powers. It could be used but treated with respect or neglect. One current example of this process is the introduction of the new Maruti cars with high acceleration and speed. People who drive them are often heard saying 'What can we do? Car runs fast.' They see themselves as being controlled by the quality of the machine rather than controlling its quality for effective and efficient driving.

In the area of production management, this has created major dilemmas. Organizations in general seem to make poor investments in both regular and preventive maintenance of technology. In our assessment, replenishment of technology is not seen as part of a manager's responsibility. Owing to the attribution of mystic qualities to technology, the belief is that it is supposed to replenish itself. In many public sector organizations some highly expensive technology lies around in a broken down condition or very often is kept under lock and key and rarely used. This is frequently noticed in research laboratories, educational institutions, and also some households. The value dilemma in the relatedness with technology is often reflected in organizations having a technology but not deploying it effectively for efficient performance.

Another aspect of the introduction of technology is related to the size of the organization. Increase in size made many organizations adopt structures based on Western models. Until the mid-1960s, most organization design was based on departmental structures. Only after the introduction of management education did corporate structures designed along the lines of divisions emerge. However, these structures rarely materialized. Operationally, in many organizations, the structure and roles continued to operate with a departmental rather than a corporate framework.

Cognitively, the managers understand the corporate structure and the nature of the new organizations. But in actual role taking they continue to work with the attitudes and orientations of familial structures and systems rooted in the traditional ethos. On the whole, despite design and structural changes, integrative and negotiative corporate processes do not emerge. Managers continue to operate in the role of sons, cousins, and uncles and continue to view the chief executive in the role of a patriarch and expect him to be charismatic.

Summary and conclusions

Exploration of Indian agrarian society and its influences on the emergent industrial scene gives rise to the following unique characteristics of the Indian context that a manager needs to understand in order to be more effective.

(1) The design of life space in the agrarian society included both the social and the work setting. Fragmenting and differentiating the two into two distinct sectors as in the West creates and generates value dilemmas in the social and work settings

as well as role taking in both systems.

(2) The social processes of relatedness coded by the caste, community, and neighbourhood are an integral part of Indian living. As such any design for organizations has to integrate these with the new inputs of formal, functional, and task-based relationships.

(3) The concept of authority in Indian tradition remains anchored in social authority. As such formal and functional authority anchored in knowledge and skills in complex technology has to be aligned with the processes of social authority.

(4) Indian managers often hold contradictory emotive and cognitive maps of people and systems. Organization designs have to be developed whereby these can be recalibrated and aligned. Without such integrating designs, organizations will continue to manage people by crisis, anxiety, or fear.

(5) Planners have to understand the psycho-cultural assumptions and philosophy of living embedded in the Indian psyche and bring forward the positive and relevant aspect of the embedded psycho-cultural assumptions in order to design relevant modalities so that energy is released to create synergy in organizations.

Part three

Developing indigenous perspectives: work motivation and organizational leadership in developing countries

Chapter eleven

Work alienation in developing countries: Western models and Eastern realities

Rabindra N. Kanungo

Introduction

In an article that appeared in *Times of India* (August 1986), a leading daily newspaper, Vasant Sathe, then a Union Minister, made a comparative analysis of India's economic performance. Referring to production in the coal industry, Sathe observed that, 'In the last 13 years of nationalisation, we have invested about Rs. 6,000 crores of public funds in the coal sector. Although the investment has increased more than hundred-fold, production has barely doubled – going up from 77 mt to 154 mt. At the same time, the wage rate has increased from Rs. 16 per day to approximately Rs. 98 per day or about Rs. 2,400 per month. On the other hand, the output-per-man-shift (OMS) in the underground mines has not only not increased but has actually gone down from 0.54 tonne to 0.52 tonne during this period.' Poor performance seems to exist in other sectors as well (e.g. in steel production), even if heavy investment in technology and equipment has been made. Since performance within any organization depends not only on financial and technological investment but also on effective management of human resource, serious attention must be paid to find out why labour productivity is low and what should be done to utilize the untapped human potential for higher performance.

Political and business leaders in India often argue that poor performance levels of Indian workers stem from their poor Protestant work ethic. But a closer look at the work ethic of Indian workers would readily reveal the inadequacy of such explanations. Understanding of the work motivation that underlies the poor performance of labour in India with the help of Western models of work ethic is too simplistic to be of any consequence. The theoretical explanations of worker motivation stemming from Western models of labour alienation are based on observations of workers in Western and developed country contexts. Such explanations therefore would have limited applicability for developing Afro-Asian and Latin American countries. Research on work alienation in these developing countries that are based on the Western models can be meaningful only when the limitations of these models are recognized and avoided. Furthermore, work alienation research in the developing world becomes more meaningful and useful when explanations of the phenomenon are sought in terms of variables indigenous to the cultural context in which the research is carried out.

In this chapter it is argued that the existing theoretical explanations of work alienation (Weber 1930; Marx 1932; Seeman 1959; Blauner 1964; Shepard 1971) and corrective management practices (Herzberg 1968; Hackman and Oldham 1976; Rabinowitz and Hall 1977) developed in the Western world have limited cross-cultural applicability. This argument is supported first by identifying the cultural bias inherent in the Western explanatory models of alienation (Kanungo 1979, 1981, 1982) and then by indicating how such a bias fails to explain adequately work alienation and its opposite work involvement phenomena in Eastern and other developing societies such as India, China, Latin America, etc. Finally the case of work alienation in India is analysed for illustrative purposes. The second part of this chapter therefore probes into the role of some critical indigenous variables responsible for the development of alienation among workers in India. The case of Indian workers provides an illustrative example of what is needed for alienation research in a developing country context: to avoid the folly of uncritically accepting the Western explanatory models and to encourage the discovery of indigenous explanations.

Critical features of the Western explanatory models

Theoretical explanations of worker alienation were first proposed by Marx (1932 [1844] and then by Weber (1930)). The conceptual models proposed by them formed the basis of much of the later thinking on the subject among both the empirically oriented behavioural scientists and practically oriented organizational change agents. According to Marx, if workers sacrifice their needs and interests and surrender their free will or control over what they do at work, they may experience alienation. The mechanization of the production process and the increased supervisory control over workers' behaviour and wages observed in the capitalist system forces workers to sell their labour for survival and to surrender their right to engage in spontaneous, free, and self-directed production activities, and thus creates alienation of labour.

Following Marx, most social scientists have assumed that the absence of worker autonomy and control in the work place is a necessary and sufficient condition for labour alienation. Such an assumption is based on an uncritical acceptance of Marxian views regarding labour and the essence of human nature. But the validity of this assumption has been questioned on the ground that the essential nature of human beings and the role of labour in a worker's life, as conceived by Marx, does not hold true in all parts of the world. In the light of current behavioural and motivational theories, the Marxian emphasis on worker autonomy and control appears both 'humanistic' and 'individualistic' in orientation. Like many assumptions in humanistic psychology (such as Maslow's [1954] need hierarchy notion), Marxian emphasis on autonomy and control suffers from problems of empirical validation and strong cultural bias (see Kanungo 1982 for details).

Weber's treatment of the concept of work alienation is very similar to that of Marx. Both believed that the individuality or personal worth of workers is determined by their labour, and that alienation results from working conditions that deny the expression of individuality. But Weber went a step further in asserting the historical antecedents of work alienation. Study of the Protestant religion convinced Weber (1930) that the ethical system of Protestantism trains people to be individualists and to believe in the goodness of work. Principles within the Protestant faith, such as 'God helps those who help themselves' or 'Work is its own reward' promote in people a high degree of individualism, a craving for intrinsic rewards and industriousness. Like Marx, Weber emphasized the freedom to make one's own decisions, to assume personal responsibility, and to prove one's worth through achievement at work, and saw loss of individuality as the necessary condition of work alienation.

Translated into motivational terms, both Marx's and Weber's emphasis on the individuality of the worker imply that if the work set-up cannot provide an environment that satisfies the needs for individual autonomy, responsibility, and achievement, it will create a state of alienation in the workers.

Most contemporary formulations of work alienation, in both the psychological and the sociological literature, have followed the Marxian/Weberian models (for an exhaustive review, see Kanungo 1979, 1981, 1982). Almost all the formulations emphasize lack of intrinsic need satisfaction as the basic condition for work alienation. The exclusive emphasis on intrinsic need satisfaction as a precondition for worker involvement (or for better quality of working life) reflects a strong cultural bias in the Western models. This was initiated by Marx and Weber through their observation of individualistic societies

195

in which the need for personal achievement, control, and autonomy are considered to be people's most central and salient needs.

The same emphasis persists in the works of contemporary Western organizational theorists. For instance, after reviewing the current psychological literature on job involvement, Rabinowitz and Hall (1977: 284) conclude that, among other things, job-involved workers believe strongly in the Protestant ethic, have strong growth or intrinsic needs, and have stimulating jobs that give them a high degree of autonomy and control. Similarly, contemporary organizational sociologists believe that workers experience alienation when they engage in job activities that are not rewarding in themselves, that do not express their unique abilities and potentialities, nor permit control, but are simply instrumental in satisfying extrinsic needs such as for money, security, etc. (Seeman 1959; Blauner 1964; Shepard 1971).

Another line of sociological research in the area of 'individual modernity' tends to echo the above viewpoint. Inkeles and Smith (1974) consider an individualistic orientation to be one major characteristic of 'modernity'. Other recent studies (e.g. Orpen 1978) have shown that 'modernity' implies acceptance of Protestant work ethic ideals and an emphasis on intrinsic work values. In contrast, 'traditionality' implies familism (a form of collectivistic orientation), limited personal aspiration, and less emphasis on intrinsic work values. Using the dichotomy of 'modern versus traditional', Inkeles and Smith (1974) have argued that the development of 'modernity' characteristics among workers is essential for the effectiveness of work organizations.

To summarize, Western models of work alienation rest on two basic premises. First, work-alienating attitudes are formed as a result of past socialization training that does not emphasize Protestant ethic norms. Second, alienation at work stems from a lack of intrinsic need satisfaction on the job.

If one accepted these premises, it would imply that many Third World countries would be doomed to suffer from mass work alienation, because these countries neither subscribe to the Protestant ethic norms nor consider intrinsic need satisfaction to be the main purpose of work behaviour. In Western models of work alienation therefore it is argued that the only hope for these countries rests on changing their ways through incorporating Western work ideologies such as Protestant ethic norms into their socialization process and adopting job-design and participative leadership concepts that emphasize the intrinsic need satisfaction of workers in the work place (Herzberg 1968; Lawler and Hackman 1971; Hackman and Oldham 1976).

Limitations of the Western models

This position taken according to Western models is not tenable on two grounds. First, one can argue that satisfaction of intrinsic needs at work may be *a sufficient but not a necessary condition* for work involvement. Work involvement does not necessarily depend on job characteristics that allow for satisfaction of needs for control and autonomy. It must be emphasized that workers have a variety of needs, some more salient than others. The saliency of the needs in any particular person is determined by his or her past socialization in a particular culture, and is constantly modified by present job conditions. Different groups of people, because of their different socialization training or cultural background, may develop correspondingly different need-saliency patterns. They may value extrinsic and intrinsic job outcomes reflecting these diverse factors. A specific set of needs (e.g. growth needs, such as self-esteem and autonomy) may be salient in one group of workers, but not in another group. This may result in different self-images in the two groups and consequently in different job expectations in the two groups. A group of workers that considers control and autonomy to be the core of their self-image may get involved in jobs that are perceived as offering an opportunity for exercising control and autonomy. Predictably, they may become alienated from jobs that are perceived as providing little freedom and control. However, such job characteristics may not be a crucial consideration in the determination of the job involvement or alienation of some other groups, which may view security and social solidarity needs as the core of their self-image.

Also, we should not overlook differences in people's self-concepts. The industrially developed societies of the West may socialize their citizens to believe that all that counts in one's life is to have individual liberty or freedom. Workers belonging to these societies may therefore feel that working life is of little worth without freedom and control. In the developing societies, however, economic and social security are often considered more important to life than are freedom and control at the work place. Thus, workers in these societies may find work very involving if it guarantees such security, but may not care very much for freedom and control in their jobs. In these societies, people may value equality more than liberty as the guiding principle of working life. The data from the study by Inkeles and Smith (1974) of six developing countries (Argentina, Bangladesh, Chile, India, Israel, and Nigeria) seem to provide indirect support for this contention and to contradict the commonly held notion among organizational theorists that assembly-line and large-scale production factory systems necessarily create worker alienation.

The second reason for the non-tenability of the Western models lies in the faulty assumption that Protestant-ethic-type socialization training is the only appropriate way to achieve greater work involvement and consequent industrial development. Moreover, it must be pointed out that socialization of the Protestant ethic variety is not the only type of training that increases work involvement. Any type of training through which people realize that their work role can fulfil their salient needs will increase work involvement. This can be illustrated by comparing Eastern and Western cultures.

First, let us consider the socialization process in many Western cultures. These cultures value individualism and promote in their members greater saliency of autonomy and personal achievement needs. The Protestant work ethic in such cultures trains people to believe that work can satisfy these salient needs and can provide opportunities for the expression of one's individuality. Therefore, work should be valued as being good and central to one's life.

In contrast, consider socialization in many developing countries. Cultures in these countries promote in their members a sense of collectivism and saliency of social and security needs. In these cultures religious preaching about achieving universal brotherhood of mankind and religious practices advocating the value of sacrificing self-interest for the benefit of others have a different socializing influence. People in these cultures develop a belief in the centrality of work not because work can promote personal achievement but because it can fulfil the collectivist goals of brotherhood and sharing in life. The Hindu religion, for example, encourages a form of work ethic that considers work as central to one's life but maintains that it must be performed as a duty in the service of others (family members, friends, relatives, even strangers), and not for one's personal achievement. Social scientists (e.g. Mehta 1976, 1978) have noticed the presence of this desire for collective rather than individual success among Indian workers. Those workers who believe that work can achieve a sense of collectivism and also fulfil salient social and security needs might therefore show the same level of work involvement as a Protestant. In Chinese society, the influence of Confucianism has created an altruistic set of values directed toward achieving common good rather than individual achievement. 'Chinese cultural tradition fosters the internalization of self discipline and self restraint. These traits imply the moral obligation of one's deferential compliance with parents, elders, and other senior's wishes ... there is always moral commitment to the collective goal which strives at excellence, dedication and involvement, notwithstanding how resentful or onerous the task is to the individual' (Chao

1988: 3). Similar collectivist orientation with emphasis on familism, group loyalty, and affective reciprocity forms the basis of worker involvement in many developing countries in Africa and Latin America.

The above examples demonstrate that people belonging to a non-Western culture tend to develop different salient needs as a result of being influenced by different cultural and group norms. The socialization training in any given culture that emphasizes the instrumentality of work roles in satisfying people's culturally determined salient needs is primarily responsible for the development of work involvement.

Search for indigenous factors

If Western explanatory models of alienation are inadequate in the context of developing nations because of cultural differences, then it is appropriate to look for explanations within the cultural milieu of these nations. In this section we explore the nature and causes of alienation of workers in India and describe a set of indigenous explanatory variables that are very different from the variables suggested by Western models. The causes of worker alienation in the Indian context can be identified both in the past socialization process of workers (i.e. to reveal the historical or predisposing cause) and in their present perceptions of the need-satisfying potential of the job, illustrating the contemporary or precipitating causes. Let us analyse these two sets of causes of worker alienation in India.

Indian socialization influence

The early socialization or conditioning process involves the influence of different social institutions such as family, educational institutions, religion, and political atmosphere. As individuals learn modes of thinking, feeling, and performance they are shaped by such ideological and cultural influences. Early interactions with social institutions and their specific representatives form the basis of many enduring psychological characteristics of future personality. The influences of socialization in India produce three types of behavioural dispositions (or ethics) that are particularly relevant in the context of work motivation. These dispositions will be referred to as (a) a personal ethic of helplessness, (b) an organizational ethic of personalized relationships, and (c) an idealized family-centred work ethic.

Workers at all levels of organizations in India seem to manifest a personal sense of helplessness. In their day-to-day work and in non-work spheres of life, they exhibit a passive attitude towards their environment. They feel that they can do nothing (in a direct manner) to change their environment. They have inculcated an external orientation, i.e. a belief that the external environment controls them rather than that they control their environment. Thus they become insecure and demonstrate a strong need for dependence on others to reduce their feeling of insecurity. As individuals, they feel that they are insignificant powerless particles of humanity and therefore believe in the futility of their actions. These beliefs create an attitude of fatalism and they become indifferent to work and work organizations. As individuals, therefore, they do not strive for challenge and excellence, but rather remain content with status quo and mediocrity. They become the victims of 'What can I do?' and the *chalega* type syndrome. (*Chalega* is a common vocabulary often used to express ready acceptance of status quo and mediocrity.)

Some social scientists (Weber 1958; Kapp 1963) have argued that the passive helplessness attitude of the Indian worker may result from the influence of Hindu doctrines of (a) Moksha (salvation) through renunciation of all material possessions (Sanyas) as an ultimate goal in life and (b) the illusory nature of the material world (Maya) and the experiences of present life resulting from the actions in previous life (the 'law of Karma' in an endless cosmic causal chain). Although such beliefs may play a role in the development of certain attitudes towards life in general (such as contempt for competitive acquisitiveness or equanimity in the face of extreme sufferings and hardships in life), they are certainly not the sole reasons for the helplessness feelings in a worker's day-to-day life. The helplessness feeling and the attitude of fatalism or external locus of control (Rotter 1966) orientation are acquired primarily through socialization practices related to action-contingent reward allocation in family, school, work organizations, or other social institutions. This point will be discussed later in the chapter.

The organizational ethic of Indian workers is also shaped by a strong sense of insecurity and dependence on others. Their work relationships are personalized rather than contractual. They work for their superiors, friends, and relatives, rather than for accomplishing the task or organizational goals under contractual obligations. Personal loyalty takes priority over organizational efficiency. Within the organization, seeking and maintaining personal status becomes the primary objective for which organizational interests can be sacrificed. Most supervisors provide personal rather than institutional leadership. Their leadership behaviour is directed towards maintaining their status or saving their skin by pleasing everyone, by avoiding conflicts or confrontation, and by not taking any risk that might rock the boat even if such actions are desirable for protecting the organizational interest.

Indian workers also manifest a family-centred work ethic. Most workers believe that work is necessary and good, primarily for maintaining one's family and providing for the well-being of aging parents, spouse, and children. Work for the sake of personal mastery over the job or for a personal sense of task accomplishment is somewhat alien to many. They have an idealized form of work ethic, however, derived from the Bhagavat Gita. They tend to subscribe in the abstract to the norm: 'Your right is to work only. But never to the fruit thereof. Let not the fruit of action be your object. Nor let your attachment be to inaction.' Such abstract principles are hardly ever practised in real working life. Duties are performed generally in the family context, but the same sense of duty does not prevail at the work place. In fact, Indian workers subscribe more to leisure and to family ethic than to work ethic. They are more familiar with the *sneha* (fondness), *shradha* (affection), and *aram* (relaxation) culture than with Karma culture. There is an emphasis on idle leisure pursuits that satisfy security and affiliative needs rather than creative leisure pursuits that achieve work objectives; on maintaining status positions rather than task goal accomplishments; on performing socially approved duties in interpersonal contexts rather than in job contexts. These are the typical characteristics of the Indian personality, and constitute disguised manifestations of a feudalistic temperament that prevails among most Indian workers.

Four key elements in the socialization process in India are responsible for the formation of the three types of ethic that we have identified. First, the *authoritarian practices* in the family, the educational system, and the religious institutions act to create a strong sense of dependence. This is reinforced by the hierarchical authority structure in all these institutions. Those who are in a position of authority tend to overcontrol their subordinates through the use of formal authority or rule-minded supervision. Unconditional obedience by surrendering to authority is considered a virtue. Personal initiative, originality, and independence in thinking and decision making in every sphere of life meets with social disapproval. As a result, independent critical thinking and reasoning (i.e. to solve one's own life problems) diminish. Positional or status authority rather than personal informed reason forms the basis of blind conformity and compliance.

Second, the *reward systems* within Indian social institutions tend to promote helplessness and external orientation. Very often people in positions of authority (parents, teachers, political leaders) promise valued rewards for the desired behaviour of subordinates but do not furnish these rewards. Such broken promises create a state of uncertainty of goal attainment, a deep sense of insecurity, external orientation, powerlessness, and, finally, low self-reliance. Furthermore, pervasive attitudes of negativism (searching only for what is wrong with an individual) and pessimism about outcomes of every action on the part of superiors discourage risk taking and responsibility-seeking behaviour, eventually leading to passivity in one's dealings with the environment.

Third, *family and religious traditionalism* of the Indian culture has created a time perspective that has an emphasis on the past rather than on the present. Emotional gratification of one's desire to maintain self-esteem through the recollection of past achievements is quite a commonplace happening. In a sense, most individuals live physically in the present, but psychologically in the past, and are unconcerned about the future. Emphasis on the past and a lack of futuristic orientation leads to a lack of planning while trying to achieve task goals. Thus jobs are handled as they come up, and problems are seldom anticipated in advance in order to make adequate preparation to solve them. Without prior preparation to solve anticipated problems, most problem solving behaviour becomes chaotic, unplanned, and unorganized. Failures to solve problems are then attributed to the complex and unanticipated nature of the problem, rather than to the lack of futuristic thinking of the individual.

There is another aspect to the Indian time perspective. Time is often considered in an abstract philosophical way as being eternal, i.e. ever present but never passing. Thus, delays in actions or slowness at work are easily tolerated as normal. Deadlines, time targets, punctuality, etc. are meaningless. People are very much used to taking in their stride the familiar 'foot dragging' bureaucratic response: action/decision will be taken in 'due course' of time.

Finally, the tradition of *joint family systems* creates problems of meeting obligatory demands from relatives, friends, superiors, co-workers, and subordinates. Such demands often conflict with organizational and task requirements. For instance, jobs are offered to candidates not on the basis of their job competency but on the basis of demands from superiors, relatives, and friends. Conflicting demands from other significant persons lead to misplacement of priorities in job activity and mis-allocation of resources. Planning becomes disrupted and personal effectiveness is lost. In addition, under the constant influence of conflicting demands, the individual experiences dissonance and, to reduce such dissonance, develops hypocritical habits of 'showing an honest face' but actually doing something else. Pressure from other relevant persons in a tradition-bound family culture forces the individual to sacrifice organizational and task objectives for the sake of maintaining personalized relationships. The work ethic is sacrificed for the family ethic.

Employees' on-the-job work experience

Besides the above-mentioned predisposing socialization influences, work alienation also results from the work experiences within organizations. Employee work experiences that contribute to work alienation can be divided into three broad categories: those related to the nature of the tasks performed on the job (task-related experiences), those related to the nature of the rewards or the compensation system (reward-related experiences), and those related to the nature of the superior–subordinate relation (supervision-related experiences). Employees' work behaviour is mainly determined by these three sets of job perceptions: the *requirements* of what the employees are expected to do on the job, the *returns* of material, social, and psychological benefits that the employees will receive in return for their work, and the manner in which the employees are treated by their superiors.

Task-related experiences

Work motivation suffers if there are no clear job expectations regarding what the employee is supposed to do on the job, and whether he can get what he values most through his job behaviour for the satisfaction of his important needs. No one will perform adequately on the job if job clarity is lacking and if he is unable to satisfy his pressing needs.

Many employees do not have clear task objectives. Very often, they have a confused knowledge of what their responsibilities are, what task goals or targets they should be aiming for, what paths or procedures they should be following to reach such targets, and how they are moving on these paths. Lack of job clarity in the employee's mind is the fault of management. Managements fail to develop adequate job descriptions and job standards which might clarify employees' duties and responsibilities. Supervisors fail to provide their subordinates with concrete task goals and specified time periods for completion of the job.

Furthermore, neither supervisors nor subordinates receive proper feedback of work progress because of the absence of a systematic reporting system and feedback procedures. Reporting and feedback systems at work are absent, and the employees know it. When standards of performance are an unknown quantity in the organization (in the minds of all employees including management), the problem of increasing motivation for improving performance becomes meaningless. Employee motivation and performance can improve only when the employees have a clear job perception with regard to what is required of them for attaining very specific task goals within some prescribed time by following some well-tested paths (i.e. a work method). Task clarity, goal specificity, and a targeted time for task completion constitute the minimal conditions for improved work motivation and performance.

Reward-related experiences

Even if job clarity is a necessary condition for worker motivation and productivity, it is not sufficient. What is also needed is to provide employees with job outcomes or rewards and compensations that the employees consider relevant for satisfaction of their needs. It must be kept in mind that not each and every reward is effective in inducing greater work motivation among employees. *Rewards valued highly* by employees are more effective than less valued rewards. An employee who values job promotion more than an increased salary will not be motivated by more money. Managements must determine how the employees value various rewards before utilizing them for increasing motivation.

Several other characteristics of rewards also come into play. For instance, while receiving a reward, if an employee perceives the situations to be inequitable by comparing himself with coworkers, his work motivation will be lowered. If an employee finds that a junior coworker with an inferior work record gets a promotion along with him, then promotion as a reward will act to lower rather than increase his motivation. Thus perceived *equity of a reward* is an important source of increased work motivation.

Another important characteristic of rewards that makes them motivationally effective is *contingency on job behaviour*. A reward that is received as a result of high performance is more effective in inducing high performance in the future than a reward that is not dependent on performance. If the money one gets at the end of the month is not dependent on one's day-to-day job performance, an increase in salary is not going to increase motivation for higher job performance. On the other hand, since the receipt of one's salary depends on one's being present on the last day of the month, the attendance record on that day will be higher than on any other day of the month.

In addition to the perceived value or importance, the equity among coworkers, and the contingency of job outcomes, two other reward characteristics seem to influence the motivation of employees: *reward visibility* or concreteness and *reward immediacy* following job performance. A job outcome that is highly concrete and tangible becomes more visible and salient in the minds of employees. Such outcomes, such as money, tend to be pursued with greater vigour or create higher levels of work motivation than less tangible outcomes like job autonomy or job responsibility. Finally, an outcome or reward that immediately follows high performance is more effective in maintaining the performance than a reward that is delayed. Recognition of one's work immediately after its accomplishment is more motivating than its recognition 2 years later when the employee has already forgotten that for which he is being rewarded.

In many Indian organizations, compensation schemes are set up and administered without any consideration of their value, equity, contingency, visibility, and timing. Employees are hired with the understanding that they receive a compensation package that is largely time based rather than performance or skill based. Employees know that their skills and performance have no relation to the salary and benefits they receive from the organization. Many so-called performance- or merit-based rewards are clearly perceived as arbitrary and inequitable since the employees work in an inadequate (mostly nonexistent) appraisal system. They are often ill informed about the reward system and consequently perceive a state of randomness or arbitrariness in reward allocation. Since job performance does not bring the sought-after reward, they feel impotent in controlling the reward through their job behaviour and consequently develop apathy towards their job. They withdraw their energy from the job and engage in organizationally dysfunctional activities (gossiping, ingratiating behaviour to supervisors, etc.) hoping that such activities will bring in the valued rewards (status in the eyes of coworkers, or perhaps a promotion or accelerated salary increment from superiors). Organizationally dysfunctional behaviour among Indian employees is so pervasive that, just as black market money is crippling the Indian economic system, blackmailing at work (through deliberate inefficiency and apathy) is destroying the moral fabric or Dharma and Karma ethic of the Indian society.

Supervision-related experiences

In addition to the lack of task role clarity and inadequate reward system, many Indian organizations emphasize *bureaucratic practices* with excessive reliance on rules and regulations. Such practices create an organizational norm that is perceived by employees as cold and impersonal. Workers in these organizations see themselves as legalistic robots guided by rules and regulations of a depersonalized organization. An impersonal and legalistic environment alienates workers from both their job and the organization. Organizational interests are seen as separate and distinct from the interests of the

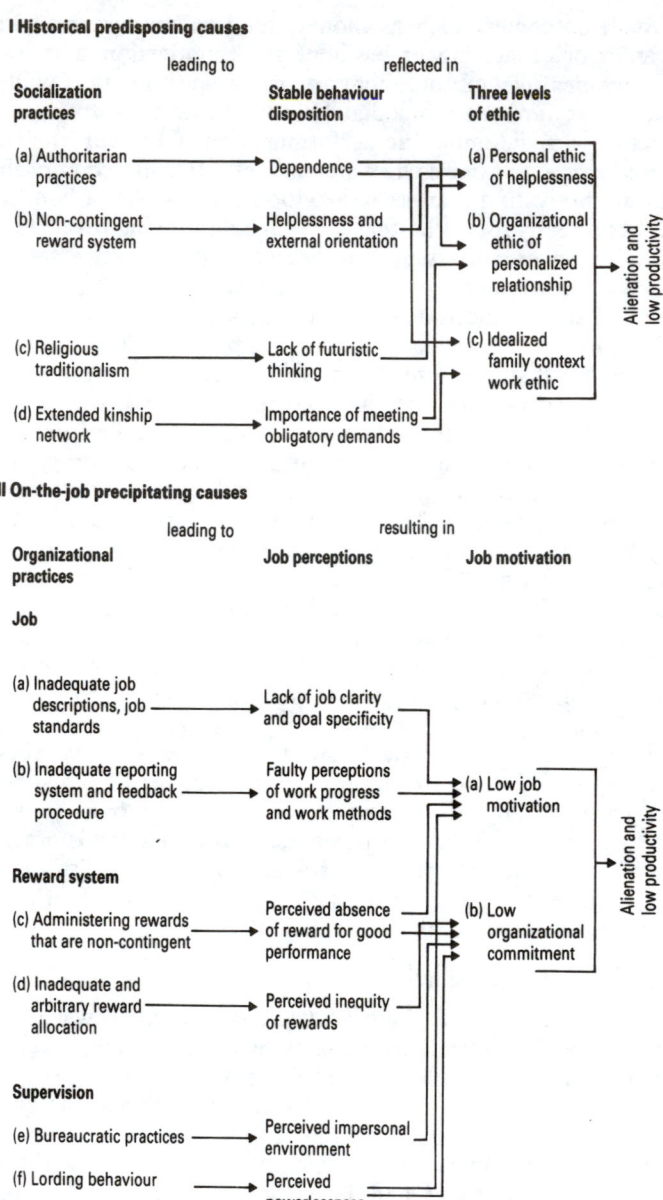

Figure 11.1   An explanatory model of worker alienation in India

workers, and workers' behaviour is often directed towards meeting their own interests even at the cost of organizational interest.

Supervisors and executives within organizations who engage in such bureaucratic practices are often more interested in lording power over others than in achieving organizational objectives through their subordinates. Such lording behaviour of people in positions of authority within organizations is often manifest in the forms of personal and public criticism of employees, condescending or patronizing attitudes towards subordinates, maintaining a certain psychological (and physical) distance from subordinates, and using rigid, legal, and coercive styles of supervision. As several researchers (Kipnis 1976; Ashforth 1986) have argued, through lording power over others, supervisors and executives use power for personal aggrandizement and for devaluing the worth of other employees. Employees in subordinate positions in turn feel low in self-esteem, powerless, and alienated at work.

Conclusion

The indigenous variables responsible for worker alienation in the Indian context are summarized in Figure 11.1 These variables are divided into two broad categories: predisposing (cultural) and precipitating (organizational) factors responsible for worker alienation. Identifications of these two types of factors in other developing countries should help us understand worker alienation in those countries better than the existing Western models. Attempts at de-alienation in a developing country context therefore have to deal systematically with the indigenous cultural and organizational practices rather than blindly following prescriptions derived from the Western models. Changing certain accepted cultural practices through intervention at the societal level is often a very difficult and slow process. However, attempts for reformative changes at the macro level should be one of the major goals of development projects in Third World countries. These attempts over a period of time tend generally to alter the prevailing culturally determined attitudes (such as authoritarianism, traditionalism, etc.) that contribute to work alienation. But with these changes work organizations must also bring about appropriate changes in their practices if worker alienation is to be avoided.

References

Ashforth, B. E. (1986) 'The experience of powerlessness in the operating core of the machine bureaucracy', unpublished doctoral dissertation, University of Toronto.

Blauner, R. (1964) *Alienation and Freedom: The Factory Worker and His Industry*, Chicago, IL: University of Chicago Press.

Chao, Y. T. (1988) 'Corporate culture and Chinese management', keynote speech, International Symposium on Social Values and Effective Organization, 26–30 November, Taipei, Taiwan.

Hackman, J. R. and Oldham, G. R. (1976) 'Motivation through the design of work: test of a theory', *Organizational Behavior and Human Performance* 16: 250–79.

Herzberg, F. (1968) 'One more time: how do you motivate employees?', *Harvard Business Review*, January–February: 53–62.

Inkeles, A. and Smith, D. H. (1974) *Becoming Modern: Individual Change in Six Developing Countries*, Cambridge, MA: Harvard University Press.

Kanungo, R. N. (1979) 'The concepts of alienation and involvement revisited', *Psychological Bulletin* 86: 119–38.

Kanungo, R. N. (1981) 'Work alienation and involvement: problems and prospects', *International Review of Applied Psychology* 30: 1–16.

Kanungo, R. N. (1982) *Work Alienation: An Integrative Approach*, New York: Praeger.

Kapp, W. K. (1963) *Hindu Culture, Economic Development and Economic Planning in India*, Bombay: Asia Publishing.

Kipnis, D. (1976) *The Powerholders*, Chicago, IL: University of Chicago Press.

Lawler, E. E. and Hackman, J. R. (1971) 'Concept profits and employee satisfaction: must they be in conflict?', *California Management Review* 14: 46–55.

Marx, K. (1932) 'Economic and philosophical manuscripts', in K. Marx and F. Engels, *Gesamtausgabe*, vol. 3, Berlin: Marx-Engels Institute (first published in 1844).

Maslow, A. H. (1954) *Motivation and Personality*, New York: Harper.

Mehta, P. (1976) 'From economic to democratic commitment: the role of worker participation', *Vikalpa* 1, 4: 39–46.

Mehta, P. (1978) 'Objective and subjective factors in employee satisfaction', *Indian Journal of Industrial Relations* 2, 13: 433–44.

Orpen, C. (1978) 'The work values of western and tribal black employees', *Journal of Cross-Cultural Psychology* 9, 99–112.

Rabinowitz, S. and Hall, D. T. (1977) 'Organizational research on job involvement', *Psychological Bulletin* 84, 265–88.

Rotter, J. B. (1966) 'Generalized expectancies for internal versus external control of reinforcement', *Psychological Monographs* 80, 1: 1–28.

Seeman, M. (1959) 'On the meaning of alienation', *American Sociological Review* 24: 783–91.

Shepard, J. M. (1971) *Automation and Alienation: A Study of Office and Factory Workers*, Cambridge, MA: MIT Press.

Weber, M. (1930) *The Protestant Ethic and the Spirit of Capitalism*, London: Allen & Unwin.

Weber, M. (1958) *The Religion of India: The Sociology of Hinduism and Buddhism* (trans. and ed. H. H. Gerth and D. Martindale), Glencoe, IL: Free Press.

Chapter twelve

Holistic strategies for worker dis-alienation in developing countries

Kalburgi M. Srinivas

Introduction

The developing countries are in the throes of a change the like of which they have never seen before. Economic order, political systems, technology of production coupled with ever-increasing population pressures and scarcity of employment as well as resources are leading to higher degrees of complexity in social organizations. The old order is disappearing. Their religious and moral systems, strong family ties and bonds, approved cultural authoritarianism and paternalism, closely guarded sex roles, and a deep sense of in-group loyalties are all slowly being challenged by increased levels of education, mass communication, and science and technology among other factors. These not-too-long-ago ascriptive societies are striving to become achievement-oriented societies.

But the new order is not yet firmly in. And there is much confusion, anxiety, apprehension, and uncertainty both at individual and at macro levels. Thus the notion of alienation may not be limited to the analysis of contemporary industrially developed societies but is equally applicable in discussions of the problems of the developing countries. In a review of psychological and cultural issues of development in Africa, Phillip Kingsley (1980) noted that alienation may be a more serious problem in the Third World than in that part of the world where there has been more technological advancement. Thus we may justifiably regard alienation as 'the signature of our epoch', to borrow Seeman's (1971) phrase. Furthermore, several empirical studies and theoretical arguments lend support to the idea that alienation is a cross-cultural phenomenon applicable to the developing countries (see for example Zurker *et al.* 1965; Simpson 1970; Tomeh 1974; Lau 1980; El Batavi 1981; Kanungo 1982).

While the forces of transition may themselves be a source of alienation, the resulting alienation may keep people locked in their traditional social patterns, defeating the avowed goals of enhancing their quality of life. Thus it is doubly important that the issue of preventive as well as therapeutic approaches to alienation be addressed in the developing countries. Seventy per cent of the world's population lives in these countries. Thus the issue at hand is nothing less than the designing of human futures.

A note of caution is in order here. The developing countries are often referred to as if they are homogeneous in their social, economic, political, legal, and cultural environments. Nothing could be further from the truth. In fact the Third World countries are more heterogeneous in all the above dimensions than the developed countries taken together. This must be kept in mind in the following discussion of alienation in the Third World. Strategies of de-alienation need to be specific to suit each situation. Accordingly, I shall not go beyond a general framework.

Having said that, it must be recognized that the so-called cultural differences may be exaggerated, as suggested by Negandhi (1983) based on his years of research on cross-cultural management. He says, 'One should not overly get excited about observed national differences, unless they are large in magnitude when compared to observed differences in a given country.... Intracountry differences within its ethnic and occupational groups are often as large or larger than inter country differences.' This line of thinking suggests that perhaps we can consider the developing countries as a whole, at least to a point, which is what I shall do below in presenting an approach to de-alienation in the Third World.

The problems of developing countries

Generally, the problems of the developing world are portrayed as those of population explosion, malnutrition, unemployment, housing, drinking water, inadequate income, and so on. The development strategy has centred around seeking to meet *basic needs*, defined as the minimum standard of living or consumption with respect to food, water purification, shelter, clothing, adequately remunerated employment, access to essential services such as health, education, sanitation, and transportation, along with a healthy, humane, and satisfying environment, where individual freedom is a right and where opportunities abound for popular participation in decisions that affect the lives and livelihood of people.

Laudable as these goals are, they primarily emphasize physical well-being. Such basic-needs-based approaches have several problems. First, as attempts to improve the quality of life, they leave out an important aspect of life – work life. Indeed, work is an important aspect of life even in the Third World (Applebaum 1984a, b). Any effort to improve the quality of life ought to include efforts to improve work life. It would indeed be naive to assume that work life would automatically improve to a desirable degree if the quality of non-working life is improved. The conventional wisdom fails to recognize the interlinkages between the physical and the psychic or assumes too much in terms of a direct and immediate connection. It also fails to recognize that increased psychic well-being spurs self-initiatives towards further gains in physical comfort and well-being.

Second, the basic needs strategy has also often been couched within a national industrialization scheme with a focus on macroeconomic growth. The pattern pursued towards this end has more often than not assumed that quality of life is not attainable except in the long run. It has held that higher levels of employment and improved standards of living (significantly, the term used is not *quality* of life) for all would in due time result from economic growth. 'True development' has become confused not merely with economic development but with modernization. True or real development is more than economic development, more than modernization. It caters to the spirit as well as the body; it attends to the psyche as well as the physical well-being. Given the poor evaluation obtained by the 30-odd years of history the 'basic needs' strategy's assumptions are highly questionable.

Third, the tragedy of underdevelopment lies as much or more in the poverty of opportunity as it does in economic poverty. Underemployment, with its constrained opportunities, is as serious a problem as the lack of employment. It has been recognized that the measures aimed solely at decreasing unemployment will worsen the situation all round (see for example Galenson 1971; ILO 1976); that the sense of impotence, helplessness, and insignificance experienced by the underemployed is not conducive to national productivity (Sablo 1971). The needs of the underemployed must be attended to; the releasing of pent-up aspirations, talents, and desires at work must therefore be a part of development. Such is not the case in the *basic needs* strategy.

Moreover, the conventional approach to development is also largely an activity of the 'experts', the development planners and administrators, notwithstanding the goals of wider participation (ILO 1976). The developees remain largely outside the planning process and the implementation of the plans, despite the popular participation goal. As such the developees' mental maps do not change very much or soon. Alienation is a mental thing. Until and unless the one that is afflicted is actively involved in overcoming the affliction (like a patient in psychotherapy) there is not likely to be significant de-alienation or real development.

Finally, one of the pressing needs of the developing countries is political stability and the institutionalization of democracy. The processes of a conventional approach to development are not helping to institutionalize democracy at the grass roots. And democratic ideals not taught at a practical level are likely to remain only abstract ideals and not take root. Work places where most people spend a good part of their working life can indeed become fertile soil for the seeds of democracy. Participative decision making and a consultative management style at the work place can impart a sense of potency to the workers which can be expected to have a healthy spill-over into the community, thereby helping to institutionalize the democratic way of life, which is one of the cherished objectives of these nations.

Thus the *basic needs* strategy of development currently being followed in the developing countries is not without problems, problems that may in fact be unnecessarily delaying a speedy realization of an enhanced quality of life for the population. Real development calls for attention to increasing the quality of working life, which is a large part of people's daily life. Real development includes attention to the mental health aspects of life. Human needs must be attended to in the work place as well as at the community level.

Worker needs in the developing countries

The productivity of labour in developing countries has indeed been low. Complaints are often heard of a labour force that is lazy, uncommitted to work life, indifferent to the product at which they labour, and frequently absent. The workforce in the developing world is often portrayed as content to have employment – *any* kind of employment – rather than face the threat of hunger from unemployment. Unfortunately, this is a caricature of an extreme kind. True, there is a high degree of unemployment in these countries. But still, the majority are employed, and a significant proportion of them underemployed, as was noted earlier. Attending to the needs of this majority is very important, and contrary to common belief it does not have to be at the cost of the 'yet to be employed'.

Studies across many developing countries have shown that their workers desire *quality employment*. For example, Negandhi's (1975) study of six countries showed that the employees, like their counterparts in developed countries, want not only higher wages and job security but also opportunities for advancement, fair treatment, better working conditions, and benefits. They prefer participative leadership and involvement in decision making within their organizations. International differences in this respect were marginal at best. Slocum (1971) in his study of Mexican workers found that, in addition to mere job security, esteem, autonomy, and self-actualization needs were very much on their minds. Desai's (1968) study of blue collar and white collar employees in India revealed that both groups preferred higher wages, better fringe benefits, and impartial policies on promotion and reward systems. Kakar (1971) found that, despite a national culture involved with rigid hierarchical relationships, Indian managers who were perceived to be helping and exerting low control elicited higher levels of subordinate performance and satisfaction than authoritarian managers – a clear illustration of what the workers respond to.

Howell *et al.* (1975) using Porter's need satisfaction measure showed that the order of need importance among Liberian workers is relatively the same as that of American workers. In a recent study Kanungo and Misra (1988) have demonstrated similar need patterns in the work context among Canadian and Indian managers. In their study of twenty-five countries including a number of Latin American countries Sirota and Greenwood (1971) noted 'considerable similarity in the work goals of employees around the world and that national differences regarding job related objectives were not nearly so great as some might think'.

While what has been cited above may not be exhaustive, it will suffice to illustrate that human work needs, such as those formulated by Thorsrud (1972), are universal:

(1) the need for the content of a job to be reasonably demanding of the worker in terms other than sheer endurance, and yet provide a minimum of variety (not necessarily novelty);

(2) the need to be able to learn on the job and to go on learning (neither too much nor too little);

(3) the need for some minimal area of decision making that the individual can call his own;

(4) the need for some minimum degree of social support and recognition in the work place;

(5) the need for an individual to be able to relate what he does and what he produces to his social life; and

(6) the need to feel that the job leads to some sort of a desirable future (not necessarily promotion).

When such needs are attended to, such attention serves as a curative to as well as a preventive of alienation, as the cases to be cited later have shown.

A contrast of strategies

In the developed countries there are institutional mechanisms, strategies, and specific activities aimed at reducing alienation arising out of one source or another. For example, political parties seek to increase voter turnout at rallies and elections through media blitz designed to increase voter consciousness, or through accentuation of issues of interest to the local voters. Alcoholics Anonymous, Weight Watchers, and Family Crisis Centres serve to decrease alienation that has specific origins. Church organizations engage in door-to-door visits and spiritual telethons that seek to increase attendance and religious affiliation of the population. Work organizations, who have the most to lose from workforce alienation, introduce specific programmes and engage in internal rearrangements that seek to increase worker *involvement* through such arrangements as

(1) reduction of work hours,
(2) reduction in shift work,
(3) flexible working hours,
(4) reduction in unpleasant and tedious jobs,
(5) job-sharing arrangements,
(6) optimum job pace,
(7) ergonomic and socio-technical job design,
(8) increased worker control and autonomy,
(9) sharing of information with workers on market conditions and company performance,
(10) quality circles,
(11) worker input and participation in decisions, and
(12) quality of work life programmes.

In contrast with these mechanisms and incentives, the developing countries do not have specific institutional programmes designed to increase involvement of any target populace, except perhaps in the religious aspects. However, there are a number of community-level activities mounted and sponsored by government as well as non-governmental agencies. As noted before, this *basic needs focus* is generally designed to increase

(1) levels of employment and income,
(2) medical care and health services,
(3) nutritional and adequate supply of food,
(4) decent and hygienic housing,
(5) safe drinking water supply,
(6) family planning,

(7) transportation services, and
(8) literacy, vocational training, and education.

Inasmuch as these efforts may be considered to contribute towards enhancement of one's self-image and 'success definition', we may regard them as perhaps weak and by no means *direct* and *explicit* strategies for individual involvement away from alienation. These strategies, then, may be conceived to be at one extreme of a de-alienation strategy whose other extreme is characterized by the specific activities and efforts illustrated in the case of more developed countries.

The problem with the basic needs focus is that it is not founded on any inclusive conceptual framework other than good intentions to better things – better defined in operational terms of physical comfort. A conceptual model that offers a solid philosophical base for development thrusts is that of Maccoby (1975). It recognizes the *organizational* *context* and the *individual context* to be complexly interlinked. It also recognizes the economic, political, and social forces in society. The model is based on four dimensions.

(1) Security: the need to feel secure of life and limb, of income and livelihood, of job continuity, of shelter.
(2) Equity: the need to experience fairness in compensation received for output, in rules and regulations under which one functions; a need to feel not discriminated against.
(3) Democracy: the need to feel free to think as well as openly express one's critical views; the need to feel that one is not limited in terms of opportunities available to oneself.
(4) Individuation: the need to feel stimulated towards the realization of one's creative potential, to keep on experiencing learning, to experience autonomy, and to feel one's unique niche in the social fabric of society.

The Maccoby model's fit to the issue at hand is more fully evident in the following quote from his colleague Neal Herrick:

> We have reason to believe that a system based on these principles would develop in the worker a sense of hope, activeness and productiveness. Many of the symptoms of discontent, mental illness, and despair would, we believe, dissolve. It is important to note here that many attempts for change are made in the erroneous belief that certain symptoms have a single cause, and if one changes the cause one cures the symptom. This kind of thinking is based on a mechanical model of cause and effect, which does not take into account the fact that individuals live in systems. In a social system

every factor is related to every other factor. If you change one factor, others tend to be affected. It is well to note that changing one principle without paying attention to others might lead to results that are very different from the ones we envisage. For example a system of total security and certain equity without individuation or democracy might result in dependent and fearful workers ... security, democracy and equity without individuation may be experienced as alienation....

(Herrick 1975)

In fact, much empirical evidence exists to support the Maccoby model's contention that work and non-work lives are less separated in the developing countries (except perhaps in the upper echelons of society) than they are in the developed countries. For example, Mehta (1976, 1978) notes that work and non-work are related in the minds of workers: 'Job satisfaction is a function also of lack of general amenities such as lack of adequate water and canteen facilities, of lack of medicine and health care provision, as well as inadequate compensation and inadequate benefits.' Applebaum (1984a) also cites evidence to illustrate the lack of separation of work life and non-work life in developing countries. Thus, a de-alienation strategy would have to be an integrated one that fights work place alienation as well as that which arises in other arenas of workers' lives – an approach that accommodates this low degree of separation between work and non-work. Such an approach, designated the 'macro-environment-conscious work-centred focus', is presented below.

A macro-environment-conscious work-centred strategy

Stated simply, this is a position midway between the two extremes described above. It is 'work-centred' in the sense that efforts are made to satisfy the work needs of employees and to free them from work alienation. It is 'macro-environment-conscious' in the sense that non-work life needs of employees are also attended to from inside the work place. It is holistic and views employees as whole persons, and seeks to do what is needed in order to make them 'fully functioning' human beings. For instance the creation of employment is accompanied by creation of working conditions that promote autonomy, participation, and growth; establishment of 'quality circles' is accompanied by provision of medical services, safe drinking water, and decent housing; job redesign programmes are accompanied by vocational training programmes. In other words, improvements in work life and non-work life proceed simultaneously. The initiatives under this strategy emanate in the work place and extend outward in a ripple effect. Why should they emanate in the work place? Because work places are the microcosm of an achievement-based new order that the developing nations are seeking to build to replace the old ascription-based order. Initiatives centred in the work place create a sense of identity with such a futuristic new order. Spill-over effects from this learning which is centred in the work place can only be beneficial to the community as a whole.

It must be noted that what is suggested here is not something that management *gives* to workers. It is something that management *does in collaboration* with workers. There is learning and growth in this very process of the two parties working jointly together, to mount de-alienation/development programmes. In other words, what is being said here is that an organization concerned with the efficient and effective production of essential goods and services cannot afford to ignore the macro-environmental problems of its workforce. Nor can community developmental efforts afford to postpone concerns for organizational effectiveness and efficiency. The development planners need to accept the fact that these two kinds of developmental efforts are systematically inseparable, and any effort to force a separation as the basic needs approach effectively does, cannot but render developmental outcomes to nought. Because the work-centred strategy parallels the Third World's lack of separation between work life and non-work life, its chances of realizing the real developmental objectives, as well as decreasing worker alienation, are greater.

Several close examples of the approach suggested here are available. In Kenya (Henley 1977), Zambia (Crosby 1976), and Argentina (Miller *et al.* 1966), the boundaries of the personnel function have been extended beyond the organization. The personnel department, for example, has welfare, social, and political activities that extend well beyond the organization's boundaries into the surrounding community. In Brazil, Freire (1972) initiated a 'consciousness raising' approach to education wherein education was woven around the immediate needs of true learners, rather than education in the abstract. In a more recent Chinese example, population control was linked with productive employment, provision of health care, shelter, functional literacy, provision of opportunity for the poor to raise their level of consumption, and the availability of potable water (cited in De 1981). Szal (1979) gives examples from a Chinese commune and from Vietnamese agricultural cooperatives wherein the members were involved in participative decision making with noteworthy consequences. Maturu (1979) gives several examples of attention to worker nutrition at the work place in Guatemala, Costa Rica, and

Vietnam as a consequence of which the workers were much 'energized', both physically and mentally, and work output was enhanced. Sharma *et al.* (1978) report on work in the Indian Postal System wherein the workers not only increased their levels of output but also experienced increased satisfaction and a relief from a sense of confinement and inhibition, and voiced a desire for more opportunities for growth. Furthermore, evaluations showed a reduction in interpersonal tensions, an increase in cooperation as well as a sense of pride among workers. Success has been reported in similar work-centred projects in banking, heavy electrical manufacturing, leather processing, chemicals and fertilizer manufacturing, etc. This was also shown in Zambia in trucking and cement and fishnet manufacturing firms (Kanawaty *et al.* 1981). More limited success has been reported in some Peruvian efforts directed at worker-owned production and in work cooperatives (Neffa 1981).

Of course, the circumstances of different nations and different sectors within a country are likely to be different, as we noted earlier. Accordingly, what has been advocated above is only a framework proposal. It needs to be adapted to suit individual countries and individual companies. Resource constraints to mount these innovative work arrangements may require organizations to join together in consortiums.

When workers are responded to at the work place, when they get a feeling that they have potential, that they can affect and change things around them for the better, they can then be expected to exercise this potency at the community level for making intelligent and mature decisions and to become self-reliant.

Some likely problems attending implementation

There is no doubt that the kind of development thrust indicated in this chapter requires an effective, decentralized, democratic administrative structure within organizations. Developing countries are in a situation of rapid change and need more adaptation than is permitted by the rigid bureaucratic models developed in the West (Thompson 1964). Non-conventional administrative procedures are called for, and this may be the largest stumbling block to the implementation of work-centred approaches to development.

Some other reasons for caution are suggested by Kiggundu and his colleagues (1983) based on their examination of the applicability of management theories to the developing countries.

• Developing country organization members have a deep personal insecurity dominated by formalism, ritualism, paper fetish, and amoral familism.

- Caste systems, religious taboos, differing concepts of time, deep-rooted traditions of centralization, and informality present obstacles.
- Trade practices, friendship patterns, cultural norms, and patriotism may interfere with attempted innovations.
- The extended family concept and kinship relations, the authority of elders, and collective responsibility may deter individual self-reliance and ambition.
- The 'smoothing mode' of conflict resolution and closer emotional interactions may lead to disguising problems rather than negotiating solutions.
- Corruption, élitism, and status related to personal and group alignment rather than merit may lead to lowered morale and ambition.
- The shortage of skilled labour and skilled professionals (amidst abundant labour supply) along with low levels of education in management may make change difficult or impossible.
- Infant industries, monopolistic practices, weak capital markets, and inadequate infrastructure may also contribute to a slow rate of growth or improvement.

However, Negandhi (1983) holds that many if not all of the so-called 'cultural factors' have to do with economic and political factors rather than culture. He lists factors of ownership, the prevalent seller's market conditions, extensive government regulation, and lack of experience in delegation of authority as explanatory variables. For example, the seller's market provides less incentive to owner–managers to delegate authority; the positive profit picture is also taken as a sign of one's success as a manager.

Worker responses may be the most favourable factor for the proposal presented here. Prayag Mehta (1976, 1978) notes from his research in India that workers have a social achievement motivation (versus individual achievement motivation). They show a desire for collective success, a desire for raising overall productivity and production, a desire for national/social prosperity, a desire for a better life for the community, a desire for safety for everyone, and a concern for improvement of general conditions and standard of living. These reflect a desire for some kind of super-ordinate achievement goals. Kingsley (1980) has noted similar orientations among African workers. With such worker orientations, it should not be difficult to obtain worker collaboration and participation. Nonetheless, it is not going to be easy, and it should not be easy. Development efforts pose numerous challenges and meeting these challenges is no easy task.

Conclusion

The approach presented here is formulated on rational as well as value-based considerations. Examples of successes in proceeding along these lines already exist, and social scientists have a role to play along with economists and administrators to move away from conventional approaches to development towards de-alienation strategies.

Does this suggestion smack of the paternalistic management of yesteryear? Not at all. Under the paternalistic blueprint, all the control and decision making rested with management, who could take away at any time what they had previously given. In the present case we suggest that the efforts be truly joint efforts between labour and management to create work involvement.

The developing countries should seek to avoid the nineteenth-century models of industrial organization and the dehumanizing values embodied in them. They should develop an organic pattern of work life with holistic and flexible work roles. In the words of Trist (1975) they should 'skip a century'.

The future depends upon the choices made now. Robertson (1983) outlines five value-oriented choices in the designing of human futures: business as usual; disaster; the totalitarian-conservatist future; the hyper-expansionist (HE) future; and finally the sane, humane, ecological (SHE) future that is self-fulfilling. The worker de-alienation strategy proposed here falls within this sane alternative.

We conclude this paper with a little poem that expresses the value premise here:

> No one should have to go to work in anguish;
> No one should have to go joyless to work
> just to earn a living;
> No one should be deprived at work of the right
> to think and act like a human being; and
> No one, not even in the Third World, should be
> deprived of the feeling that one has human value.

References

Applebaum, H. (1984a) *Work in Market and Industrial Societies*, Albany, NY: State University of New York Press.

Applebaum, H. (1984b) *Work in Non-market and Transitional Societies*,

Albany, NY: State University of New York Press.

Crosby, J. (1976) 'Personnel management in a developing country', *Personnel Management* 8, 9: 19–23.

De, N. R. (1981) 'A perspective on global planning for development', presented at the QWL and the 1980s, International Conference, Toronto, September.

Desai, K. G. (1968) 'A comparative study of motivation of blue collar and white collar workers', *Indian Journal of Social Work* 28, 4: 379–87.

El Batavi, M. A. (1981) 'Psychosocial stressors in working life: problems specific to developing countries', in Lennart Levi (ed.) *Society, Stress and Disease: Working Life*, vol. 4, pp. 12–13, New York: Oxford University Press.

Freire, P. (1972) *Cultural Action for Freedom*, Harmondsworth: Penguin.

Galenson, W. (ed.) (1971) *Essays on Employment*, Geneva: ILO.

Henley, J. S. (1977) 'The personnel professionals in Kenya', *Personnel Management* 9, 2: 10–14.

Herrick, N. Q. (1975) *The Quality of Work and its Outcomes*, Columbus, OH: Academy of Contemporary Problems.

Howell, P., Strauss, J., and Sorensen, P. F. (1975) 'Research note: cultural and situational determinants of job satisfaction among management in Liberia', *Journal of Management Studies* 12: 225–7.

ILO (1976) *Employment, Growth and Basic Needs – A One World Problem*, Report of the Director General of the ILO prepared for the World Employment Conference, June.

Kakar, S. (1971) 'Authority patterns and subordinate behaviour in Indian organizations', *Administrative Science Quarterly* 16, 3: 298–307.

Kanawaty, G., Thorsrud, E., Semiono, J. P., and Singh, J. P. (1981) 'Field experiences with new forms of work organization', *International Labour Review* 120, 3: 263–77.

Kanungo, R. N. (1982) *Work Alienation: An Integrative Approach*, New York: Praeger.

Kanungo, R. N. and Misra, S. (1988) 'The bases of involvement in work and family contexts', *International Journal of Psychology* 23, 3: 267–82.

Kiggundu, M. N., Jørgensen, J. J., and Hafsi, T. (1983) 'Administrative theory and practice in developing countries: a synthesis', *Administrative Science Quarterly* 28: 66–84.

Kingsley, P. (1980) 'Adaptation to new technology: some cultural and psychological issues in technological development', *African Social Research*, December: 783–809.

Lau, F. M. (1980) 'Social integration, alienation and leisure activity among workers in Singapore', *National Taiwan University Journal of Sociology* 14, November: 143–65.

Maccoby, M. (1975) 'Changing work: the Bolivar project', *Working Papers for a New Society*, 3, Summer.

Maturu, N. R. (1979) 'Nutrition and labour productivity', *International Labour Review* 118, 1: 1–12.

Mehta, P. (1976) 'From economic to democratic commitment: the role of worker participation', *Vikalpa* 1, 4: 39–46.

Mehta, P. (1978) 'Objective and subjective factors in employee satisfaction', *Indian Journal of Industrial Relations* 2, 13: 433–44.

Miller, D. C., Chammorro, E., and Agulla, J. C. (1966) 'Community power perspectives and role definitions of North American executives in an Argentine community', *Administrative Science Quarterly* 10, 364–80.

Neffa, J. C. (1981) 'Improvement of working conditions and environment: a Peruvian experiment with new forms of work organization', *International Labour Review* 120, 4: 473–90.

Negandhi, A. R. (1975) *Organizational Theory in an Open System: A Study of Transferring Advanced Management Practices to Developing Nations*, New York: Dunellan.

Negandhi, A. R. (1983) 'Management in the Third World', *Asia Pacific Journal of Management* 1, 1: 15–25.

Robertson, J. (1983) *The Sane Alternative: A Choice of Futures* (3rd edn), Minneapolis, MN: River Basin.

Sablo, Y. (1971) 'Sectoral employment growth: the outlook for 1980', in W. Galenson (ed.) *Essays on Employment*, Geneva: ILO.

Seeman, M. (1971) 'The urban alienations: some dubious theses from Marx to Marcuse', *Journal of Personality and Social Psychology* 19 (2): 135–43.

Sharma, K. C., Singh, H., and Deish, K. (1978) 'Participative redesign of the work system', HRD Series 3, Dept of Personnel and Administrative Reforms, Ministry of Home Affairs, Government of India, New Delhi.

Simpson, M. E. (1970) 'Social mobility, normlessness and powerlessness in two cultural contexts', *American Sociological Review* 35: 1002–13.

Sirota, D. and Greenwood, J. M. (1971) 'Understanding your overseas work force', *Harvard Business Review* 49: 53–60.

Slocum, J. W. (1971) 'A comparative study of the satisfaction of American and Mexican operatives', *Academy of Management Journal* 14, 1: 88–97.

Szal, R. J. (1979) 'Popular participation: employment and the fulfillment of basic needs', *International Labour Review* 118, 1: 27–38.

Thompson, V. A. (1964) 'Administration objectives for development administration', *Administrative Science Quarterly* 9: 91–101.

Thorsrud, E. (1972) 'Policy making as a learning process', in A. B. Cherns, R. Sinclair, and W. J. Jenkins (eds) *Social Sciences and Government: Policies and Problems*, London: Tavistock.

Tomeh, A. (1974) 'Alienation: cross cultural analysis', *Journal of Social Psychology* 94: 187–200.

Trist, E. (1975) 'Planning the first steps toward quality of working life in a developing country', in L. E. Davis and A. B. Cherns (eds) *Quality of Working Life: Problems, Prospects and the State of the Art*, vol. 1, New York: Free Press.

Zurker, L. A., Jr., Meadow, A., and Zurker, S. E. (August 1965) 'Value orientation, role conflict and alienation from work: cross cultural study', *American Sociological Review* 30: 539–48.

Chapter thirteen

Performance management in developing countries

Manuel Mendonca and Rabindra N. Kanungo

Introduction

In many developing countries, both the public and private sector organizations have been targets of criticism for their poor management practices, bureaucratic inefficiencies, and low levels of productivity. For instance, in India the deplorable productivity levels in the coal, power generation, and steel industries came under a scathing attack in two lengthy articles by Vasant Sathe, a former Union Minister for Energy (*Times of India* 4 and 5 August 1986). The problems of low productivity in Indian public sector organizations have not been due to the lack of economic, technological, or human resources, but rather to ineffective management practices, particularly in the management of human resources. In his insightful analysis of the Indian situation, Sathe concluded that:

> 'We should firmly insist that the entire workforce, from management down to the last employee, will be collectively responsible for the production and productivity of the unit. A new participatory work culture would thus have to be established. The management must be given continued authority without any limitations of tenure or age, the only criterion being merit and the capacity to deliver.... Gunah pujasthanam. Gunishu nacha lingam nacha vayah' [It is merit alone that should be worshipped – neither gender nor age is relevant].

A year earlier, participants at a seminar of senior-level executives, administrators, and consultants, unanimous in their findings of increasing inefficiency, low morale, and low productivity among Indian workers, concurred with the view that what is happening 'publicly' in the public sector is happening 'privately' in the private sector. Declining work motivation in developing countries like India is indeed endemic and prevents the benefits of the exceptional achievements in science and technology, medicine and health, food and agriculture from reaching the teeming masses – particularly in the rural areas. The problem of low work motivation is so enormous and overwhelming that it seems to paralyse the will to act of even the best-intentioned executives. Addressing the work motivation issues, Kanungo and Misra (1985) have spelt out a practical approach which demands a systematic analysis to identify

the likely behavioural problems at each stage of the process of human resource management: manpower planning, recruitment, induction and training, job maintenance, performance improvements and employee development; and

the past socialization process of the workers and their present perceptions of how the job can satisfy their needs.

Following the analysis, the approach outlined basic action steps to either prevent or address the behavioural problems that have been identified. Of course, the action steps are an ongoing process which simply will not take a vacation! Critical to this approach, however, is the step which requires the development of mechanisms to monitor and evaluate employee performance constantly. Such an evaluation will provide management with the basis that will facilitate the development of human resource systems – selection, career development, and compensation – that support the strategic business objectives of the organization. The employees too have a substantial stake in performance appraisal. It provides feedback on performance, specifying areas which need improvement, and indications of whether they will receive the expected salary increase or promotion. For these reasons the importance of performance appraisal is receiving increasing attention; and organizations, in both the public and private sectors, see the need to revamp their performance appraisal systems for better organizational effectiveness. The list of organizations in the forefront of this effort to modernize their personnel function reads like a *Who's Who* of business and industry in many developing countries (e.g. India, Singapore, Malaysia, Philippines, Pakistan, Indonesia, and Sri Lanka). There is an awakening in these countries to the tremendous potential of performance appraisal programmes to increase productivity and pave the way for employee growth and development.

Performance appraisal is inherent to the fundamental responsibility of the manager but is often brushed aside for other 'more pressing' organizational problems which, more often than not, crop up precisely because of inadequate attention to this basic managerial responsibility. In developing countries there is the additional 'catch-

22' situation. On the one hand, effective performance appraisals presuppose the existence of certain conditions and norms in the organization but the cultural baggage of the employees, in most cases, is incompatible with these norms and conditions. On the other hand, the performance appraisal programme itself provides a perfectly natural vehicle and the least disruptive approach to managing the cultural changes necessary for organizational effectiveness and employee satisfaction. Fortunately, a great deal is known today of the determinant of a successful appraisal programme, but its treatment in the literature can be broadly grouped into two categories. One category consists of articles which critically analyse the appraisal mechanics and forms to the exclusion of almost all other aspects of the appraisal process. The other uses the recipe approach – a specific plan, complete with forms and scoring manual – touted as a panacea for the motivational ills of the employees. Both formats are of little use to the practising managers: the former is much too abstruse, and the latter is an insult to their intelligence.

The purpose of this chapter is to bring together the current knowledge of the determinants of a successful appraisal programme in a manner that the practising manager in developing countries can use to develop a system which is conceptually sound and meets the needs of both the organization and the employees. Specifically, the chapter will discuss the strategic and process issues of performance appraisals and the nature and mode of cultural changes that must be considered by the organization and employees to ensure that the cultural 'fit' reflects the aspirations of these two partners, who alone can make or mar the appraisal system.

Performance management – the process and essential preconditions

The process

The management of performance in any organization is an on-going cyclical process. It begins with the definition of the subordinate's job, unless the job is so simple that there is absolutely no doubt in anyone's mind as to what is the expected job behaviour. In this first step, the manager must *identify* all the important aspects of the job and *clarify* how it is related to the goals of the organization. One way of identifying job objectives that are concrete and appropriate to organizational goals is to view the recipient of the job's products as the 'customer' of that job. In this approach, the managers assist their employees to identify the 'customers' of their output. For example, the sales analyst prepares the monthly sales statistics which are routed to the sales manager, the marketing manager, and senior managers. The sales analyst sees each recipient as a 'customer' and becomes conscious of the job's responsibility to satisfy the specific needs of the customers. The customer approach enables the employees to experience the significance of their tasks and promotes, in varying degrees, identification with the organization's goals. These outcomes are ensured only if the process of job definition is a joint effort of the manager and the employees which leads to an agreed understanding of and commitment to the appropriate job behaviours.

The second step of the cycle is the *setting of expectations*. The first step spelt out what needs to be done. The second step specifies how well the tasks must be done. It sets the standards by which the job performance will be appraised. Goal-setting theory (Locke and Bryan 1968), abundantly supported by empirical evidence (Locke *et al.* 1981), stipulates that employee performance is greatly enhanced when the assigned goals are difficult, but attainable; specific, but appropriate to the goals of the organization. This step also establishes the performance period – usually 6 months to a year for non-managerial jobs and 2 years and more for managerial jobs, the rationale being that it takes much longer for performance results to become visible in the latter case than in the former.

The process of performance appraisal, despite the most sophisticated attempts to introduce objective procedures, will always remain a subjective process and, as such, highly vulnerable to fallible judgements even with much goodwill. Therefore the participation of employees in the establishment of standards and measures of performance is crucial. The knowledge and expertise of both the supervisor and the employees contribute to performance standards and measures that are reasonable, realistic, and appropriate. This is not to suggest that subordinates, left to themselves, would set unrealistically low standards. In fact, there is considerable evidence that subordinates often tend to set unrealistically high goals (Lawler 1977). The joint mutual influence process, in addition to injecting realism, would ensure manager–subordinate agreement and give the subordinate 'ownership and control', which go a long way towards generating the trust, acceptance, and commitment so necessary to this highly subjective system (Locke and Latham 1984).

Before we proceed further, it is useful to illustrate these two steps which constitute the foundation of the appraisal system. Let us consider the job of a salesman. Based on his own knowledge and experience and that of his salesmen, the sales manager lists all the job behaviours which result in successful sales performance, e.g. developing a prospects list, setting up appointments with customers, demonstrating products, customer follow-up, responding to customer complaints/enquiries, communications with the sales manager, developing budgets, sales reports, training juniors, initiating new sales approaches. These behaviours are then arranged in the order of how critical they are to increasing sales. Specific measures such as five customer demonstrations per week, ten new appointments every month, sales report by the first day of each month, etc. are assigned to each behaviour and become the standards and measures of performance. The deliberations of the manager and the employee at this stage of the cycle have the potential to generate, often unwittingly, considerable mistrust and conflict. Preoccupied with 'productivity', the manager sets the performance goals (expectations) in terms of some measure of productivity. The employee, on the other hand, intent on reaching these goals performs all the required behaviours only to find his efforts thwarted by environmental or other constraints entirely beyond his control. Both the manager and the employee will be spared this needless frustration if they recognize the fundamental difference between 'performance' and 'productivity' (Kanungo 1986).

'Performance' refers to an employee's actual manifest behaviour at work. 'Productivity', on the other hand, is the result, in terms of output, of that behaviour (i.e. performance). However, this behaviour involves the employee's interaction with the other inputs of the social system (coworkers, supervisors, subordinates), the technical system (materials, tools, machines, transforming process used), and the environment (market, economy, regulations). Thus, while performance depends upon the employee's knowledge, skills, ability, and motivation, productivity depends not only on the employee's performance but also on the socio-technical system and the environment. The salesman in our earlier example, despite an excellent performance, could lose to a competitor if the plant is unable to guarantee delivery as per the customer's schedule.

Another important aspect of the manager's role, then, in this stage of the performance management cycle is to work at identifying and removing the environmental constraints. If this is not possible, the appraisal programme must provide for an adjustment mechanism to recognize performance which meets the predetermined standards but fails to achieve the desired level of productivity owing to factors beyond the control of the employee.

The third step of the performance management cycle is *monitoring the performance*. During this phase, the manager provides informal on-going feedback, which is to be viewed not in terms of fault-finding but rather as on-the-job coaching. When managers function as coach, they seek to help employees grow and reach desired performance levels. Coaching involves knowing how well the employees are performing relative to performance standards in terms of specific measurable behaviours, and discussing areas for improvement. The coach gives praise for work well done and offers constructive criticism when appropriate. In the latter case, the manager cites specific behaviour with specific suggestions on how to correct the performance problems. Performance standards can never be etched in stone; their validity always assumes a relatively stable environment. The manager who functions like a coach will be sensitive to changing environmental factors and will make suitable adjustments to the performance standards. Perhaps the shortfall in performance is because the employee is deficient in certain skills. The coaching approach will cause the manager to be immediately aware of such deficiencies and provide remedial measures, e.g. training. In their coaching stance, managers are careful to create an open relaxed atmosphere which encourages employees to seek guidance in sorting out priorities or in resolving problems.

The fourth step is the *formal appraisal review*, at the end of the predetermined performance period, during which managers record their assessment of the individual's performance. This phase usually poses the greatest problem for most managers as it demands that they play two apparently conflicting roles – as coach and judge. The most frequently recommended approach to this phase is termed the 'problem-solving' approach because its focus is on the identification and removal of obstacles to good performance such as inappropriate or obsolete work procedures, lack of resources and certain skills, and lack of a clear understanding of the job role and requirements. Based on a joint discussion between the manager and the subordinate, it permits a mutual exchange of information which helps to correct each other's information gap. It increases the subordinates' trust in the fairness of the process because they are now certain that the manager does indeed have all the information needed for a reasonable assessment. Furthermore, it provides an opportunity to discuss the short- and long-term career objectives of the subordinates, as well as their training and development needs. The problem-solving approach creates a climate of mutual trust, is non-threatening, and therefore makes the appraisal review the ideal event to discuss and set goals for the next performance period. In this approach, managers function as both coach and judge, but the obvious emphasis is on their mentoring role as they seek to nurture the subordinates' strengths and minimize the negative effects of their weaknesses, if these cannot be completely eliminated.

Managers can choose from a wide variety of techniques to rate employees' performance; some organizations combine techniques or use different techniques to rate different categories of employees. However, it must be emphasized that the criteria for the choice of the technique must obviously be its capacity to capture employee performance in terms of the predetermined job behaviours. The use of personal traits to appraise performance should be avoided unless these are critical to the performance of the job, in which case the traits should form part of the performance standards. For example, good salespersons or employees who are members of a work team need to be high on the personal trait of 'ability to work with others'. On the other hand, bench scientists who work by themselves may not need that personal trait. However, if personal traits are critical to the job, then the rating format should encourage the manager not merely to record observations in terms of the presence or absence of the traits but to illustrate them more specifically with examples of the job behaviours observed. For instance, if the manager rates a foreman 'low' on 'resourcefulness' then it will help that foreman improve his performance if the manager recorded an example of a behaviour reflecting a lack of initiative and its consequence for the organization such as: 'Your attention to the high rate of equipment failure would have impelled you to alert the maintenance department in time to prevent a needless shut down for 3 days.'

It must nevertheless be recognized that the rating instrument is not an end in itself but a means to bring together in one medium information which supports the problem-solving method discussed. Any displacement of the means–end relationship which results in the mechanics of the instrument being accorded a more important role than the process which it is designed to support will certainly not contribute to the effective management of performance.

If the performance review is to aid in performance management, the assessment recorded should provide information which facilitates equitable compensation decisions and identifies training and development needs. When managers ensure equity in compensation decisions, they unleash the tremendous motivational power of the compensation programme, with two positive consequences, among many, that inevitably follow. First, the correct and desirable performance behaviours are reinforced which greatly increases the probability that such behaviours are repeated in the future. The employees get a clear, direct, and unambiguous message of the type and level of performance behaviours expected from them. Second, the satisfaction that follows equitable compensation increases the value that employees place on the rewards they receive from the organization. The empirical evidence is overwhelmingly conclusive that employee motivation is high when rewards are contingent upon performance behaviour and are valued by the employees (Kanungo and Mendonca 1988).

Identifying training and development needs is the necessary, but not sufficient, first step to improving performance. It must be followed through with appropriate programmes which remedy specific performance deficiencies or provide opportunities for the acquisition or enhancement of certain skills and abilities. This activity is especially critical to organizations which compete in a highly dynamic and rapidly growing industry.

Essential preconditions

The four steps of the performance management cycle that we have described constitute a process that is integral to an effective organization. It links the different organizational systems, builds teamwork, and develops employees. However, the effectiveness of this process is largely dependent on certain preconditions without which the performance management process is a meaningless exercise in futility which will do more harm than good to both the employees and the organization.

The first precondition is that managers recognize that an organization is not composed of automatons whose successful functioning depends upon endless elaborate rules and control systems. An organization is a dynamic social system of living human beings with specific aptitudes, abilities, motives, and aspirations. The tremendous potential of this social system cannot be tapped by developing hierarchical power structures with a bewildering array of committees, subcommittees, position titles, and sycophantic relationships. Rather, it can only be done by a clear articulation of the vision for the organization – its mission and purpose – that will excite and challenge its employees, most of whom would welcome an opportunity to use their talents and abilities for the mutual benefit of themselves and the organization. Managers, then, need to look upon their employees as a vital resource and to understand how varied talents, aspirations, and behaviours affect productivity.

The second precondition is closely related to the first. Since employees are a vital resource, then the expenditures relating to employees such as recruitment, compensation, training, and development can only be looked upon as an 'investment' much like, if not more critical than, the expenditures on capital assets. In reality, most managers regard their employees as an 'expense'. Although they bemoan constantly, in union negotiations, press briefings, and even at cocktail parties, that employee expenditures are enormous and steadily rising, yet the managers seem blissfully content in doing absolutely nothing about them. When managers are allowed to believe that employees are a necessary and an inevitable expense, then this belief seems to provide them with an immunity from being held responsible for the impact of the enormous labour cost on the profitability of the organization. Of course, any question on low profitability is invariably explained by factors other than the employees' poor performance. Such a rationalization becomes a great cover-up for the managers' abdication of their responsibility to 'manage' employee performance towards organizational objectives. On the other hand, when managers regard their employees as an 'investment', then logically there follows the implicit obligation to get an adequate return from this investment which leads to a conscious deliberate action plan to manage employee performance, to establish specific job objectives, and to set in motion the process, described in this chapter, to evaluate employee performance and to coach and develop employees towards the attainment of the job objectives.

The absolutely essential need to view expenditures relating to employees as an 'investment', to be managed as such, is especially pertinent to the public sector enterprises in developing countries where providing 'employment' *per se*, without regard to organization objectives, seems to have become an end in itself – almost an implementation of a social policy. Another caveat is also in order: the mere change of the name of the personnel function to the Department of Human Resources will not ensure that the employees are, in fact, treated and managed as a vital resource. An executive in an Indian organization once quipped: 'HRM is so important to our organization that the total investment for this function amounts to the cost of one name-plate: Manager-HRD.' Even establishing a specific government ministry of human resources will not, by that action alone, guarantee results, as can be seen from the Indian experience.

How does an organization promote the idea that the employees are its most important resource investment? It obviously begins at the top and forms an integral part of the organization's culture – its core beliefs and values. Top management's strong commitment to this view should be unequivocally communicated throughout the organization. A practical approach which works, if consistently followed, is to reward managers for developing their subordinates. Managers, like their subordinates, do respond to rewards and punishments. It often happens that managers' efforts in employee development are not only not rewarded but are, in fact, penalized. For example, when managers take seriously their responsibilities as coach and develop their employees, they often find a high turnover of their well-trained employees through transfer to better positions in other departments. Nevertheless, managers are still held responsible for meeting departmental goals although they now have to function with new inexperienced employees. With this experience, it is unlikely that these managers will continue to invest, as before, the needed time and effort in employee development. Hence, rewarding managers for employee development is the third precondition for successful management of employee performance. Implicit in this condition are the concomitant conditions that managers are trained with the necessary skills in using the system of performance management.

It is important to recognize at this stage that while the effectiveness of the performance management process depends upon the preconditions just discussed, the success of the organization's efforts both to create the necessary preconditions and to implement the process will, in the final analysis, hinge on the organizational climate and internal work culture. In an extensive study of performance appraisal practices Lawler *et al.* (1984) found that when the organizational climate was one of high trust, support, and openness it had a significant positive impact on the performance appraisal process. In a supportive and trusting climate, senior managers, through personal examples, can transmit the appropriate appraisal behaviour which can then be emulated by managers at all levels in the organization.

Lawler's findings also suggest that in performance appraisal it is more fruitful to emphasize, in addition to the appraisal process, the organizational culture that influences the process. Top management will be seen as taking performance appraisal seriously if they spend the time and effort to fit it explicitly to the prevailing culture (norms, values, beliefs) and human resource strategies of the organization. The question of cultural 'fit' is most vital. The success of programmes, techniques, and processes, particularly those relating to the social system, presupposes an internal work culture whose norms, beliefs, and values are conducive to and supportive of the required attitudes and behaviours. Programmes that are highly successful in the industrialized developed countries can, and often do, fail in the developing countries not because of any deficiency in or unsuitability of the programme but because these ready-made programmes were uncritically adopted without any regard to their congruence with the internal work culture.

The performance management programme is indeed a powerful tool for organizational effectiveness in developing countries as well. However, it is necessary to identify the critical features of the work culture in developing countries which facilitate or hinder many organizations from realizing the full benefits of the performance appraisal process. What are these cultural constraints? How can they be overcome? These important questions are addressed in the next section.

Culture and its role in performance management

In discussing the role of cultural variables in effective performance management, we shall explore the characteristics of the socio-cultural environment and the work culture of organizations as discussed in Chapter One. Socio-cultural norms, values, and belief systems of developing countries are likely to influence the appraisal process, positively or negatively. Of course, it is not desirable, even if it were feasible, nor necessary for an organization to resort to policies and practices which would coerce the employees into giving up their deeply held cultural values and beliefs. We shall, instead, propose organizational interventions which, through their synchronization with the employees' cultural beliefs and values, facilitate the performance management process.

The socio-cultural environment in developing countries is characterized by a relatively high uncertainty avoidance, low individualism, high power distance, low masculinity, and low abstractive thinking (see Chapter One). Each of these cultural dimensions represents a set of underlying beliefs and assumptions of people which they carry with them when they join an organization. These belief systems of organizational members, in turn, influence the internal work culture. Thus the employees' cultural baggage eventually transforms into the dominant work culture of the organization. For illustrative purposes, the role of cultural variables will be discussed by reference to organizations in India.

The relatively high 'uncertainty avoidance', the first characteristic of the Indian socio-cultural environment, involves the unwillingness of employees to take personal initiatives on the job since such initiatives are neither encouraged nor rewarded within organizations. Employees are dependent on the authority structures and develop an external orientation, i.e. a belief that the external environment controls them rather than that they control their environment. During early socialization, whether at home or at school, achievements are taken for granted and go unrewarded, but mistakes are invariably singled out for special attention. Any attempt to try something new is not only not supported but is viewed with great pessimism and scepticism which soon discourages future attempts. As a consequence, the upbringing which promotes the passive and almost unquestioning acceptance of one's lot in life eventually leads to fatalism – the *chalega* type syndrome (see Chapter Eleven). Such an attitude is not conducive to risk-taking, to meeting challenges, and to striving towards excellence. It is obviously an obstacle to effective performance management which requires employees who are open to and participate in the setting of challenging and difficult goals.

The second characteristic, relatively low individualism, is inevitable in the highly collectivistic nature of Indian social institutions. The hierarchical structures in almost every social institution lose no opportunity to remind individuals that unconditional obedience to authority is a virtue. The individual derives his identity as a member of a family, a caste, a community, whose norms and values take precedence over those of the individual. This group identity is zealously protected often with extreme social sanctions against any member whose thought and actions conflict with the group norms and values. Hence, the family, caste, community dominate the individual. Unlike in Western cultures, work to the individual is not an act of self-fulfilment or self-expression, but is primarily a means to maintain his family and to provide for the well-being of aged parents, spouse, and children. Therefore, when job tasks are performed, the individual's priority and concern is not the accomplishment of job objectives as such, or the fulfilment of the contractual obligations that arise from the fact of employment. What are more salient to the individuals are the personalized relationships generated by the job. They work for their superiors, friends, and relatives rather than for accomplishing the task or organizational goals under contractual obligations. It is easy to see the dysfunctional effects of collectivism on the performance management process which relies for its success on the individual's being motivated by the personal sense of task accomplishment and, of course, the rewards that accompany it.

The relatively high power distance, the third characteristic of the Indian socio-cultural environment, is also inevitable from the hierarchical authority structures which pervade most social institutions. As discussed earlier, the obedience is demanded not on the basis of any rational argument or thesis but simply by virtue of the authority of the position or status. In fact, the logic seems to be that if the reason for an order or command was explained, then such explanation would be misconstrued by the individual as a sign of weakness on the part of the superior. An individual brought up in such authority structures will tend to regard his manager as a 'whimp' if he fails to exercise his authority. He will have difficulty in seeing his manager as a partner and in developing the relationship of joint problem-solving so essential to successful performance management. Furthermore, the attachment to groups such as one's caste or community tends to arouse doubts of equitable treatment by the supervisor who belongs to a different caste or community. The mistrust and suspicion generated by caste and communal affiliations seriously jeopardize the appraisal process.

The fourth characteristic, relatively low masculinity, refers to the extent that the individual's behaviour is driven by feelings; low masculinity denotes that feelings play a dominant role in decision making and in relationships. In an organizational setting, the behaviour of members low in masculinity will be driven by feelings rather than task considerations. The attachment to family, caste, and community, discussed earlier, also operates to produce this characteristic. The highly developed family-centred work ethic does create a sense of duty to work, but this duty assumes meaning and urgency only as a way to fulfilling one's duty to the family, caste, or community (see Chapter Eleven). Satisfaction of affiliative needs takes precedence over satisfaction derived from achieving work objectives. Performing socially approved duties in the interpersonal contexts, again, takes precedence over duties arising from contractual obligations.

The predominance of feelings and interpersonal considerations, then, places participants at a disadvantage in the performance management process which demands a relatively objective and rational focus on job tasks and goals, and on action plans to meet them. Considerable interpersonal relations are involved in the process as participants jointly define job objectives, set performance expectations and evaluation measures, determine resources needed in terms of time, materials, authority, training, etc., and establish feedback mechanisms. However, the low masculinity characteristic could contaminate the interpersonal process as work relationships are personalized rather than contractual and as the feedback provided is misconstrued as attacks on the person rather than on the behaviours observed. Furthermore, the evaluation of performance will always be problematic because the worker believes that expressions of affection and personal loyalty to the superior (just like the loyalty to the head of the joint family) are more important and expected than efficient and effective contributions to achieve job objectives.

The last characteristic, relatively low abstractive thinking, highlights the ambivalence of the values of the Indian worker. Low abstractive thinking denotes that, in their approach to the job, the workers are not guided by a work ethic relevant and appropriate to the job or by abstract principles governing their job behaviours. Instead, their job behaviours are very much determined by the immediate context that is salient to them (high associative thinking). Thus their behaviours reflect a sense of always living in the present, and since the 'present' is constantly changing, employees who are high on associative thinking (i.e. low abstractive thinking) will prove to be highly unpredictable as far as the required job behaviours are concerned. The following two incidents cited by Tandon (in Nigam 1984) illustrate the operation of this cultural variable:

An aircraft component manufacturer had assigned to its most

competent machinist a three-day job that was most critical to the overhaul of an aircraft engine. In the midst of the operation, the machinist absents himself for four days without informing anyone. Queried on his return, he explains that he was responding to his uncle's request for help.

In a well-managed, modern plant in Bombay, 35% of the workers are invariably absent during April and May when production is at its peak. Reason? To assist their families in the villages in the usual chores before the monsoons.

Undoubtedly, the low abstractive thinking is incompatible with the performance management process which requires that employees abide by a specific set of guidelines or principles in the work place. Setting specific goals to be attained by specific time targets and developing specific action plans are all contrary to a lifestyle that does not emphasize future planning but prefers to handle jobs as they come without any thought to anticipating and preparing for likely future problems. Such an approach is ideally suited for 'management by crises' but utterly inadequate for performance management.

We have reviewed the impact of several cultural dimensions on the performance management process, but our focus has been primarily on the employees. In the next few paragraphs it would be useful to consider the impact of these dimensions on managers – their philosophy, beliefs, and practices as they relate to performance management. The characteristics of management values and the climate of beliefs stemming from the cultural dimensions in developed and developing countries are summarized in Chapter One. To avoid repetition, we shall focus only on some relevant characteristics and discuss their genesis and likely impact on performance management in the Indian context.

Indian organizations are often managed as closed systems that are barely responsive to environmental changes. The genesis for this can be attributed to the all-pervasive authoritarian structures which, along with the historic influences – pre-colonial and colonial times – have caused the evolution of a feudalistic temperament in many managers who regard their departments as petty fiefdoms. Of course, such an approach may not have a drastic effect on their business as long as they are in the seller's market, which seems to be the case for the larger organizations. But the feudalistic temperament of the managers discourages risk taking and entrepreneurial activities. Most organizations do not reward risk taking and entrepreneurship. The compensation is usually determined by considerations such as age, seniority, and rank, rather than by performance (Tandon 1982).

In family-owned and managed companies the professional managers, although designated as such, are in fact bureaucrats when one considers that the entrepreneurial decisions rest with the family, somewhat akin to the Government Ministry in relation to a public undertaking. Finally, the feudalistic temperament promotes the maintenance of the status quo, rather than the entrepreneurial spirit which is essential for any development effort.

Directly flowing from the feudal concept is the managers' concept of human nature as expressed by Theory X (McGregor 1960). The workers are viewed as lazy, steeped in the 'aram' culture, uninterested in work, and with limited creative potential. Since managers are persuaded that workers cannot be entrusted with responsibility, no attempt is made to enrich their jobs. On the contrary, workers are controlled by an elaborate system of rules, procedures, and regulations. The human relationships between managers and employees are characterized by both the authoritarian and paternalistic style of management. The manager is the father-figure of the joint family system and similarly demands and expects unquestioning obedience and loyalty from the workers. The notable difference is that in the joint family system the decision of the father is generally consistent with his view of the best interests of the family. In the organization, in contrast, seeking and maintaining personal status becomes the primary objective for which organizational interests can be sacrificed, because most managers provide personal rather than institutional leadership (McClelland 1975).

The decision-making process reflects the tradition-bound dogmatism of the social institutions. Accordingly, the test of organizational policies and procedures is not a rational consideration of their appropriateness, necessity, and validity but rather the simple fact that these policies and procedures have always existed – 'this is the way it has always been done here'. Tradition, then, establishes the major decision rule: 'Elders and seniors are always right.' In family-owned organizations, the deleterious effects of tradition are compounded by the practice of appointing a family member as head of the organization without any regard to the individual's competence, thereby creating a unique management style derisively referred to as 'management by chromosomes'. The owner justifies this approach by saying: 'Whom can I trust more than my sons, my kith and kin; surely not strangers?' (Nigam 1984: 22).

Despite the outward appearance of a tranquil solidarity, the joint family system is often a hot-bed of intrigue and scheming by different factions led by different uncles. This experience of groupism often gets transferred to organizations in the private sector but almost always in the public sector. One can almost describe the government undertaking as a gigantic joint-family whose feuding members seek security in their own group defined in terms of castes, regionalism, etc. Influenced by modern management thought and practices as a result of their exposure to multinational corporations, business schools, and management journals, managers today readily concede that merit, fairness, and justice in business operations are important values. They even develop policies to support these values but, by a strange twist of logic, they expect that family, caste, and communal considerations should prevail in decisions relating to tenders, contracts, and recruitment (Nigam 1984).

The administrative practices inherited from the colonial civil service have caused managers to evaluate decisions in the light of past precedents, which is appropriate for the maintenance of the status quo – the fundamental objective of the Indian Civil Service. But managers need to focus on the future, to be proactive, if they are to seize upon the opportunities likely to develop. The focus on the past makes them too rigid to respond to rapidly changing technology, product mix, competitors, and even the changing nature of their employees.

Finally, we need to consider certain norms that pervade management philosophy and beliefs. One such belief is the orientation of the organization based on some dogmatic sloganeering. The private sector is profit oriented, whereas the public sector is socially oriented. Therefore a manager who is competent in one sector cannot be competent in the other sector. In the public sector, profit is such a dirty word that in one government undertaking questions were raised when it made a profit. Of course, the Managing Director was never questioned in all the previous years when the organization suffered enormous losses (Nigam 1984). The extent of the sloganeering can be gauged from the practice in public sector organizations in the area of staffing, which is often based on 'status' than on 'need'. For example, it is not uncommon for a senior managerial position to be provided automatically, regardless of need, with a staff of a private secretary, a personal assistant, a typist-clerk, four peons, and a chauffeur. In bureaucratic parlance, this complement of staff is referred to as the 'sanctioned strength' (of employees) that is attached to a position. Perhaps this practice facilitates the budgeting process and may even be thought of by some politicians as a quick-fix to the unemployment problem. Nevertheless, such a practice suggests that employees are not looked upon as a vital resource but merely as some decorative accoutrement to the manager. This suggestion together with the belief that human beings have a fixed potential and are not malleable, which is frequently encountered among managers in developing countries (see Chapter One), would explain why no planned programmes or efforts are even considered, let alone initiated, to develop and fully tap the potential of the employees. The prevalence of these norms not only does not impel managers to develop their employees but, in fact, underscores the futility of any efforts in that direction. Consequently, the question of rewarding managers to develop their employees simply does not arise.

In summary, the management philosophy and climate of beliefs is characterized by the rigid maintenance of the status quo, heavy reliance on bureaucratic practices, ecosystem distrust, narrow in-groups, high power distance to hang on to one's own resources, and short-term gain perspectives. Many of these characteristics tend to have a negative impact on the performance management process and also are unfavourable to creating in the organization the preconditions necessary for it.

Organizational intervention to ensure cultural fit

Several cultural constraints that hinder the effective implementation of the performance management process have been identified in the previous discussion. We now propose a *modus operandi* for each step of the performance management process to ensure that it removes these constraints and builds upon those cultural beliefs and values which have the potential to facilitate that step of the process. In developing these proposals, we briefly review the major activities of each phase of the process, indicate the specific manner of conducting these activities, and discuss the underlying rationale, as summarized in Table 13.1. We shall conclude this section by considering the training and development that will be necessary to initiate and effectively sustain the proposed interventions.

The first step of the performance management process is definition of the job. The attitude and behaviour of managers are critical at this stage because it offers them the opportunity not only to provide direction and establish expectations but also to set the tone for the manager–subordinate relationship and, generally, to create the climate in which these activities will be conducted.

It is the paramount responsibility of managers to define the job, i.e. what needs to be done, as clearly and unambiguously as possible for their employees. In a work culture characterized by 'uncertainty avoidance', managers are not naturally inclined to fulfil this responsibility. Managers are reluctant to spell out objectives for their subordinates in specific terms, sometimes because they themselves have not received clear-cut objectives from their superiors. At other times, they are apprehensive that such a definition would make them

Table 13.1 Suggested managerial conduct (attitudes and behaviours) during the performance management process to overcome inhibiting effects of the work culture

Process steps	*Uncertainty avoidance*	*High power distance*	*Low masculinity*	*Low abstractive thinking*	*Low individualism*
			Cultural variables		
Job definition	The manager clarifies departmental and job objectives in specific measurable terms	The manager establishes his subordinates' job objectives	Objectives: meeting needs of individual, organization, community; personal duty rather than contractual obligation		
Establishing performance standards	The manager sets difficult, but attainable, goals (according to competence)	The manager builds upon subordinate trust and acceptance of job content	Performance goals meet the above criteria	Performance goals are specific and clear and involve observable job behaviours	The process used promotes employees' belief in their capabilities
Monitoring the performance	The manager identifies controllable factors and empowers the employee to focus on these in attaining job objectives	The manager adopts the role of coach and mentor to his subordinates	The manager highlights the impact of performance (positive and negative) on people inside/outside organization	The discussion between the manager and the subordinate focuses on behaviours in the light of agreed performance goals	The manager provides constructive feedback geared to performance improvement and the individual's development
Formal appraisal review	In summative evaluation, the manager recognizes uncontrollable factors which impeded performance	The manager continues his role of coach and mentor	The manager recognizes and rewards successful performance at organization's community events	The manager and the subordinate establish specific clear performance plans for following year	The manager formulates specific action plans for employee development and removal of contextual obstacles to good performance

Note: To ensure the effectiveness of the activities in each phase of the process, the manager must adopt the nurturant-task leadership style.

accountable for their decisions should these turn out to be incorrect. The high tendency to be risk averse seems to pervade all levels of the organization. However, the 'high power distance' characteristic of the culture underscores the significance of this managerial responsibility because the employees expect it of their managers. But managers should recognize that, because of the 'low masculinity' characteristic, the employees expect the job to be defined not as a set of contractual obligations but rather as a personalized relationship. In other words, employees perform tasks not because these are contractually prescribed in a job description but because they see it as fulfilling a personal obligation to the manager – out of a sense of personal duty towards their superior.

How can managers meet the challenge posed by these conflicting demands? First and foremost, they should clarify in their own mind the objectives of their unit in relation to the overall objectives of the organization. They then take a good hard look at each job to determine what its contribution ought to be to fulfilling the unit's objectives. Second, the job objectives are communicated to the employees in such a manner that they are seen by the employees as an opportunity to fulfil the duties arising from their work relationships with the manager and colleagues, inside and outside the work unit. This can be achieved by expressing the job objectives as meeting the needs of the user of the product or service which results from the job. At the same time, the job objectives are also placed in the broader organizational context to encourage the employees to become aware and appreciate the potential of their jobs to contribute to organizational goals which, ultimately, impact on the well-being of not only the organization but also the larger external community, be it the neighbourhood, region, or country. It is also desirable to include in this picture the organization's contribution, if any, to a body of knowledge in a specific discipline or expertise in some area of technology or management.

Defining the job in terms of its specific context tied to the broader organizational context will increase task identity and significance (Hackman and Oldham 1980) because the employee now sees his job as an opportunity to fulfil his obligatory duty towards people and thereby to satisfy the 'relationship or people orientation' which is perceived to be more salient and important than the mere fulfilment of contractual obligations. The management style of the supervisor plays a crucial role in the success of the interventions being discussed. Firm structured direction, consistent with the 'high power distance' characteristic of the work culture, can and ought to be tempered by a nurturant-task leadership style (see Sinha 1980 and also Chapter Fourteen) which draws upon familial and cultural values like affection, dependence, and the need for a personalized and mutually supportive relationship. The dependence of the employee upon the supervisors is not a parasitic dependence. Rather, it is more akin to the dependence of the chela on the guru, which is based on trust and has the potential of being 'nurtured' into a 'dependable' relationship (Sinha 1986). Like the chela, the employees trust the manager, at least initially, and are receptive to any effort by the manager which enhances their belief in personal efficacy – that they are able to perform the job tasks. When managers communicate the job objectives clearly, leaving no room for role ambiguity or role conflict, they have eliminated a contextual factor which has been found to lower the self-efficacy belief of the employee (Conger and Kanungo 1988). A clear job definition, then, will contribute to the employee's belief in internal control which will be fostered and reinforced even more in subsequent phases of the process.

The second step of the performance management process, establishing performance standards, calls for a considerably greater involvement by the employee in the process, particularly the goal-setting process. Employee participation in setting specific and difficult goals is essential if goal setting is to improve performance (Locke and Latham 1984). Several characteristics of the work culture operate against this process: 'high uncertainty avoidance' inhibits employees from risk taking; 'low masculinity' sees goals in terms of people orientation and not as contractual obligations; 'low abstractive thinking' is not conducive to norms that emphasize planning such as setting specific goals, target dates, and action plans; 'low individualism' does not give the individual a personal sense of task accomplishment.

Although the goal-setting process appears to founder on the rocky obstacles of the work culture, yet the process offers managers committed to nurturant-task leadership an opportunity to help their employees, who are dependent on them, to cope with the demands of the job. Building upon the employee trust and acceptance of the job content and its organizational context, developed in the previous step, the managers will continue their efforts in empowering the employee. Specifically, their role in goal setting will be to propose goals that meet job objectives but which initially are sufficiently small and within the existing competencies of the subordinates to be executed successfully (Beer 1980). As the employee experiences success, tasks with gradually increasing complexity and responsibility are assigned, which makes the employee feel more capable. The manager can also point to the successful performance of coworkers with similar skills, qualifications, and experience. Such vicarious experiences do serve to increase the employees' belief in their capabilities (Bennis and

Nanus 1985; Bandura 1986). Words of encouragement and similar forms of social persuasion that the employees can perform are also likely to enhance their belief in their abilities (Conger and Kanungo 1988; Bandura 1986). However, the effect of both vicarious experience and verbal persuasion in strengthening the individuals' belief in their self-efficacy are likely to be weaker than that resulting from the individuals' own task accomplishments (Conger and Kanungo 1988). Throughout the process the employee is assured of all resources and support necessary to achieve the goals. The process of setting goals that are specific, appropriate, and difficult, but within the individual's level of competence, in an atmosphere of trust and support, both personal and organizational, reduces uncertainty avoidance, fosters a greater sense of internal control, and sets the stage for the individual to experience a personal sense of task accomplishment which will reduce the negative effects of low individualism. The relationship and group orientation will be met by highlighting the connection between the goals and unit's objectives, and the impact on the department if the goals are not attained.

The third step, monitoring the performance, makes considerable demands, primarily on the manager's skills in giving feedback and coaching the employees. During feedback the manager is perceived as a 'judge', and during coaching as a 'friend, philosopher, and guide'. Balancing these conflicting roles is enough to test the mettle of any manager. But it does seem to be a formidable task in a work culture whose characteristics, particularly the high power distance, are not exactly supportive of the feedback and coaching that are so crucial to the success of the process. A special effort by the managers, entirely at their own initiative, is absolutely mandatory. The nature of the effort is, in fact, a continuation of the nurturant-task leadership prescribed for the entire process.

The subject matter for the feedback will be the specific observed behaviours viewed in the light of the agreed behavioural objectives. However, an exclusive focus on past behaviour could degenerate into a sterile exercise in fault-finding. As the variances between the targeted goals and actual results are noted, the focus should shift immediately to a discussion of what the employee can do and how the manager can assist the employee to attain the job objectives. These discussions will identify the causal factors that are controllable and uncontrollable, and will zero in on the controllable factors to determine the additional efforts and actions that are needed, such as training in problem-solving, technical assistance, information, role clarity, adequate resources, elimination of dysfunctional policies and procedures, etc. Through the positive, encouraging, and constructive tone of these discussions, managers will convincingly demonstrate to their employees their full confidence in the employees' competence to perform at the organizationally required level. According to Bandura (1986: 400), 'people who are persuaded verbally that they possess the capabilities to master given tasks are likely to mobilize greater sustained effort than if they harbor self-doubts and dwell on personal deficiencies when difficulties arise'. Furthermore, the employees' personal competence beliefs are also affected by their emotional arousal state – depression and self-doubt – which can be quite high during feedback sessions when performance is below target. The negative effects of aversive beliefs can be reduced if the manager brings into the discussion external and unstable factors such as task difficulty, inadequate support systems, unforeseen factors, etc. which also contributed to the inadequate performance (Weiner 1985).

Such an on-going dialogue, which provides emotional support and creates a supportive and trusting atmosphere, removes the need for the employee to adopt a 'defensive' posture and is very effective in strengthening the self-efficacy beliefs which, in turn, help to reduce the negative effects of high power distance. Regular periodic feedback will increase the employees' personal sense of task accomplishment and reinforce their belief in internal control. The continuing focus on job objectives and their impact on departmental and organizational goals will satisfy the relationship or people orientation and, at the same time, promote abstractive thinking.

The last step of the process, formal appraisal review, assesses the performance but also identifies the obstacles to good performance. At this stage, the thrust of the manager–employee dialogue is to evaluate the results of the efforts at the end of one time period in order to develop, for the next time period, action plans which will build on the experience of the past.

The characteristics of the work culture, which act as inhibitors in the previous steps, will continue to influence the efforts in this step as well, but, we hope, to a much lesser degree because of the manager's efforts to build upon the positive potential of the cultural beliefs and values of the employees. Thus, the adoption and implementation of the nurturant-task leadership style and process throughout the previous phases would have enhanced abstractive thinking by its focus on performance objectives; reduced uncertainty avoidance by providing specific direction in terms of achievable job objectives, agreed performance standards, and problem-resolution orientation; reduced power distance by its nurturant, supportive, and trusting climate; promoted the relationship or people orientation by placing job objectives in a personalized context, as a personal contribution/obligation to the manager, the end-user of the job's products/services, the organization, and the community-at-large; and enhanced social achievement orientation (Mehta 1978) by its empowering strategies which strengthened the employee's beliefs in self-efficacy and provided opportunities to experience significant personal accomplishment for the collective good.

In the continuing dialogue of the previous phases, both the manager and the employee would have had opportunities to review performance and work towards the removal of obstacles to good performance. The major concern in the last step is to record the summative evaluation of the performance, to propose appropriate development measures, and to initiate plans to identify and remove the remaining obstacles to good performance. Whatever the appraisal instrument used, the rating of personal traits should be avoided, unless these traits are essential for job performance, because their use needlessly creates an ego-defensive orientation and takes the focus away from job behaviours that are critical to performance. Also, a needless obsession with personal traits will be contrary to the strategies proposed in the previous phases to re-orient the employee to think and function in terms of goals and behaviours that are job related, and to create a trusting and supportive climate necessary to effective performance management.

An element that is pivotal to improved employee performance is the individual's belief in his self-efficacy, a sense of personal mastery – the 'can do' attitude. The recording of the performance, then, should ensure that the employee's self-efficacy belief is not damaged. If the employee, who has the capacity to perform at a given level, puts in a performance below that level, then both facts, along with an agreed explanation for the failure, should be recorded, especially in situations where the goals are expressed in terms of productivity measures. For example, if the deadline was not met by an employee the manager could still reinforce the self-efficacy belief by recording: 'Although you missed the deadline, I am pleased at the tremendous effort you put into the project. As discussed, paying attention to the following [*specific remedial action*] will ensure your success the next time.' One cannot overemphasize the need for the manager and employee to come to an agreed understanding of the performance as well as of the remedial/development plans to improve performance. Such an understanding reflects a union of purpose and effort between the manager and the employee, and it is greatly facilitated by the various strategies proposed in each phase.

In identifying the obstacles to good performance, the manager should also look at the contextual factors: organization, supervisory style, reward systems, and job design. These factors, in addition to their potential to impact on the entire performance management process, have been found to be particularly potent in affecting the self-efficacy beliefs of the employees (Conger and Kanungo 1988). In terms of organizational factors, managers should consider whether their departments are experiencing major changes or transitions brought on, for example, by significant technological changes which seriously affect job definition and role clarity and may require skill levels beyond existing competencies. A supervisory style other than the nurturant-task leadership is not conducive to overcoming the negative effects of the work culture. The reward system should provide rewards that are valued by employees and should be tied to competence and to the performance of behaviours that meet job objectives. The fairness of the system needs to be probed to ensure that ingratiating and/or dysfunctional behaviours are not rewarded. Also, when the job objectives are met, this accomplishment should be appropriately recognized at special events to which family members are invited, and in company publications. In the area of job design, the supervisor should take care to see whether role ambiguity, role conflict, and role overload are present.

Preparing for performance management

In this section we propose some initiatives which organizations in developing countries can take to prepare their managers and employees for the installation and implementation of the performance management programme.

The managers must function as nurturant-task leaders for the entire duration of the performance management process and must be provided with the opportunities, resources, and organizational support to develop the attitudes, behaviours, and interpersonal skills (e.g. feedback, coaching, and empowerment) needed for their formation and growth as nurturant-task leaders. As noted previously, managers are called upon to be mentor and coach to their employees. In the Indian context, for example, these roles are vividly illustrated by the guru–chela relationship. The chela is socialized to look up to his guru for wisdom, direction, and reassurance. The guru, on the other hand, is acutely conscious of his responsibility to develop his disciple gradually into an autonomous person – a vital link in the conservation and transmission of the spiritual heritage. The guru humbly acknowledges that he is not the source of wisdom but rather an instrument, often an imperfect one, of the Almighty. Therefore, in his relationship with the chela, the guru does not presume to have all the answers but invites the chela to ponder, together with him, the eternal verities. Through this empowerment process, the Indian sages and gurus, down the centuries, have been transforming the almost helpless, ignorant, and totally dependent disciples into confident independent teachers in their own right, deeply steeped in the ancient wisdom, lore, and traditions.

Managers have a similar task ahead of them – to empower their employees who are socialized to be dependent upon them and, indeed, expect from them direction, guidance, and support. The specific attitudes and activities required of the manager have been discussed, illustrated, and explained at each step of the performance management process. The actual practice of the proposed activities will, undoubtedly, enhance the manager's facility and skills. Nevertheless, formal training programmes are necessary for the development and maintenance of these skills.

A suggested content of the programme would be as follows.

(1) An understanding of
the role of the performance management process in achieving job objectives; and
the rationale underlying the attitudes, activities, and behaviours of each phase of the process
(2) Individual/group tasks and activities designed to improve and enhance interpersonal communication – specifically the following skills.

Active listening: a manager with this skill 'actively tries to grasp the facts and the feelings in what he hears, and he tries, by his listening, to help the speaker work out his own problems' (Rodgers and Farson 1989: 133). Of course, active listening does not preclude managers from adopting a directive role when they perceive that the employee is, in fact, looking for direction.

Feedback: it helps employees consider changing their behaviour to meet job objectives, provided that the feedback is descriptive rather than evaluative, specific rather than general, well-timed, directed towards behaviour which the employees can do something about, and is given in a trusting and supportive atmosphere (Mill 1989).

Empowerment: an empowering manager through a variety of strategies and techniques creates conditions which develop and enhance the employee's belief in personal efficacy and, as a consequence, increase his motivation for task accomplishment. Empowerment also involves the removal of conditions which lead to the employee's experiencing a sense of powerlessness with its consequence of reducing his motivation for task accomplishment (Conger and Kanungo 1988).

(3) Reading and formal education in behavioural sciences. The former is most effective when the concepts and processes dealt with in the material are discussed with peers in an attempt to develop practical applications. Formal education could take the form of university extension programmes or seminars.

The thrust of the training programmes is to instil in the managers an awareness of their responsibility to *manage* the performance of their employees and to equip them with the skills they need to increase the employees' self-efficacy beliefs that they can, in fact, perform the objectives of their jobs.

The training of employees would be part of the organization's socialization programme with a focus on three areas:

(1) technical training to assist in a better performance of current job tasks;
(2) education in organizational policies and procedures;
(3) induction into the organizational culture which considers all employees as members of a family engaged in providing mutual support and assistance in order that the organization can fulfil its obligations to its customers and the larger community.

The performance orientation of the organizational culture can also be promoted through the various socio-religious festival events that are closely associated with the life of organizational members in developing countries. For example, in India, most organizations celebrate the Ganesh or Durga Pooja festivities which also include the participation of employees' families. These events are ideal forums for praise and encouragement of exceptional performance by individuals, groups, and departments. Such recognition takes on added significance when it is done in the presence of family members and becomes a powerful impetus which promotes organizational cohesiveness and loyalty and contributes to strengthening the self-efficacy beliefs of employees through both enactive attainment and the vicarious experiences of observing the job successes of coworkers.

Conclusion

In every developing country, there is a great desire to share in the benefits which science and technology can bring. However, in the final analysis, all plans and resources committed to the realization of these hopes and aspirations will only be successful to the extent that each organization meets its objectives. In practical terms, the country's development hinges on the organization effectively managing its human resources which, in turn, highlights the managers' responsibility to manage the performance of their employees, consistent with the job objectives and the overall goals of the organization.

In this chapter we have discussed the entire performance management process, providing at each step of the process the theoretical support for the 'know-how' and illustrations of specific actions required by both the manager and the subordinates. We recognize that the characteristics of the work culture in developing countries are likely either to facilitate or inhibit the implementation of the process. Therefore, we have identified these characteristics and have proposed concrete organizational interventions to take advantage of the 'facilitators' and to overcome the debilitating effects of the 'inhibitors'. The interventions proposed are specific not only for each phase of the process but also for the formation (training and development) of both managers and employees to prepare them adequately to implement the process.

In our discussion, we have consciously stayed away from using the word 'programme' to describe the performance management process. The modern connotation of 'programme' suggests a beginning and an end, a time duration that is short, and often denotes the quality of a 'fad' that soon disappears like the morning mist at the first rays of the rising sun. We see performance management to be inextricably tied to the manager's function to 'manage' his employees, as a vehicle to ensure the attainment of the departmental objectives. We see performance management as an opportunity for managers and employees to be engaged in a partnership of purpose, direction, and effort as they strive to fulfil both personal and organizational objectives. Finally, we do not see performance management as a set of simple, easy, and uncomplicated routines. Instead, we see a set of challenging tasks which demand considerable intellectual, emotional, and physical energy as both managers and employees, at *all* levels (obviously including top management as well), bring to bear on the fulfilment of these tasks their time, talent, and skills, and, above all, their total commitment and dedication. It is not easy ... but the numerous benefits to employees and the organization make the effort worthwhile.

References

Bandura, A. (1986) *Social Foundation of Thought and Action: A Social-cognitive View*, Englewood Cliffs, NJ: Prentice-Hall.
Beer, M. (1980) *Organizational Change and Development*, Santa Monica, CA: Goodyear.

Bennis, W. and Nanus, B. (1985) *Leaders*, New York: Harper & Row.

Conger, J. A. and Kanungo, R. N. (1988) 'The empowerment process: integrating theory and practice', *Academy of Management Journal* 13: 471–82.

Hackman, J. R. and Oldham, G. R. (1980) *Work Redesign*, Toronto: Addison-Wesley.

Kanungo, R. N. (1986) 'Productivity, satisfaction and involvement: a brief note on some conceptual issues', *International Journal of Manpower* 7: 8–12.

Kanungo, R. N. and Mendonca, M. (1988) 'Evaluating employee compensation', *California Management Review*, Fall: 23–39.

Kanungo, R. N. and Misra, S. (1985) 'Declining work motivation in India', *Indian Management*, May: 1–14.

Lawler, E. E. (1977) 'Reward systems', in J. R. Hackman and J. L. Shuttle (eds) *Improving Life at Work*, Santa Monica, CA: Goodyear.

Lawler III, E. E., Mohrman, A. M., and Resnick, S. M. (1984) 'Performance appraisal revisited', *Organizational Dynamics*, Summer: 20–35.

Locke, E. A. and Bryan, J. F. (1968) 'Goal-setting as a determinant of the effect of knowledge of score on performance', *American Journal of Psychology* 81: 398–406.

Locke, E. A. and Latham, G. P. (1984) *Goal-setting: A Motivational Technique That Works!*, Englewood Cliffs, NJ: Prentice-Hall.

Locke, E. A., Shaw, K. N., Saari, L. M., and Latham, G. P. (1981) 'Goal-setting and task performance: 1969–1980', *Psychological Bulletin* 90: 125–52.

McClelland, D. C. (1975) *Power: The Inner Experience*, New York: Irvington.

McGregor, D. (1960) *The Human Side of Enterprise*, New York: McGraw-Hill.

Mehta, P. (1978) 'Work motivation in Indian public sector: some conceptualization', presented at the Seminar on Alienation, Efficacy, Motivation and Employee Participation, National Labor Institute, New Delhi, 17–18 March.

Mill, C. R. (1989) 'Feedback: the art of giving and receiving help', in R. N. Kanungo and A. M. Jaeger (eds) *Introduction to Organizational Behavior: Selected Readings*, 2nd edn, pp. 125–6, Littleton, MA: Copley Publishing Group.

Nigam, R. K. (ed.) (1984) *The Management Philosophy of Prakash Tandon: Reflections on General Management Issues and Problems of the Public Sector*, New Delhi: Documentation Centre for Corporate and Business Policy Research.

Rogers, C. and Farson, R. E. (1989) 'Active listening', in R. N. Kanungo and A. M. Jaeger (eds) *Introduction to Organizational Behavior: Selected Readings*, 2nd edn, pp. 127–39, Littleton, MA: Copley Publishing Group.

Sinha, D. (1986) *Psychology in a Third World Country: The Indian Experience*, New Delhi: Sage.

Sinha, J. B. P. (1980) *The Nurturant-Task Leader*, New Delhi: Concept.
Tandon, P. (1982) 'Hierarchical structure and attitudes toward risk in state-owned enterprises', in L. P. Jones (ed.) *Public Enterprise in Less-developed Countries*, Cambridge: Cambridge University Press.
Weiner, B. (1985) 'An attributional theory of achievement motivation and emotion', *Psychological Review* 92: 548–73.

Chapter fourteen

A model of effective leadership styles in India

Jai B. P. Sinha

The model

Although it is generally agreed that the effectiveness of a leadership style is contingent on both task and subordinate's characteristics, the former has been found to be less crucial than the latter (Hassan 1985). India has a collectivistic culture (Hofstede 1980) where maintaining relationships is more important than task accomplishment (Kakar 1978). Hence, the nature of the superior–subordinate relationship is presumed to have a direct bearing on the effectiveness of leadership styles. There are three specific expectations of subordinates which are reported to be pertinent:

(1) a preference for a personalized over a contractual relationship with the leader (Dayal 1976);
(2) a tendency to depend on a leader for guidance, direction, and support (Sinha 1970); and
(3) a willingness to accept the superior status of the leader, i.e. a preference to work in a superior–subordinate rather than a peer relationship (Kothari 1970).

Not all subordinates in Indian organizations share these preferences and expectations. Yet those who do work more effectively under a nurturant-task (NT) leader (Sinha 1980, 1984). A nurturant leader 'cares for his subordinates, shows affection, takes personal interest in their well being, and above all is committed to their growth' (Sinha 1980: 55). In order to be effective, however, he makes his nurturance contingent on the subordinate's task accomplishment. He structures his and his subordinates' roles in such a way that the subordinates understand and accept the goals and the normative structure of the group and develop commitment to them. The nurturant-task leader guides and directs them to work hard and to maintain a high level of productivity. Those who do meet his expectations are reinforced by

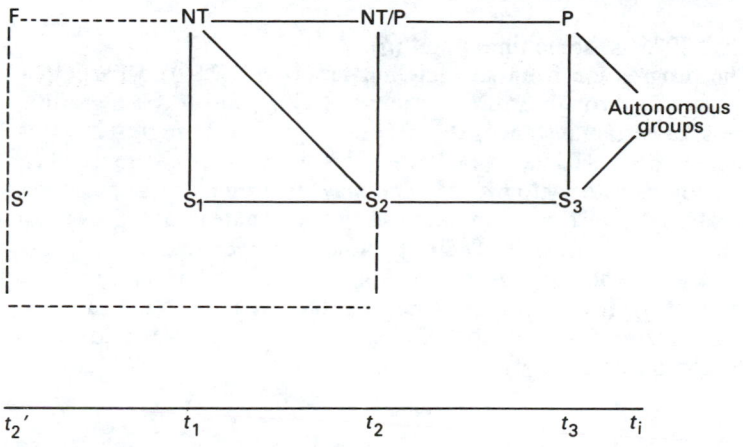

Figure 14.1   Model of effective leadership style

Note: S, subordinate; F, authoritarian; NT, nurturant-task; NT/P, combination of nurturant-task and participative; P, participative; *t*, time point. Solid lines indicate positive nature/direction of relationship, and broken lines indicate negative nature/direction of relationship.

nurturance. In the process, there develops a relationship of understanding, warmth, and interdependence, leading to higher productivity and better growth of both the subordinates and the leader.

Over a time period, the nature of relationship changes (Figure 14.1). Initially (at t_1) the subordinates (S_1) depend heavily on the leader not only for guidance and direction but also for support and encouragement. But as they work hard, they develop self-confidence through gaining experience in handling tasks and higher levels of skill. They start enjoying hard work without continuous patting on the back. They need less direction and guidance. They are in a position to assume responsibility and enjoy their independence. Instead of dependence they need more autonomy and participation in decision making (S_2 at t_2). If the leader responds to this altered level of skill and expectations of the subordinates by reducing his close direction but retaining warmth and personal care, and by delegating more responsibility and autonomy but keeping an eye on their performance (nt/p at t_2), the subordinates feel more encouraged and involved and therefore make greater efforts to increase productivity. The growth and work involvement in the subordinates and the corresponding shift in the leader are postulated to let the subordinates S_3 become fully prepared for participation to which the leader might respond by being participative (P at t_3). There is a possibility, although still distant, that they might even create an autonomous group

253

(Herbst 1976) at some time point (t_i).

The progression from strongly nurturant-task (NT) to participative style (P) through a mix of the two (*NT/P*) has to be a gradual process. In certain instances the process may become regressive. It is possible that an NT leader, because of his successful experience at t_1, may become fixated into his style and may insist on closer supervision and paternal affection even when the subordinates have grown up and do not relish his style. Their resentment may be taken as a threat by the leader who might regress towards an authoritarian (F) stance (Nandy 1975). If he does, he would disrupt the interaction process, and all – the leader, the subordinates, and the group – would suffer (F–S' combination at t_2').

The empirical evidence

Over forty field and experimental studies on leadership in Indian organizations have been conducted by Sinha, his associates, and several other researchers (see Sinha 1980, 1984). Further studies on leadership are in progress in India that attempt either (a) to map the overlaps or distinctiveness of various leadership constructs such as the authoritarian, nurturant-task, and participative styles, and initiating structure versus consideration, task versus people orientations, or (b) to test the model presented earlier in a contingency framework. The evidence by and large supports the model and shows its usefulness in work organizations. A brief review of some of the findings reported earlier (Sinha 1980, 1984) and some new findings are presented in this chapter.

Relationship between the styles

Some scholars (e.g. Nandy 1976) seemed to believe that any emphasis on performance is a reflection of secondary authoritarianism and that an authoritarian leader is likely to show affection and protectiveness under favourable conditions. By implication, the nurturant-task style is a façade of an authoritarian leader and it might wear off under stressful conditions.

Sinha (1980) argued that while authoritarian and nurturant-task styles may share a preference for structure in leader–subordinate relationships, they do differ in emphasis on *self* versus *people* and *task* orientations. An authoritarian leader is essentially self-oriented whereas the nurturant-task leader is primarily concerned with his subordinates and their performance. Two studies (Sinha 1980: 171–

92) were conducted to examine the contention. In both studies a group leader was instructed to behave with his subordinates in authoritarian, nurturant-task, or participative manner. The subsequent ratings by the group members, who were blind to the experimental manipulations, perceived the nurturant-task leaders as similar to the authoritarian leaders on being strict, in pushing their ideas through, and in controlling the member's ideas and activities. The nurturant-task leaders, however, were also close to the participative leaders in encouraging the members to contribute to the group task for which they were given due credit. The most striking finding contrasting the three leadership styles was that participative leaders were perceived as being interested in group members' participation, authoritarian leaders in maintaining their leadership, and the nurturant-task leaders in getting work done.

A number of studies (Sinha 1980, 1984; Ansari 1987; Sinha *et al.* 1988), disclosed moderate to very high correlations between nurturant-task and participative styles and moderately positive to negative correlations between nurturant-task and authoritarian styles. In almost all cases the inter-style correlations were smaller than the reliability coefficients indicating that the styles indeed manifested distinct, although overlapping, configurations of leadership acts. The overlap between the nurturant-task and participative styles was taken to argue that both are people oriented, except that the former is more paternal than fraternal in its flavour.

Sinha and Sinha (1984) also examined the shift in authoritarian, nurturant-task, and participative leadership under non-stressful to stressful conditions. The findings revealed that while the participative style was weakened and the authoritarian style strengthened under the stressful conditions, the nurturant style remained more or less the same. Because the three styles are postulated to reflect a broad developmental continuum (Sinha 1980), the possibility of a regression in nurturant-task and participative styles under stressful conditions is not totally ruled out. However, such a regression cannot be taken for the non-entity of either participative or nurturant-task style.

The factor analyses of multiple leadership acts did not always yield quite neat structures. In one study (Sinha 1984: 90) factor analysis provided three distinct factors: subordinate-based participation, leader-centred nurturance, and authoritarian styles. These factors had meaningful correlations with several other types of leadership behaviour. For example, nurturance compared with the participative style had higher positive correlations with guidance and encouragement and negative correlations with power. Participative style was strongly related to friendly orientations and unexpectedly it was also related to direction. Authoritarian style had strongest correlations with power, distance, and discipline. Hassan (1985) found a general factor, people-oriented style, which was related to the nurturant-task style (factor II) and the participative style (factor III). Authoritarian style became fragmented into three other interrelated factors. However, they were all orthogonal to the first three factors. In another study (Singh 1985), the nurturant style was the tenth factor and included some items from the participative style. Verma (1986) found that the items of nurturant-task style became fragmented into subordinate growth orientation (factor I), directive leadership (factor IV), and caring type (factor VI). And yet, none of them became mixed with the specific factors of authoritarian style. Probably these studies should have extracted second-order factors in order to obtain a clearer view of a style's configurations.

More recently Ansari (1987) factor analysed the ratings by subordinates ($N = 440$) of the leadership styles of their immediate superior. He found very distinct nurturant-task (factor I), participative (factor II), bureaucratic (factor III), and authoritarian (factor IV) styles. Ansari's empirically derived factors included exactly those items which were theoretically expected to load on them. Thus the theoretically conceived factor structure was fully validated. Ansari had an advantage over others partly because he had a larger sample size which gives more reliable factor structure and partly because he used subordinates' perception which has been found to be less contaminated by social desirability effect than the self-ratings by those who were in leadership positions (Sinha 1980).

Relationships of nurturance and task styles with other currently available leadership styles were examined in two separate studies. Smith (1986) had samples of managers from the UK ($N = 74$), Japan ($N = 98$), and India ($N = 57$) who responded to Blake Mouton's Managerial Grid, the Ohio State Initiating Structure and Consideration scales, and Sinha's (1980) paternalism (nurturant and task styles) items. Verma (1986) had 216 Indian managers who completed Sinha's and the Ohio State scales. The findings are reported in Table 14.1. Indian samples in the above two studies are referred to as IND 1 and IND 2 respectively.

Table 14.1 shows the styles to be highly intercorrelated in all three countries. However, it is worth noting that nurturance had higher correlations with 9, 9 than with paternalism and with consideration than with initiating structure in all countries. While consideration was by and large more closely associated with nurturance, initiating structure was more strongly related to task-oriented style. Compared with nurturance, task orientation was indeed more closely associated with paternalism (except in the UK). In sum, the coefficients of

Table 14.1 Relationship among leadership styles in three countries

	Nurturant	Task oriented
Managerial grid (9,9)		
UK	0.64**	0.23*
JAP	0.58**	0.33**
IND 1	0.64**	0.70**
Paternalism (9+9)		
UK	0.38**	0.23*
JAP	0.37**	0.42**
IND 1	0.35**	0.56**
Initiating structure		
UK	0.39**	0.46**
JAP	0.39**	0.47**
IND 1	0.27*	0.47**
IND 2	0.67**	0.62**
Consideration		
UK	0.58**	0.00
JAP	0.52**	0.28**
IND 1	0.61**	0.50**
IND 2	0.47**	0.51**

Source: Smith (1986)

Note: UK, $N = 74$; JAP, $N = 0.98$; IND 1, $N = 57$; IND 2, $N = 216$; **$p < 0.01$; *$p < 0.05$.

correlation validated the task-oriented style of leadership and further indicated that nurturance and consideration, despite their culture-specific differences, shared the people orientation of the leaders.

Testing of the model

The earlier studies (Sinha 1980, 1984) reported a number of instances in which the nurturant-task leadership was found to be associated with the effectiveness of subordinates, departments, and the organization. There was also evidence that the nurturant-task style of the heads of education departments was related to the educational climate which was conducive to the quality of education. In another study, the nurturant-task style of college teachers resulted in a greater commitment of students to education.

These studies, however, did not exactly test the model. The model required that the subordinates must be identified as those who were high and those who were low on being prepared to participate on the basis of their preferences for dependence and a personalized relationship, and status consciousness. It was in the latter group that the nurturant-task (NT) leader was postulated to be effective. For those who were prepared to participate, participative (P) leaders were expected to be more effective. An experimental study was conducted to test the model. Twenty two-person groups of those freshmen who were highly prepared and twenty two-person groups of those who were not so prepared to participate were randomly divided into four treatment conditions each having two phases of leadership: NT–NT, NT–P, P–NT, and P–P. A senior class student played the leadership roles in both phases. The findings showed that the groups were most effective under a participative leadership when it was preceded by a phase of nurturant-task leadership. In contrast, nurturant-task leadership following a phase of participative leadership was the least effective.

An earlier reported field study also supported the model (Sinha 1984). When subordinates were perceived to be neither efficient, nor dedicated to work, nor willing to work without supervision the leadership reported that they were likely to use either authoritarian or nurturant-task style. However, the same leaders conceded that authoritarian style was likely to be ineffective and would cause dissatisfaction among the subordinates. They felt that the nurturant-task style, on the other hand, would lead to greater effectiveness. The participative style would be effective if the subordinates were efficient, dedicated to work, and willing to work on their own.

This study suffered from a limitation, i.e. it had only the leader's perspective. The leaders rated subordinates' preparedness to participate, the likelihood of their employing one or the other style, and the stipulated effectiveness of a particular leadership style under the circumstances. Subordinates' views and perceptions were not taken into account. Hence, two studies (Sinha *et al.* 1988) were conducted to test the model from the subordinates' point of view. The first involved 140 managers from a private sector manufacturing organization. The managers rated their immediate superior on the leadership styles scale and also rated their own performance. They also reported the extent to which they preferred (a) to maintain a personalized relationship with their immediate superior, (b) to seek his advice and direction in job and personal matters, and (c) to respect his higher status. The three preference scores were combined to yield a composite score of subordinates' preparedness to participate and to assume responsibilities for the task. A higher score indicated that the manager was less prepared to participate and assume job responsibilities. The managers (in the subordinate's role) were categorized as those ($N = 60$) who were high on preparedness and those ($N = 80$) who were low. Their effectiveness ratings were correlated with their perception of the styles of their immediate superior. The results revealed that the managers who preferred dependence and personalized relationship and respected their immediate superior were more effective under the nurturant-task superior. The task-oriented leader was more effective overall, but the participative style was unrelated to effectiveness in both conditions.

In the second study, effectiveness of the leader was decomposed into five components: (a) getting work done by the subordinates; (b) influencing his immediate superior in the matters in which he was right; (c) maintaining a good relationship with his subordinates; (d) enjoying the trust of his immediate superior; (e) achieving success in his career. A sample of sixty-six managers from a private manufacturing organization rated the leader's effectiveness on the five indices. They made forced choice ratings between nurturant, participative, task-oriented, and nurturant-task-oriented styles of their leader. They also showed their preference for a personalized and dependence relationship and their respect for the immediate superior. Following the procedure of the preceding study, they were grouped as those who were high ($N = 31$) and low ($N = 35$) on preparedness to participate. Five indices of effectiveness and their composite effectiveness scores were correlated with leadership styles separately for high and low prepared groups. Again, it was the nurturant-task style which was related to the composite effectiveness scores ($r = 0.32$, $p < 0.05$) and the extent to which the leaders maintained a good relationship with subordinates ($r = 0.37$, $p < 0.05$) under the low prepared to participate condition. The participative leader had the trust of the subordinates ($r = 0.32$, $p < 0.05$). Surprisingly the nurturant-task style was not found to be effective in getting work done. The participative style was not effective on any other indices of effectiveness in either group of subordinates. A psychometric limitation of the study was the forced choice ratings of leadership styles which creates problems of interpreting the measure. Secondly, single item measures of the preferences for dependence, a personalized relationship, and status differential may not provide a sound basis to identify those who were prepared and those who were not prepared to participate.

Therefore another study (Prasad 1989) was designed to overcome these limitations. The study was similar in procedure to the preceding two studies (Sinha *et al.* 1988) with the modification that all three sets of variables – leadership styles, leader's effectiveness, and subordinate's preparedness to participate – were measured through multiple items. A sample of 223 middle-level managers in a large engineering organization participated in the study. They judged the extent to which their immediate superiors were nurturant, task oriented, nurturant-task oriented, and participative in their leadership styles. For each style, ten behavioural statements were rated on a five-point scale of how frequently the behaviours are engaged in by the leader: never (1), rarely (2), sometimes (3), usually (4), and always (5). The effectiveness measures were identical with those employed in the second study. Subordinate's satisfaction with job, pay, organization, work climate, and immediate superior was also rated on a five-point scale of very dissatisfied (1), dissatisfied (2), so-so (3), satisfied (4), very satisfied (5). The scores were added to derive a composite score of satisfaction. The respondents also rated their life satisfaction using the same five-point scale.

The degree of preparedness to participate was indicated by scores on (a) preference for personalized relationship, (b) preference for dependence relationship, and (c) ready acceptance of the leader's superior status, each having ten items. The items were rated on a five-point scale of quite false (1), false (2), doubtful (3), true (4), and quite true (5). Scores were added across all thirty items to derive a composite score of preparedness to participate. Low scores meant

Table 14.2 Relationship between leadership styles and effectiveness and satisfaction under the condition of low preparedness of the subordinates to participate

	Styles			
	Nurturant	*Task oriented*	*Nurturant-task*	*Participative*
Effectiveness				
1. Getting work done	0.20*	0.26**	0.53**	0.15
2. Influencing superior	0.22*	0.24*	0.41**	−0.13
3. Maintaining relation with subordinates	0.21*	0.19*	0.46**	0.13
4. Enjoying trust of superior	0.25**	0.26**	0.47**	0.15
5. Success in career	0.20*	0.06	0.45**	−0.12
6. Composite effectiveness	0.20*	0.23*	0.45**	0.13
Satisfaction with				
1. Job	0.25**	0.24*	0.45**	0.29**
2. Pay	0.16	0.23*	0.46**	0.17
3. Organization	0.22*	0.23*	0.41**	−0.02
4. Work climate	0.20*	0.29**	0.38**	0.05
5. Immediate superior	0.21*	−0.02	0.15	−0.04
6. Composite satisfaction	0.25**	0.27**	0.40**	0.17
7. Life satisfaction	0.26**	0.24*	0.39**	0.12

Source: Prasad (1989)

Note: N = 112; **p <0.01; *p <0.05.

greater preparedness to participate. The sample was divided into high preparedness ($N = 111$) and low preparedness ($N = 112$) to participate on the basis of median split. The indices of subordinate's effectiveness and satisfaction were correlated with their superior's leadership styles separately for the high and low preparedness groups of subordinates. The findings are reported in Tables 14.2 and 14.3.

Table 14.2 shows that the participative style was found to be unrelated to the indices of subordinate's effectiveness and satisfaction (with only one exception). That is, the subordinates who were *not* prepared to participate and perceived their leaders as participative were neither effective nor satisfied. In contrast, the subordinates under nurturant, task-oriented, and nurturant-task-oriented leaders were effective as well as satisfied. In fact, on all indices (except one, i.e. satisfaction with immediate superior), the coefficients were larger for the nurturant-task-oriented style than for either nurturant or task-oriented leadership. In other words, the managers who preferred a personalized and dependence relationship, readily ac-

Table 14.3 Relationship between leadership styles and effectiveness and satisfaction under the condition of high preparedness of the subordinates to participate

	Styles			
	Nurturant	*Task-oriented*	*Nurturant-task*	*Participative*
Indices of effectiveness				
1. Getting work done	0.09	0.26**	0.26**	0.23*
2. Influencing superior	0.23*	0.09	0.32**	0.30**
3. Maintaining relation with subordinates	−0.02	0.10	0.15	0.28**
4. Enjoying trust of superior	0.03	0.05	0.25**	0.35**
5. Success in career	0.10	0.03	0.25**	0.11
6. Composite effectiveness	0.09	0.08	0.26**	0.30**
Satisfaction with				
1. Job	0.11	0.29**	0.21*	0.24*
2. Pay	0.06	−0.05	0.16	0.14
3. Organization	0.18	0.11	0.26**	0.30**
4. Work climate	0.04	0.12	0.14	0.25**
5. Immediate superior	0.11	0.05	0.24*	0.21*
6. Composite satisfaction	0.22*	−0.07	0.25**	0.26**
7. Life satisfaction	0.26**	0.24*	0.39**	0.12

Source: Prasad (1989)

Note: $N = 111$; **$p < 0.01$; *$p < 0.05$.

cepted the superior status of their immediate superior, and were working under nurturant-task-oriented superiors (but not under participative leaders) were effective as well as satisfied.

The picture was quite different for those who were indeed prepared to participate (Table 14.3). For them, the participative superiors were, as a whole, more effective. These superiors helped managers maintain a good relationship with subordinates who enjoyed the trust of their superiors. The subordinates under the nurturant-task leaders were equally effective in getting work done, influencing their superiors, or achieving success in their career progression. The participative superiors were also more conducive to satisfaction except in the matters of pay and influencing the immediate superiors. The subordinates under task-oriented leaders were effective in getting work done and had greater job satisfaction. Nurturance without a blend of task orientation was by and large ineffective.

Conclusions

The evidence on the whole substantiates the model. There are still gaps, however, which warrant further investigation. We have yet to establish the external validity of the model. Sinha (1980) provided some supportive case studies, but the real test of the model requires a longitudinal study in an organizational setting where a nurturant-task leader may be induced to shift towards participative style through the phase of a blend of nurturance-task and participative orientations. The impact of such shifts needs to be systematically assessed.

The correspondence between the self-rating of managers in the leadership position and the perception by their immediate subordinates has yet to be fully examined. The information that we have collected so far shows a discrepancy. Leaders tend to present themselves in a socially desirable fashion. Subordinates disagree with them. Probably, unobtrusive observations of leader's and subordinate's behaviours and the subsequent scaling of such behaviours might provide a more sound basis to check the validity of the leadership styles scale.

The applicability for the model to the various types of organizations also needs to be ascertained in future research before managers can confidently implement the model in their organizations.

References

Ansari, M. A. (1987) 'Managing people at work: leadership styles and influence strategies', Department of Humanities and Social Sciences, IIT, Kanpur.

Dayal, I. (1976) 'Cultural factors in designing performance appraisal system', SRC Industrial Relations and Human Performance, New Delhi.

Hassan, A. (1985) 'Subordinate and task characteristics as moderators of leadership effectiveness', Ph. D thesis, Patna University.

Herbst, P. G. (1976) *Alternatives to Hierarchies*, Leiden: Martinus Nijhoff.

Hofstede, G. (1980) *Culture's Consequences*, Beverly Hills, CA: Sage.

Kakar, S. (1978) *The Inner World: A Psycho-analytic Study of Childhood and Society in India*, New Delhi: Oxford University Press.

Kothari, R. (1970) *Politics in India*, New Delhi: Orient Longman.

Nandy, A. (1975) 'Master builders', *The Sunday Statesman*, 7 September: 12.

Nandy, A. (1976) 'Adorno in India: revisiting the psychology of fascism', *Indian Journal of Psychology* 51: 168–78.

Prasad, J. (1989) 'The NT style: a test of the model of effective Indian leaders', Working Paper, Magadh University, Bodh Gaya.

Singh, C. B. P. (1985) 'Behavioural strategies in power relationship', Ph. D. thesis, Patna University.

Sinha, J. B. P. (1970) *Development Through Behaviour Modification*, Bombay: Allied Publishers.

Sinha, J. B. P. (1980) *The Nurturant Task Leader*, New Delhi: Concept Publishing.

Sinha, J. B. P. (1984) 'A model of effective leadership styles in India', *International Studies of Management and Organization* 14, 2–3: 86–98.

Sinha, J. B. P. and Sinha, T. N. (1984) 'Stress as a factor of shift in leadership styles', *Journal of Social and Economic Studies* 1, 3: 243–52.

Sinha, J. B. P., Pandey, D., Pandey, S. K., and Pandey, R. L. (1988) 'Effective leadership styles in Indian work organizations', *Management Review* 3, 1: 1–13.

Smith, P. B. (1986) 'Relationships among leadership style measures', personal communication, University of Sussex, UK.

Verma, N. (1986) *Leadership Styles in Interpersonal Perspective*, Delhi: B. R. Publishing.

Chapter fifteen

Management of development in tribal cultures: ideology and leadership

Sitakant Mahapatra

In this chapter we seek to isolate some of the crucial issues relating to economic development in India's tribal societies. Change and modernization in this context has been slow and halting. The awareness of the peculiar cultural uniqueness of these societies and its crucial role in designing, implementing, and managing development has been far from satisfactory among planners, economists, and development administrators. The comparative irrelevance of economic categories and fiscal policies, the intimate linkage between culture and management, and the crucial role of the traditional culture-leaders are some of the issues discussed broadly in this chapter. It is felt that although the observations are based on experience of field work in Eastern India and among selected tribal societies they have a wider relevance to the whole business of initiating and managing change in 'other cultures' in other parts of the world. They are offered here not as final solutions to a continuing problem in Third World development but as questions which need to be continuously asked and to which honest answers need to be sought by all concerned.

The tribal context

Tribal cultures account for 7.76 per cent of India's population. They number 52.3 million as per the 1981 Census. They are largely concentrated in ten states of the Central Highlands, the Chhotnagpur plateau, the Eastern Ghats in Orissa and Andhra Pradesh, and the western parts of the country. These regions account for about 85 per cent of the total tribal population in the country. The northeastern states account for the remaining 15 per cent.

Tribal cultures occupy around 18.7 per cent of the total geographical area of the country, usually in the difficult and inhospitable terrain in the hills and valleys. The soil is generally of low productivity. The tribal communities of India vary widely in their degrees of isolation, levels of acculturation, numbers, and ethnography. There are about 250 tribal communities in India, speaking 105 languages and another 225 subsidiary dialects. As far as numbers are concerned the tribal communities range all the way from the Santals, the Bhils, and the Gonds who number more than 4 million each to small groups like the Chenchu who number less than 100 or communities like Mankirdia and Tharua who number less than 1,000 each. Obviously their social and cultural values, their life styles, and the pace of modernization and economic development vary very widely. The tribal communities range all the way from hunters and gatherers to settled peasant cultivators. Agriculture is mostly at the subsistence level, often based on slash and burn techniques or shifting cultivation. A recent study conducted by the Administrative Staff College of Hyderabad reveals that production from land is very inadequate to maintain a household at subsistence level. They therefore have to depend on gathering minor forest produce for maintaining a reasonable economic balance and to supplement the meagre produce from the land. Geographically isolated, they live in areas which have little outside communication and poor infrastructural facilities. Their economy is only slowly becoming monetized. Enrolment in schools is low and the drop-out rate is very high. The percentage of literacy compares very unfavourably with the general literacy except in Meghalaya and Assam (northeastern states) where the tribal cultures are more Westernized and Christianized than in the rest of the country.

Many of these tribes possess a well-knit socio-cultural system, strong kinship bonds, a stable village organization, and a fairly high level of performing arts. They also fabricate many exquisite art objects in metal, bamboo, timber, local grass, and leaves of trees. The textiles produced manually in small looms and their pottery are of a very high order of excellence. They also have a high level of plastic arts. Their wall decorations with mural paintings, using local earth colours and other supplemental primary colours, are also of a very high level of sophistication and complexity. The Saora pictograms painted on walls by the priest Kudan have attracted world-wide attention.

The Santals of Eastern India build houses which are well known for their symmetry, cleanliness, and elegance, and they paint the walls with floral motifs and geometrical designs. Most of the tribal communities have a vast repertory of songs and dances linked to ritual performances at the recurring festivals of the agricultural cycle and occasions of life crises or rites of passage such as birth, marriage, death, and attainment of puberty. The oral poetry of the Indian tribes reveals a high degree of competence in using language, a preference for use of symbols even in matter-of-fact day-to-day social communication, and an attitude of celebrating life even in the midst of poverty and deprivation. They reveal a sense of gratitude for the fact of being alive and a mood of acceptance of life on its own terms almost in an existential way. There is no fashionable despair, cynicism, or turning back on life.

Thus a fairly high level of social and cultural expression coexists with economic backwardness and isolation in the tribal world of India.

Tribal attitude to development schemes

In more than one forum of scholars, economists, and administrators we find a rhetorical prescription of what the nature and direction of development in these societies should be. It is time that we started at the other end and asked what the tribes themselves want to be and what can be our role in articulating these aspirations and helping achieve their realization. There is a continuous and significant problem of perception here. In the Third World the development model generally revolves around the city, the emerging pockets of culture-élites, the *nouveau riche*, the articulate minority that has access to power, both political and economic, to decision making and to the media. The problem is compounded by language. Most tribal societies are small encysted societies – except for the Santals, Gonds, Bhils, and those communities living in the northeast. The tribal languages are mostly oral and not understood by those who have to do with their development. Mercifully many among their men folk are bilingual and understand the language of the state or local area in which they are situated. The cultural distances, however, are enormous. A communication gap is only natural and often consultation with the local tribal population is inadequate, jerky, and discontinuous, if not totally absent.

In every society there is a will for betterment of the neighbourhood, its infrastructural adequacy, and the income of individual families. This is articulated through organizations – political, economic, and professional. The society seeks validation of its aspirations through group decision and group action. The rank path of politics is the new path to economic development and conferment of benefits. It is generally perceived by the members of a society that in today's world political authority holds the key to economic decision making and therefore that, to bring about economic change and modernization, access to and control over political authority is a prime need.

In tribal societies, while there is evidence of sizeable energy, enthusiasm, and informal capacity for socio-cultural organizing, there seems to be a total indifference when it comes to political and/or economic organization. The same society which looks at all aspects of organizing the ritual–festival celebrations, the celebrations concerning life crises such as birth, marriage, and death and prescribes elaborate mechanisms to organize all aspects of each ritual – fund raising, functional differentiation, religious litanies, priesthoods, singing and dancing, etc. – is singularly indifferent to and incapable of organizing itself for achieving political and economic ends. Some have looked upon this as an inevitable part of the moral basis of a poor society (Banfield 1968). Often it exhibits little enthusiasm for the form and content of the new political and economic system. No doubt the members of the society are familiar with the socio-cultural, the ritual–religious, functions through an intimate process of time-honoured socialization. However, the experiments of political decentralization, the Panchayati raj system (a form of local self-government) under which the hierarchy begins at the village level and climbs up through Panchayat (roughly a group of about ten contiguous villages) and the Panchayat Samiti (or the community development block) to the state legislatures, is somewhat unfamiliar. The development functions are mostly undertaken through the community development block which is headed by a Block Development Officer. This is the level where the Panchayat Samiti comes into the picture. It has a role in deciding on different development needs and programmes, fixing and assigning priorities, seeking funds, and articulating aspirations, grievances, and demands. In turn, it is expected to collate and compile the needs of different Panchayats which are supposed to do likewise in respect of the villages in their charge. The ward member of the village, the sarpanch (head) of the Panchayat, and the Chairman of the Panchayat Samiti are thus the elected new functionaries of the new grass root political system in a democratic society. The system has been in operation from the early 1950s and with varying degrees of success. In tribal areas, however, there is a general indifference (part of it understandable in their socio-cultural milieu) to this system. Apart from the more general reason of the lack of acquaintance or familiarity, there seems to be a deeper sociological reason. The rhythm of life still moves faster in ritual, cultural, and social levels – in festivals, in performing arts, in plastic arts, in religious celebrations – and less in the drab routines of political and economic operations, even when the contours of the new elective system and its access to economic well-being are perceived. Here the relative roles of the traditional hereditary leader and the modern elective leader is very important and at least in respect of one society – the Santal, which happens to be one of the largest in the country, their population being around 4.6 million in the 1981 Census – it has been found to be rather ambivalent. The complex nature of the ambivalence, hesitations, and contradictions has been more fully explored in the book *Modernization and Ritual* (Mahapatra 1986).

The new political institutions were to be associated with the normal developmental activities in the locality. These consisted of minor road constructions, excavation of drinking water wells, construction of primary schools, and execution of minor irrigation projects including tanks, cross bundhs, and irrigation wells. A number of activities related to the extension of modern agricultural practices – the distribution of fertilizers and undertaking the demonstration of new techniques in selected plots for popularizing the new methods of cultivation. Besides this, the Panchayats and Panchayat Samitis were often called upon to be associated with other activities such as the public distribution of consumer goods, initiating small industries, health and sanitation programmes in the local areas, and so on. At the Panchayat Samiti level, there was a Block Development Officer, a number of Extension Officers, and the Gram Sevaks (village-level workers). The Gram Sevak was the lowest public functionary in this structure, and he was in charge of a small group of villages.

Needless to say, these new political institutions, which were introduced throughout the country, were new and strange to the tribal world. It was no longer possible to function in the closed world of the tribe and its well-recognized preferences and value systems. The institutional framework itself presupposed choice of functionaries on the basis of certain criteria to be evolved. Association with the outside world, and most of the government officials were bound to be outsiders, gave rise to unfamiliar and strange forebodings.

Evolving mechanisms to find out what would be the acceptable goal in any particular field of development was another situation to be faced. This was a complex problem for the tribal leader. Take the example of the digging of a drinking water well in a particular village, when there would be conflicting claims for its location. Someone had to decide its location. This and other developmental projects involved a choice of alternatives, and ascertaining what was not only practicable in terms of finances available but also acceptable to the local people. This involved decision making, and this type of decision making was essentially different from the type of decision making with which the hereditary tribal leader and the tribal people were acquainted.

Further, the lurking suspicion that the new political set-up might 'contaminate' and spoil the poor *Adivasi* (tribal person) is quite common, though it is rarely expressed. The concept of *diku* (outsider) becomes identified with the operation of the new political system, and a sense of fear and suspicion remains at the back of the tribal person's mind.

The hesitation to participate fully and positively in the new system has implications for the entire developmental process. The idea that in a vast and complex social situation the development process must depend upon the 'indigenous developers' has received a jolt, for 'indigenous developers' are not forthcoming. The authorities in charge of running the Panchayati raj bodies have tried to bring about a marriage of the traditional authority and the new political system. Those who are acceptable to the authorities and are sometimes 'sponsored' as candidates for the Panchayati raj bodies, and eventually get elected uncontested, are rarely persons who command the respect and loyalty of the community. They are rarely effective in enlisting popular support or in expressing the genuine aspirations of the locality. This only leads to confirmation of the tribe's belief that the new leaders are more likely to be the 'yes men' if not the henchmen of the *diku*, and to that extent they can never serve the interests of the community.

To sum up, the tribal attitude to the new political system is never straightforward. It has certain inherent contradictions which were perhaps natural. Broadly speaking, the three phases in tribal attitude to development schemes may be described as below. In the first phase the tribal society hesitated regarding the utility of the new political system and expected too little of it. In the second phase it accepted the system and expected too much from it which naturally led to disappointment. And in the third phase, there was a grudging acceptance with the pragmatic approach of reconciling to the inevitable and realizing from it whatever possible.

Management of economic development in tribal cultures

Development implies the improvement of general living conditions in an area and of the community inhabiting that area. It therefore has the twin aspects of infrastructural growth – more roads, more schools, more hospitals, etc. – and larger familial incomes. They involve, in turn, resource mobilization, savings, reinvestment, and proper and effective utilization of resources for achieving the goals of development. These resources in a tribal world are not merely physical or financial; they are equally importantly the human resources, i.e. the resources of life style uniqueness which are often hidden away, not understood, or misunderstood by the outsider who is in charge of managing the development.

Gone are those days, luckily, when development anthropology

269

tended to look on growth, change, and modernization of traditional, ritual-based, or feudalistic social structures as inevitably contingent on an initial phase of demolition. Demolition meant eradication of superstitions, blind beliefs, taboos, inertia, the lack of entrepreneurial qualities, and the absence of the 'acquisitive instincts' and 'the willingness to work hard'. It was presumed that nothing new can grow, no development can take place, no change can be ushered in until the ground has been cleared from the century-old debris which are inevitably bottlenecks and obstacles to growth. Development anthropology has travelled a long way. It is now prepared to concede that traditional societies could have growth-positive as well as growth-negative factors and elements in its societal and individual psyche; and the skill of development management consists in properly identifying them, describing them, understanding their roots and linkages, and then going about isolating, marginalizing, or removing the negative elements while incorporating, enlisting, and productively utilizing the growth-positive elements. This is the biggest challenge to the managerial revolution so badly needed in the economic development of other cultures. In such cultures with one foot in several past centuries and another in 'today', one in complex tradition and another in new awakenings, new processes struggling to be born, utmost care and patience is necessary, first to understand the confusing contours and then to seek answers and formulations.

It may be worthwhile to look more closely into the nature of these complexities and ambivalences through certain concrete field studies and developmental work in Eastern India.

The first relates to the modernization of agriculture in Santal tribal society. It reveals how new and 'profane' technology could sometimes be antithetical to old and sacred ritual. One Santal village, after a lot of extension work and persuasion, had taken to hybrid maize. The fields were properly cultivated. The crop was coming on very well. But the Asadia festival was delayed. The village Manjhi had gone to his father-in-law's house in a village nearly 40 km away and there he lay very sick. He had not been able to decide, in consultation with the village elder, the date for Asadia, and therefore the festival had not been held. And nobody in the village would enter the field for de-weeding as the Asadia worship had not been done. Some young boys who had read up to the ninth and tenth class in high schools argued for the de-weeding to be done, but they were described as 'faithless', and finally the voice of the elders prevailed. The de-weeding was done only after Asadia. But the delay of more than a fortnight considerably damaged the crop.

It is evident that the modernization of agriculture which demands timely inter-cultural operations sometimes comes into conflict with the ritualistic basis of agriculture. Here technology and ritual must combine to create a new system of ritual, flexible and liberal enough to absorb the demands of new technology, or conversely the ritual must be restructured (Mahapatra 1986).

Another instance relates to the Kondh tribal society of Phulbani district in Orissa. This experience is in the field of horticulture on the hillslopes. Slash and burn cultivation has been the practice in this area. Anthropologists have now come to realize that this is not, after all, the very inefficient mode of production that it is sometimes made out to be. On the contrary, in a given demographic situation it was a fairly efficient mode in terms of labour productivity. For very little labour went into the process. It consisted of cutting down forest growths on hillslopes, burning them to allow weeds and undergrowth to die and the ash to mix with the soil, and then scattering a mix of seeds of different crops, sometimes as many as twelve, just prior to the monsoon. The different crops had different harvesting times. After harvest the area under crop was left out for forest growth to reclaim it.

The slope was again taken up only after 8–10 years. Over the years, with population growth and pressure on land, the vacant period has come down sometimes to as low as 3 years, and the consequences have been low productivity, a high run-off rate of top soil, etc.

On the slopes the government supervises the planting of orchards and trees. The Kondhs can cut down trees other than those bearing fruit. In fact it is a taboo to put the axe to the fruit-bearing trees. Hence it is necessary to plant such trees and not trees capable of being used only for fuel or timber. This realization has been very useful and in fact sometimes the planting of the trees, mostly done with government funds, purchasing the labour of the local population, has been deliberately initiated by invoking the spirit of the relevant gods through a sanctified ritual. This is a positive manner in which development management incorporates traditional ritual and old belief systems.

Then again it has now been realized how the manner of allocating *podu* lands on hillslopes was governed by an egalitarian principle that almost conforms to the Marxist dictum – from each according to his ability and to each according to his needs. For clearing the forest for *podu* each family contributed the labour of its able-bodied working members while it was allotted land proportionate to its size.

Thirdly in a Dongria Kondh area of Koraput district in southern Orissa one can see how bananas and pineapples have been grown for many miles on the erstwhile *podu*-ravaged hillslopes, even when there are no physical demarcations determining individual ownership and government has not yet conferred proprietary right on the

271

land with the cultivators because of a long-standing principle, since the days of the British Raj, that above a 10° slope on the hills land tenure rights cannot be conferred on individuals. Development banks always emphasize that the incentive to work and to invest cannot come, and credit flow cannot be there, until individual land rights have been assured. But development has already *happened* without much difficulty and there has not been any conflict so far in claiming the usufructs even when there are no boundaries of plots or fields. No one can say that there may not be any conflicts in future, nor that the cultivators will not feel the pressure of the 'acquisitive instinct' in demanding the conferment of individual rights. But the relevant lessons are there for us to see as far as they relate to tribal management.

In a Munda village in Orissa the Community Development Block had dug a drinking water well. For years before that the village used to get its drinking water from a hill stream flowing near the village. With deforestation the volume of water in the stream had dwindled and there was also the risk of occasional pollution of the water. They used to collect water from this stream in earthen pitchers. Now when they drew water from the deep well using the same earthen pitchers and a rope, more often than not the pitchers were broken by hitting against the sides of the well. Word went round that there was an evil spirit or *bonga* in the well that demolished the pitchers and then nobody would use the well. A resourceful village-level worker demonstrated that aluminium and brass containers were not broken up. He also demonstrated with earthen pitchers how a light skilful pulling of the rope prevented them hitting against the wall of the well. Even then the villagers were insistent that something needed to be done to appease the evil *bonga*. The village-level worker gave in, and some propitiation rites were observed, but the villagers used the new management technique that the functionary had taught them. Perhaps management is too big a word to be used for this tiny skill but in the situation of the primitive tribal world this also needs to be taken care of.

A similar experience occurred in a development programme involving upgraded hybrid cows for milk production. The tribal person gets 50 per cent as a subsidy when an upgraded milch cow is made available to him. A tribal person once complained how he had been cheated by being offered such a cow which was giving 10 litres of milk a day but within a week it had come down to a trickle. Subsequent investigation revealed that the problem was in the maintenance of the cow. For the tribal beneficiary the concept of maintaining a cow was to let it out to the nearby forest in the morning and get it back in the evening. It was offered whatever gruel and other food surplus was in the house which in any case was not much. It had not been clearly taught to him that this upgraded cow deserved pre-mixed feed at regular intervals and proper attention and maintenance. It was also not to be left out in the forest as, in another case, such a milch cow ate some leaves of a shrub which was harmful and could be saved only by surgery.

Adapting operational management techniques to tribal values is inevitably necessary for the successful implementation of the new technology. Development efforts cannot be successful unless these apparently minor and insignificant management techniques are devised to meet the needs of the tribal people.

Conclusion

The general irrelevance of political ideology is a harsh reality in underdeveloped societies where the manipulation of political power and access to it are through a host of non-ideological parameters. These range all the way from personal, factional, religious, and caste issues to issues concerning tribal group identity. Modern ideology and the political party system cuts across cultural cohesiveness. Many culture-heroes or culture-leaders have slowly come to realize that, disregarding pan-tribal solidarity, solidarity even with a particular tribal group is sometimes in conflict with the modern political ideology – that political partisanship can divide the tribal group. They have also realized that cultural solidarity can be a prisoner of political pluralism as in case of the Jharkhand movement among the Santals in India.

There is also the question of the rift and rivalry between the traditional and the modern leader. Except in those rare cases when the traditional leader himself becomes the modern leader by a transformation of roles, the new leadership has generally gone to the younger people and the traditional leadership to the older, thus with a marked role differentiation. While the new leader looks after the political and the economic issues and issues relating to development, the traditional leader looks after the ritual–religious and the socio-cultural matters. They differ not merely in age but in styles of functioning, dress, attitudes, and the idiom they use. While the traditional leader is generally steeped in the lore of the tribe and is not very articulate or communicative, the new leader reshapes his bearing so as to be acceptable to the authorities with whom he has to work and whose blessings or goodwill he must enjoy to survive and to ensure the flow of economic benefits.

The power of the new political élites is secular and is based on neither folklore nor folk religion. To continue in authority, however, it must derive strength from the matrix of a society steeped in ritual. Here is the essential contradiction in the new political élite's objective of maintaining the solidarity of the tribe and at the same time retaining his image as culture-hero to the masses within the tribal community (Mahapatra 1977).

Successful development efforts depend on bringing about a *rapprochement* between the twin approaches and the factionalism not only between the traditional and new leadership but also between ideology and culture. It has also to marry traditional attitudes in education and socialization and in the ancient lore of the tribe with the learning of small management training in respect of specific programmes. More particularly, in designing development and implementing the various schemes, it has consciously to seek a better understanding of the cultural ethos and then go about incorporating the useful positive cultural traits while marginalizing or eliminating the negative ones. It involves skill and insight. It involves patience and a capacity for synthesizing technique and tradition, culture and politics, pragmatic management, and sanctified ancient lore and ritual.

References

Banfield, E. C. (1968) *The Moral Basis of a Backward Society*, Chicago, IL: Free Press, Research Centre in Economic Development and Cultural Change, University of Chicago, 8.

Mahapatra, S. (1977) 'Ecological adaptation to technology – ritual conflict and leadership change. The Santal experience', in K. David (ed.) *The New Wind: Changing Identities in South Asia*, p. 362, Amsterdam: Mouton Publishers.

Mahapatra, S. (1986) *Modernization and Ritual*, pp. 45–6, 50, 80, Calcutta: Oxford University Press.

Chapter sixteen

Managing political modernization: charismatic leadership in the developing countries

James Woycke

Arthur Schweitzer (1984) has called the twentieth century the 'age of charisma'. Nowhere is this more the case than in the developing countries. It sometimes seems that virtually every political leader of developing countries has been described as charismatic by the media or the academic community. It is certainly true that the majority of charismatic political leaders since 1945 have been situated in the developing world. Keeping this in view, the present chapter has three objectives: first, to determine whether charismatic leadership in the developing world is situation or person specific by contrasting the behaviours and leadership effects of charismatic and non-charismatic leaders; second, to describe the relevance of charismatic leadership to the leadership needs of the developing world and to identify specific actions which charismatic leaders have taken to meet these needs; and finally, to draw some implications for managing organizations.

Charismatic leadership characteristics

Max Weber defined charismatics as those leaders who are regarded as being 'endowed with supernatural, superhuman, or exceptional powers or qualities' (Weber 1964: 358–9). Because of these powers or qualities, followers give the leader devotion, hero worship, or absolute trust. Students of charisma in organizations have elaborated on this definition (see for example Conger and Kanungo 1988). A charismatic relationship may arise in a situation of chronic or acute social stress which challenges existing norms and values and which cannot be resolved by existing social or political institutions. An individual who has faced and resolved this crisis in his own life presents his message to others, who respond positively. The leader is accepted because he is best able to articulate the felt grievances of followers and because he offers a message of hope which claims to re-establish a normative sense or order that is compatible with traditional cultural values or myths. The leader is perceived as extraordinary because of his unique message and because of the political risks involved with articulating an alternative normative order.

In the area of public sector governmental organizations, it is easy to see the relevance of charismatic leadership in the developing world, particularly in the newly independent countries. Here, foreign colonial rule weakened or displaced traditional social, economic, cultural, and political institutions, while denying local populations any opportunity to share in the new Western institutions that replaced them. After the First World War, fought in part by colonial troops and in part for democracy, nascent political movements arose which began to advocate equality and independence. After the Second World War, fought to an even greater extent by colonial troops and for racial equality, many of the discharged colonial soldiers found a social, economic, and political order which no longer corresponded with their experience or expectations. In many colonies popular leaders emerged who articulated these grievances and who quickly assumed leadership of the rapidly expanding nationalist movements.

Charismatic leadership, then, seems to fit the developing world situation well – perhaps too well. Precisely because of the ubiquity of charismatic leaders in Afro-Asian countries, it has been suggested that the developing world situation itself – the sense of normative crisis provoked by colonial discrediting of traditional institutions and values and the nationalist discrediting of colonial institutions and values, combined with the prestige associated with independence – is inherently charismatic and would endow any leader with 'situational charisma' if he happened to be in office at the right time (Runciman 1963: 154).

In order to determine whether the political leaders of the developing world possess personal charisma or situational charisma, some analytical framework is necessary to permit us to identify those variables which are associated only with personal charisma. One such framework is Toth's (1973) Charismatic Leadership Inventory, a comprehensive aggregate list of variables associated with charismatic leadership.

Toth reviewed the social science literature on charisma published before 1972. He compiled a list of all descriptive terms applied to charisma. A total of 784 statements were listed on file cards. These statements were then grouped in four broad categories derived from Vernon's Paradigm of Situational Symbolic Interactionism: leader (385), audience (169), situation (105), symbols (125). A closer examination proved many of the original statements to be redundant.

After collapsing the sample, a final total of 87 descriptors remained: leader (38), audience (20), situation (13), symbols (16). For the purpose of the present study, these descriptors were regrouped in ten major categories: (1) situational context; (2) follower predisposition; (3) leader personality; (4) leader behaviour; (5) leader–follower interaction; (6) follower response to leader; (7) follower effects; (8) leader's message; (9) symbolism; (10) oratory. Each major category contained one or more subcategories. The most salient subcategories will be highlighted in the subsequent discussion.

In order to apply this revised inventory to developing world leaders a sample of charismatic and non-charismatic leaders was selected on the basis of recent scholarly publications. Charismatic leaders were selected if they have been identified as charismatic in two or more social science articles on charisma and if they are described as charismatic in one or more scholarly biographies or monographs of the individual leaders. Non-charismatic leaders were selected if they have not been identified as charismatic in any social science literature on charisma. A final 'evening out' of the two samples was made, so that the non-charismatic set matched the charismatic set in terms of geographic region, population, territory, and chronology. Each leader held government office (after independence) for at least 5 years; most served for 10 years or more. The final sample included the following leaders:

Charismatic	*Non-charismatic*
Castro (Cuba)	Trujillo (Dominican Republic)
Peron (Argentina)	Betancourt (Venezuela)
Nkrumah (Ghana)	Vargas (Brazil)
Kenyatta (Kenya)	Tubman (Liberia)
Nyerere (Tanzania)	Mobuto (Zaire)
Nasser (Egypt)	Obote (Uganda)
Ataturk (Turkey)	Nuri al-Said (Iraq)
Nehru (India)	Reza Shah Pahlavi (Iran)
Mao Zedong (China)	Rhee (S. Korea)
Sukarno (Indonesia)	Phibun (Thailand)

For each leader one recent biography was content-analysed. Four of the non-charismatic leaders were represented by political monographs because of the absence of any full-length biography. Biographies were read *in toto* and monographs were scanned on the basis of index references for all statements describing the leadership of the subject, including the situation in which the leader emerged; the personality, behaviour, sense of purpose, leadership technique, style, and oratory of the leader; the leader's relationship with followers and subordinates; and the routinization of his leadership, including attitude and policy towards national political and economic development. All statements fitting one or more of these general descriptions were entered on file cards. These cards were then coded according to the categories in our revised Charismatic Leadership Inventory.

The results of the coding analysis are mixed. Theoretically, charismatic leaders should score higher than non-charismatic leaders in all categories, since the Inventory is derived from descriptors of charisma. But in our survey this did not occur, and some non-charismatic leaders scored relatively well on some categories. This suggests that situational charisma may indeed be a significant aspect of charismatic political leadership in the developing world. Nonetheless, eight descriptors strongly differentiate the charismatic and non-charismatic samples. It is encouraging that these eight variables are among the most central elements of charismatic leadership. The following are the eight descriptors with biographical quotations to represent each of them.

Leader has magnetic or compelling personality

> Kemal was deliberate in movement. His body radiated energy, even in repose; his cold eyes gleamed with it, all-seeing and alive with the light of his contradictory moods.
>
> (Balfour 1965: xvii)
>
> He eschewed the strong-man role, as he would throughout his career, yet an aura of decisiveness surrounded him.
>
> (Page 1983: 135)
>
> Mao was unshakable. With obstinacy he set his course. Inner sparks kept him moving forward.
>
> (Terrill 1980: 93)

Leader with a sense of calling

> He was convinced that he was a born leader and could translate into action the theories he had studied.
>
> (Page 1983: 66)
>
> Arrogant British action provoked a group of army officers, led by Nasser, to band in a conspiracy. All the pent-up indignation of his adolescent nationalism now congealed in a relentless determination to rid Egypt of her British masters.
>
> (Nutting 1972: 19–20)

Leader identifies with his mission

> He did not doubt his own mission to be their leader. He was a living legend entering upon his inheritance, the messiah whose message set free all the people.
>
> (Murray-Brown 1973: 257)

> Mao felt that his own will embodied the Chinese way for his era.
>
> (Terrill 1980: 290)

Oratory

> No one who ever watched Peron perform in front of a mass audience could miss the symbiotic relationship between them.
>
> (Page 1983: 223)

> Sukarno's most noticeable skills were those of exhortation and persuasion. As an orator he could hold an audience in the hollow of his hand.
>
> (Legge 1969: 6)

Symbolism

> Jawaharlal used symbols and slogans of a new cultural awakening to preach to the masses. He talked to them using symbols and slogans they understood.
>
> (Pandey 1976: 87)

> Ideology was a manipulative device rather than the presentation of a plan of action: the slogans marshalled by Sukarno evoked a deep response for his hearers and embodied a view of the world and a set of values.
>
> (Legge 1969: 353)

Leader as source of legitimacy

> His role was that of supreme legitimator.
>
> (Terrill 1980: 375)

> For most members of the party, effective legitimacy remains the prerogative of Nkrumah, stemming from the charismatic aspects of his leadership.
>
> (Apter 1963: 297)

> Fidel's personal preeminence allowed him to bypass institutional channels for decision-making in the determination of policy and the setting of revolutionary goals.
>
> (Gonzalez 1974: 179)

> He was still there, indispensable as arbiter and unifier when critical moments came. It was a remarkable demonstration of his personal authority that even those who had taken executive responsibility from him turned to him at such times.
>
> (Legge 1969: 214)

Leader unifies followers, seeks broad support

> The *conductor* preferred to act as arbiter or peacemaker, remaining above the din of battle and maintaining the balance of forces within his movement.
>
> (Page 1983: 314)

> A part of his special power was his ability to project himself as the blender of opposing views.
>
> (Legge 1969: 356)

Followers give leader devotion, loyalty, awe

> The crowd was not preoccupied with ideologies or doctrines or propaganda, but wanted only Colonel Peron. It felt an almost religious emotion for him.
>
> (Page 1983: 136)

> It was Fidel's new political style that enabled him to capture widespread popular support and to obtain carte blanche from the enthusiastic masses in shaping the new order.
>
> (Gonzalez 1974: 50)

> Kenyatta retained an unrivalled hold over the mass of the Kikuju people. His presence drew thousands to meetings.
>
> (Murray-Brown 1973: 283)

> At none of the rallies did Mao make any kind of speech. He merely stood and raised an arm. Yet hundreds of thousands wept from joy and jumped up and down in response to his mere presence.
>
> (Terrill 1980: 318)

Leadership needs of the developing world

Charismatic leadership fulfils several important functional needs common to many developing countries. The first such need for newly independent nations is to create a foundation for *political legitimacy*. The national unit and its institutions and agencies must become accepted and legitimated by the people. At the time of independence political legitimacy is in question. Colonialism discredited traditional institutions and values, and nationalism discredited colonial institutions and values. For the moment, the personal legitimacy of the charismatic leader must serve as a substitute for institutional legitimacy. Only the leader possesses the authority to make the many rapid decisions required in the first flush of independence (Rustow 1967: 154–6). Gradually, however, the leader is able to transfer his personal legitimacy to the institutions of the new state.

> The role of the hero is first of all to be a readily available, easily understood symbol of the new nation, someone to incarnate in his person its values and aspirations. But the hero does more than symbolize the new nation. He legitimizes the state by ordaining obedience to its norms out of loyalty to his person.
>
> (Wallerstein 1961: 99)

The second functional responsibility of political leaders is *economic development*. Objectives must be determined, policies formulated, and people persuaded. Charismatic leadership can be especially important in this effort. 'What appears to set charismatic leaders apart is their strategic vision and their ability to motivate [people] to achieve ambitious goals' (Conger and Kanungo 1988: 3).

In his recent survey of economic growth in the developing world, Paul Reynolds found that political actions are the single most important factor affecting growth. Governments which favour growth, which rely on private market forces, and which possess administrative competence are more likely to achieve real economic growth than are governments which seek ideological rather than practical objectives, which interfere in economic processes, and which lack a corps of competent administrators (Reynolds 1986: 416–18).

In our sample of ten developing countries headed by charismatic leaders, only four demonstrated significant economic growth during the tenure of the charismatic leader: Kenya, Egypt, Turkey, and India (Reynolds 1986: 231, 304, 321, 329). The other countries have shown no growth or negative growth since independence (Ghana, Tanzania) or during the rule of the charismatic leader (Cuba, Argentina, China, and Indonesia). In each case political decisions have clearly affected the prospects for growth. In three countries – Cuba, Tanzania, and China – decisions to pursue some form of social revolution have disrupted market forces and discouraged foreign investment. In two countries the leader's ambition to achieve national greatness through monumental construction projects drained economic resources from essential development programmes. And in Argentina the economy was skewed to favour workers and the army – the political props of the Peron regime – at the expense of other sectors of the economy.

A few quotations from leader biographies will illustrate how charismatic leaders can help – or hinder – national development. The first step that a leader takes in the developing world context is to legitimize the new nation, new norms, and new institutions. Witness Kwame Nkrumah:

Nkrumah has become the symbol of Ghana.

(Apter 1963: 305)

Nkrumah has become the symbolic referent in which widely differing social groups find orientational identity with one another.

(Apter 1963: 305)

The legitimacy of Nkrumah has been granted to the norms around which secular role behaviour within the government must conform.

(Apter 1963: 212)

He has been able to use the legitimate organs of political rule as a vehicle for nationalism. More than anyone else he has endowed parliamentary structures with effective legitimacy.

(Apter 1963: 223)

Secondly, through the leader's actions all of the people must be made to feel themselves part of the nation:

His vision of unity was overwhelmingly important in forging the nation and developing within it a sense of identity and self-respect.

(Legge 1969: 7)

For the first time a government was treating workers with respect instead of repression. They were beginning to feel like citizens who mattered, and they owed this psychic gratification to the colonel.

(Page 1983: 72)

Thirdly, the leader must provide a vision of the future for the whole nation:

Mao was coming close to the viewpoint that a new society was the ultimate goal.

(Terrill 1980: 47)

Nasser was not satisfied with one revolution. In his view there had to be two, a political upheaval and a social revolution.

(Nutting 1972: 58)

What he had to do now called for something more – the talents of a reformer, a prophet, a statesman. Having saved his country, his next objective was to create a new country. His ambition was nothing less than to transform society – to sweep away a medieval social system and replace it by a new one based on modern civilization.

(Balfour 1965: 377)

Nyerere has always considered that his multiple role as founding father, as president of his country, and as leader of his party, must be used not only to unify, but also to innovate and modernize, politically and socially, for the public benefit.

(Smith 1971: 61–2)

It soon became evident that Peron's vision of a New Argentina was a far cry from an agricultural society. The president intended a radical transformation and firmly believed he could succeed.

(Page 1983: 169)

Sukarno's own concept was narrow, emphasizing the primacy of the political struggle for independence and ignoring questions about the form of the state and the type of society to be built when independence came.

(Legge 1969: 80)

As the last quotation illustrates, not all visions are equal. Unfortunately, the goals a leader sets or fails to set can make or break the economy of a country.

Finally, the leader must be personally and politically able to move people towards the vision of the future society; the leader must find the right mix of idealism and pragmatism to accomplish social transformation:

Nyerere sought to develop new socio-economic values within the context of a new political philosophy. He molded tribal values with modern life.

(Smith 1971: 4)

He knew he had little time to create a new country and his pragmatic approach was the one for which his life had most fitted him.

(Murray-Brown 1973: 383)

Kemal was farsighted in planning but pragmatic in execution.

(Balfour 1965: 430)

He seemed to have no grasp of economic problems and he was certainly less concerned with the content of policies than with the

techniques of politics. He was not effective as a practical adminis-
trator.

(Legge 1969: 6)

The fidelista order was politically effective but ultimately unsuited
for sustained economic development. It was unable to resolve the
growing tension between charismatic personal rule, which was of
pivotal political importance to the regime, and the institutional
requisites for rapid economic development.

(Gonzalez 1974: 145)

Charisma, then, is important for legitimating the nation, the state
institutions, and the policy objectives of the leader and his government. But, however successful these political actions may be, they do
not guarantee successful economic development. A leader must have
a vision of a country, but also of what he wants that country to be. The
leader who can envisage a long-term goal for the country and devise
short-term policies to reach that goal is more likely to succeed than
the leader with limited vision, or no vision.

Implications for management

Can a successful charismatic leader become a successful charismatic
manager? For managing it is no longer sufficient to articulate an in-
spiring vision; now the leader must implement that vision. This is the
stage of charismatic leadership which Weber described as routinization: the process whereby the leader institutionalizes his charisma.
The leader must devise new operational norms for these institutions
and demonstrate to his followers how to adopt these norms. He must
become a preacher, a teacher, and a performer: preach, in order to
persuade people to adopt new institutional norms; teach, in order to
instruct followers on how to implement these norms; and act, in
order to demonstrate through personal example how to behave in
order to achieve the desired goals.

Practical charismatic leadership, whether at the state, corporate,
or bureaucratic level, requires that the leader preach a single goal to
his followers. Successful managers 'consistently hammer away at a
theme' in order to persuade people to adopt their proposed course of
action. In our sample of Third World nations, several leaders toured
the country 'incessantly' in order to preach the need for change
(Apter 1963: 215; Balfour 1965: 364; Gonzalez 1974: 51; Terrill 1980:
162). Julius Nyerere even resigned his office as president in order to
devote himself full-time to touring and speaking throughout Tanzania (Smith 1971: 71, 82).

Secondly, the leader needs to instruct his people on how to operationalize new norms and institutions. He must explain why change is necessary, and at the same time present change in a reassuring manner by relating it to past and present circumstances, so that change becomes a new means of achieving traditional goals or that it adapts traditional means to achieve new goals. This is a patient time-consuming didactic effort, but one which even a powerful autocratic leader like Kemal Ataturk willingly adopts for the purpose of national re-education:

Kemal had to conquer the obstinate and querulous spirit of the elected representatives. Thus daily Kemal would go to the Assembly. With complete self-possession and a few brief words he would silence their murmurs. In that clear resounding voice which combined the accents of persuasion and authority, he would continue to expound his arguments, his ideas, and his demands. The charm would begin to work, their voices to acclaim him, their hands to rise in an affirmative vote. The new Assembly proved responsive to his assiduous direction. In the crucial early weeks he seldom missed a sitting, expounding measures before they were debated, making his own views clear. Once when the ayes had it, he said, 'Put down your hands. I have failed to explain this point to you.' He then did so, making it clear that he wanted rejection, and on the next vote the nays had it.

(Balfour 1965: 234, 279)

Finally, the leader must involve himself in the change process. In this way his charismatic prestige sanctions change, while his behaviour demonstrates change in action. Citing Ataturk again:

Never before had a head of state left his capital to address his subjects directly. Thus Kemal was breaking with precedent to forge a new and personal bond between ruler and ruled. Everywhere he was at pains to emphasize the democratic nature of his tour. There was to be an end to those formal ceremonial functions. He wanted to change the political structure of the country, to rouse the people to a new concept of popular sovereignty.

(Balfour 1965: 364–5, 368, 45)

To summarize, then, charismatic leaders become charismatic managers (whether managing a country or a corporation) when they have a strategic vision, are able to communicate this vision, and have the tactical ability to achieve their objective. They repeat their message on every possible occasion, relating current events to the common goal, and relating their goals to followers' objectives and experiences. All of this is capped by a pragmatic sense of timing: knowing when and how to proceed. It is not an easy formula to master, but the best leaders in developing countries have shown that it is a successful one.

Note

This chapter is based on a larger on-going study under the joint participation of Robert House, Don Spangler, and James Woycke.

References

Apter, D. (1963) *Ghana in Transition*, New York: Atheneum.
Balfour, P. (1965) *Ataturk: The Rebirth of a Nation*, London: Weidenfeld & Nicolson.
Conger, J. and Kanungo, R. N. (eds) (1988) *Charismatic Leadership: The Elusive Factor in Organizational Effectiveness*, San Francisco, CA: Jossey-Bass.
Gonzalez, E. (1974) *Cuba under Castro: The Limits of Charisma*, Boston, MA: Houghton Mifflin.
Legge, J. (1969) *Sukarno: A Political Biography*, Ithca, NY: Cornell University Press.
Murray-Brown, J. (1973) *Kenyatta*, New York: Dutton.
Nutting, A. (1972) *Nasser*, New York: Dutton.
Page, J. (1983) *Peron: A Biography*, New York: Random House.
Pandey, B. N. (1976) *Nehru*, London: Macmillan.
Reynolds, L. (1986) *Economic Growth in the Third World, 1850–1980: An Introduction*, New Haven, CN: Yale University Press.
Runciman, W. G. (1963) 'Charismatic legitimacy and one-party rule in Ghana', *Archives Européennes de Sociologie* 4: 148–65.
Rustow, D. (1967) *A World of Nations: Problems of Political Modernization*, Washington, DC: Brookings Institution.
Schweitzer, A. (1984) *The Age of Charisma*, Chicago, IL: Nelson-Hall.
Smith, W. (1971) *We Must Run While They Walk: A Portrait of Africa's Julius Nyerere*, New York: Random House.
Terrill, R. (1980) *Mao: A Biography*, New York: Harper & Row.
Toth, M. (1973) *The Theory of the Two Charismas*, Ph.D. thesis, University of Utah.
Wallerstein, I. (1961) *Africa: The Politics of Independence*, New York: Random House.
Weber, M. (1964) *The Theory of Social and Economic Organization* (trans. by A. H. Henderson and Talcott Parsons), New York: Free Press.

Chapter seventeen

Summary and conclusions: in search of indigenous management

Alfred M. Jaeger and Rabindra N. Kanungo

The purpose of this book of readings is to illustrate in great detail the uniqueness of managing organizations and people in a developing country context. The book conveys a sense of frustration with the often seemingly insurmountable obstacles encountered by organizations in the carrying out of their day-to-day operations, as well as the joys associated with success in the face of such obstacles. The obstacles have been described in different ways in each and every one of the chapters of the book. Every chapter also has descriptions of ways of successfully dealing with obstacles, in some cases even turning these obstacles into advantages. It is herein that the mission of this book is reflected: to search out indigenous approaches to management, describe them, and begin to organize them into a body of knowledge which can be shared and developed by the international management community. Hence, what we shall do in this chapter is review what has been discussed in the book, identify what patterns have emerged in the material that has been presented, and attempt to organize a base of knowledge which will be of use to managers, management researchers, and management educators concerned with the management of organizations in developing countries.

The readings in this book have been grouped into three parts, each of which represents a different perspective on the topic being considered. Part I can be characterized as taking a macro-level perspective. It contains papers which look at the properties of organizations and their behaviour in the developing country environment. Here successful organizational responses to specific difficult organizational environments are described. Part II essentially takes a comparative perspective. It examines the environmental factors, particularly the underlying cultural values, which inhibit the adoption and successful utilization of Western management practices in a developing country context. Part III describes successful indigenous approaches to management, generally on the interpersonal level. In this section, models of supervision and leadership and managing employee motivation and performance are presented which take into account the environmental and cultural variables which distinguish developing countries.

In order to pursue our search of indigenous management we must also keep in mind what we mean by management and what the task of management is. If we look at a leading American management textbook, *Management* (4th edn, 1986) by Don Hellriegel and John W. Slocum, Jr., we note that in their first chapter they emphasize the functions of management. They point out that the traditional view of management's functions includes planning, organizing, leading, and controlling. This perspective assumes a sort of sequential process: plans are made and objectives are established; a structure must be organized with which to carry out the plans; the organization must be led to achieve its objectives; throughout this process, controls must be exercised to make sure that behaviour and outcomes are within the desired range.

This conceptualization of management, although abstract, implicitly includes assumptions about the existence of the type of stable environment and about time and people found in the developed countries. The sequential process of planning, organizing, leading, and controlling may not have pan-cultural generalizability particularly in the context of developing countries. To describe management in a manner appropriate for all contexts it is more useful to examine the functions of organizations and the role of management therein.

Organizations are established to carry out tasks which could not be accomplished by one person working alone. Thus the tasks of organizations are usually more complex than those which can be accomplished by one person alone and/or involve a quantity of work beyond the capacity of a single individual. When more than one person is involved in a cooperative effort, two key organizational tasks must be accomplished for the work to proceed. The work must be divided up amongst the individuals in the organization. This division of labour pulls people apart and gives rise to a need for some coordination between the various members of the organization. Thus the management of organizations is involved with dividing up the work and ensuring that the effort of individuals is coordinated. This internal management function can essentially be characterized as making sure that 'the job gets done'.

Management of organizations is also concerned with the relationship of the organization to its environment. This means that organizations must do such things as deal with their outside suppliers, keep an eye on their competitors, and be aware of the impact of government policies and actions on their operations. Therefore management also involves dealing with the outside environment.

To understand the link between these two functions we can turn to Thompson (1967), an American organization theorist whose prime focus is on what he calls the core technology which is at the heart of the functioning of any organization. Thompson's main premise in the analysis of the relationship of organizations to their environment is that technology demands a certain regularity to function properly. Therefore, for organizations to function and to survive, the technology must be able to operate in a fairly stable environment. One of the main strategies for doing this is to buffer or protect the core technology from the fluctuations and threats in the outside environment. Thus, one other important function of management is to manage the boundary between the internal operations of the organization and its outside environment.

To summarize the foregoing discussion, we can say that the assignment of the management of an organization consists of three main tasks:

- to ensure that the core task of the organization is carried out
- to keep track of the environment so that the organization is in a position to deal with it effectively as necessary
- to protect and buffer the technical core of the organization from environmental influences which might disrupt its operations

The obstacles to effective management which are encountered in developing countries can be summarized as follows:

- deficiency of resources, financial and human
- turbulence of the environment, both for the organization and the individual
- cultural values

The deficiency of resources in developing countries simply means that they are relatively poor in comparison with developed countries. Of particular interest here, as the focus has been on behaviour rather than tangible assets, is the deficiency of human resources. What does this mean for organizations and developing country economies? A specific example can illustrate development in the face of a poverty of tangible assets. Consider Germany in 1945. Certainly it was a poor country with very few tangible assets. Its people were hungry and poorly clothed and housed, and industrial production was minimal. Nevertheless, economic development began at that time and continued to produce a spectacular success. One may argue that the large sums of money provided by the Marshall Plan are the reason for that success; however, they are of a similar order of magnitude to the external debts of developing countries, which have not made a similar impact. The key factor is really the human resources. Although Germans in 1945 did not have a lot of material possessions and comforts, the people were educated, had a knowledge of and experience with industrial production, and had a sense of confidence that an industrial economy could be rebuilt. It is the latter factor, the sense of confidence, belief in what was being done, and vision for the future which was a crucial element in this success story. It caused people to work together as it made the reasons for this fairly obvious even when the immediate rewards were not obvious or forthcoming.

How does one overcome the deficiency in human resources? The solution to the lack of knowledge and experience is time and training. Over time, experience will be accumulated by organizational members. Knowledge deficiencies can be overcome by education and training. Nevertheless, these will be wasted to a certain extent if the organizational members do not have confidence in their self-efficacy in given tasks and in the fact that their efforts will meaningfully contribute to the realization of greater organizational goals. This feeling of helplessness and the lack of self-efficacy feelings is in some ways a reflection of the turbulent environment in which not just the organizations but also the individuals find themselves.

How is this learned helplessness (see Chapter Eleven) overcome? How is confidence instilled in individuals living and working in a developing country environment? Several answers are provided in the readings of this book. One example is the strategic development organization described by Khandwalla in Chapter Two. Such organizations can be viewed as sorts of organizational role models. These organizations are often highly visible and when successful this type of organization can serve as an inspiration to other organizations and individuals. They can serve as training grounds for individuals, providing them not only with skills but also with the self-confidence necessary for functioning in a turbulent environment. The other approach to helping individuals and organizations gain confidence is through strong or charismatic leadership. This was illustrated in several of the chapters in this book. In Chapter Five, Hardy describes how a strong leader was able to build up a good research-oriented university in the face of extreme environmental pressures. Although the focus in the chapter is on the leader's dealings with the external environment, it is clear that his personality had a definite positive impact on the internal working environment of the institution. Woycke, in Chapter Sixteen, examines the role of charismatic leadership in the political modernization of developing countries. He found that charismatic leaders with visions for the future were able to have a significant impact on effecting major political changes. Here again one can argue that they created a psychological climate which allowed their followers to take actions with the belief that a meaningful result would occur. Chapter Fourteen also addresses the role of leadership. Here, Sinha describes effective leadership behaviours in a developing country context where power distance and uncertainty avoidance tend to be high. The nurturant-task behaviours he describes not only facilitate the interaction of managers and their subordinates, but also create an environment within which the subordinate can function more effectively to achieve organizational objectives.

The problems of coping with a turbulent environment have been mentioned above in a couple of cases, mostly within the context of leadership. They are also addressed in a number of the chapters in the book. How can one go about dealing with a turbulent environment? As we mentioned before, one of the important management tasks is to ensure that the organization's technical core operates in as stable an environment as possible. This can be done in two ways: by ensuring that the organization operates in a stable environment; and by buffering the technical core from environmental fluctuations.

Ensuring that the organization operates in a stable environment appears at first to be rather contradictory when one is speaking of developing countries. What we are referring to here is the organization placing itself in a position which is more stable than might generally be the case. How might this be done? Kiggundu in Chapter Three discusses various modes of structural adjustment necessary for creating a more stable environment for organizations. One way is to establish linkages with other firms in the environment and cooperate so as to reduce uncertainty. In India, for example, there are several industrial groups which control a number of firms. This cooperation spreads risk and allows sharing of resources and some economies of scale. Larger industrial groups are also more successful at dealing with the government in matters relating to customs clearance, obtaining foreign exchange, and investment permits. On a smaller scale, the family firm, or extended family firm, puts the organization in a more secure environment. Firms often deal primarily with others who are members of the same extended family. Similarly, ethnic firms often prefer to deal with other firms of the same ethnic group. In this way dealings in the environment are with other parties who can be trusted. This creates and reinforces stable relationships and thus reduces environmental uncertainty.

Another strategy for operating in a more stable environment is to develop linkages with enterprises in the developed countries. One example of this type of linkage would be the joint venture. This type of arrangement can provide improved access to technology, and know-how, financing, and markets. More informal cooperative relationships are also possible. For example, it is now not uncommon for enterprises in the Caribbean region to perform computer data entry for firms in North America. This type of linkage can be beneficial to both parties and provides the developing country enterprise with a stable income and exposure to international standards of operation. Competing directly in international markets is another way to 'escape' the turbulence of developing country environments. This is done by a number of large firms from the larger developing countries. It is also done by smaller firms, such as the software development companies in India which sell to the international market. This is not an option open to all firms. However, those that do can have a great impact on the economic and human resource development in their home countries.

The other way to protect the technical core of the organization is to buffer it from unpredictable outside influences. One way this can be done, in the language of organization theory, is to build up organizational slack. This means the accumulation of slack resources which can be utilized when resources from the environment become unavailable. In practical terms, this would mean, for example, carrying excess inventory of key goods that might become scarce or purchasing foreign exchange well in advance of when it may be needed. Another example is the common practice of firms in Brazil to help their employees with personal financial problems. For example, because of the lack of public social services, employees may have an illness in the family which puts them in a precarious financial position. The personnel departments of larger Brazilian firms regularly provide assistance to employees in such a situation, thus mitigating the impact of the employee's problems on the functioning of the firm.

The cooperative arrangements between firms mentioned earlier can also serve a buffering function. They can ensure a regularity of supply as well as regular markets for the organization's output. In this way the organization can operate without major disruptions in its operations. Environmental scanning is of prime importance in dealing with a turbulent environment. Organizations must be vigilant about finding out what is happening in the environment so as to be able to anticipate the nature and the direction of major changes. This means not only watching what is going on but also developing good sources of information. For example, larger firms in developing countries are known to be in a position to hire or retain as consultants individuals with good government connections. These individuals can sometimes influence government actions and can be good sources of information. Good and timely information is most important as only with this can organizations hope to be able to take actions which will help them to deal most effectively with the obstacles that the environment may put in their way.

Most of the chapters in this book have addressed the impact of cultural values on the management of organizations. The conceptual perspective set forth in Chapter One indeed provides a detailed model of how cultural values impact on management. Furthermore, it proposes key cultural dimensions along which developed and developing countries would differ. These differences are very significant and certainly indicate limitations to the utilization of many Western management techniques as well as being potential obstacles to effective management in general. This topic is the particular focus of Part II of this book. In Chapter Seven, Jaeger reviews a large number of American management terms and practices and identifies the values which underlie them. The conclusion is that most of these values clash with those that predominate in developing countries. Thus an unquestioning adoption of management techniques in developing countries may be of limited effectiveness and may even be counterproductive. Kiggundu in Chapter Eight does a similar analysis, with a more limited focus – that of socio-technical systems. He also finds that, in general, the socio-technical systems approach for organizational analysis and design is based on underlying values which are in conflict with those found in developing countries.

Chapters Nine and Ten are country specific, focusing on China and India respectively. Zhuang and Whitehill examine the cultural values and socio-political factors which would have an influence on the acceptance of Western management practices by organizations in the People's Republic of China. They describe numerous obstacles not just to the adoption of Western management practices but also to the management of organizations in such a way that enterprises could be competitive in international markets. Parikh and Garg perform an intriguing analysis of the role structure of traditional Indian society. They describe the centuries-old role structure of traditional society which had its origins in the village but has been carried to the cities with increasing urbanization. Roles are well defined as are the relationships and obligations between roles. Such a role structure comes from a social system which is analogous, although not identical, to Toennies (1887) *Gemeinschaft* which was prevalent in pre-industrial Europe. With the coming of industrialization in Europe, society took on the form of *Gesellschaft* which is based on reciprocal but impersonal relationships. Parikh and Garg describe in some detail the value dilemmas of individual managers caused by the forced adoption of European (British) formal organizational structures which appear to reflect the *Gesellschaft* form to which European society had moved. These value dilemmas result also in behaviours which are detrimental to organizational functioning and effectiveness. They posit this as one of the major reasons for the chronic problems of efficiency in large Indian organizations.

Despite the relatively bleak picture painted by the foregoing, a number of the authors do present us with examples of indigenous management which is effective. While we shall not do a complete review of these examples from the preceding chapters, some of the insights they have provided will be highlighted.

Rieger and Wong-Rieger, in Chapter Six, do an interesting analysis of cultural differences as they relate to and impact on organizational structures. They identify key values which will affect the way in which organizations are structured and operate. Based on the values they have defined, they posit several organizational configurations which reflect different combinations of these values. Findings from a study of examples of these configurations in the airline industry are described. Several of these configurations are ones found in American management textbooks. Others, however, such as the autocracy, the traditional bureaucracy, and the political entourage seem to be examples of unique and successful adaptations to the cultural conditions found in developing countries.

Part III deals specifically with management practices with their origins in the developing world. The focus here is on motivation and leadership, two key aspects of management and ones where some progress has been made in the development and documentation of indigenous techniques.

Kanungo in his analysis of worker alienation in developing countries proposes an explanatory model that specifies indigenous variables affecting worker motivation in India. Identification of predisposing and precipitating factors responsible for alienation in developing countries would assist in designing indigenous management techniques. The process of moving from the diagnosis of cultural variables and their impact on employee motivation to the design of culture-compatible management techniques is highlighted in Chapters Twelve and Thirteen. Mendonca and Kanungo have proposed several specific interventions in the performance management process that take into account the culture-based characteristics of workers. Going beyond the issue of developing specific culture-compatible motivational techniques, Srinivas argues in favour of developing culture-compatible holistic strategies for de-alienation among workers in developing countries. Such strategies would involve simultaneous interventions in both work and non-work spheres of life.

In the field of leadership and supervisory practices, Sinha has proposed an indigenous model that seems to fit organizations in developing countries. He has argued that in cultures with a collectivist orientation the nurturant-task and directive styles of supervision would be most effective, at least in the initial stages of superior–subordinate interaction. Once the subordinates feel confident with regard to their personal efficacy on the job, the supervisor may then change to a more participative style.

Effective management in developing countries would require, as Mahapatra in Chapter Fifteen rightly suggests, identification of both growth-negative and growth-positive culture-based elements. Management practice would then be designed to marginalize or remove the negative elements and incorporate the positive ones. Examples of such management practice are offered by Srinivas in his discussion of de-alienation strategies, by Mendonca and Kanungo in their discussion of performance management, by Sinha in his advocacy of the nurturant-task style of supervision, and by Mahapatra in his search for creative combinations of traditional rituals with technology for achieving economic development objectives.

In providing an impetus for the development of indigenous management theories and techniques in developing countries, the book opens up a wide research arena. At the level of theory building, we need to analyse the existing state of organizational functioning critically, to look for prevailing local environmental conditions responsible for both organizational effectiveness and dysfunctions, and then to develop appropriate explanatory models of organizational behaviour. At the practice level, based on the explanatory models, we need to identify clearly and to describe and operationalize both the facilitatory and inhibitory factors for achieving organizational growth or developmental objectives. Indigenous management techniques can then be designed by incorporating growth-positive factors and eliminating growth-negative factors. These techniques can then be validated in actual management practice.

References

Hellriegel, D. and Slocum, J. (1986) *Management*, 4th edn, Reading, MA: Addison-Wesley.

Thompson, J. D. (1967) *Organizations in Action*, New York: McGraw-Hill.

Toennies, F. (1887) *Community and Society (Gemeinschaft und Gesellschaft)* (trans. by C. P. Loomis), East Lansing, MI: University of Michigan Press (original work published in 1887).

Index